Guide to Play Selection

Guide to Play Selection

Third Edition

A Selective Bibliography for Production and Study of Modern Plays

Compiled by the NCTE Liaison Committee with the
Speech Communication Association and the American
Theatre Association, Joseph Mersand, Editorial Chairman

Distributed jointly by the National Council of Teachers of English,
Urbana, Illinois, and the R. R. Bowker Company, New York.

Copyright 1934, © 1958, 1975 by the National Council of Teachers of English. All rights reserved. Printed in the United States of America. A publication of the National Council of Teachers of English, 1111 Kenyon Road, Urbana, Illinois 61801. Hardbound copies distributed by the R. R. Bowker Company (a Xerox Education Company), 1180 Avenue of the Americas, New York, New York 10036.

Library of Congress Catalog Card Number 74-33724
ISBN: 0-8141-1946-8 (paper)
ISBN: 0-8352-0862-1 (cloth)

Contents

Preface

The publication of the *Guide to Play Selection,* third edition, represents a triumph of faith, hope, and charity over such obstacles as thousands of miles between members of our committee, impossible schedules in our respective institutions, and the usual drain on patience when a project takes almost a decade to complete. When the letter of June 23, 1967, arrived designating me the continuing chairman of the committee to update the *Guide,* I thought that it would be a matter of a year or two only before the task was completed. Well, actually eight years have transpired, but they were worth the waiting; for what has resulted, thanks to the energies of our committee members and the guidance of the NCTE Editorial Board, is a far better reference work than the second edition. Let me, like Elizabeth Barrett Browning, count the ways.

This is the first reference work of its kind prepared by representatives of three distinguished organizations interested in promoting all the communication arts, and especially the love and growth of the theater. Since the inauguration of the liaison committee, the Speech Association of America has become the Speech Communication Association, but Executive Secretary William Work has ever remained with our committee, to attend every annual meeting and give of his wisdom and counsel. The American Educational Theatre Association has become the American Theatre Association, and several executive secretaries have come and gone, but their interest has never waned.

The third edition features three new sections not found in the second. The introduction, "A Guide to Play Production" by Julian M. Kaufman, discusses general criteria of play selection and provides an overview of the collaborative process of producing a play, focusing chiefly on the role of the director in giving conceptual unity to the production. The section on musical plays directs its attention to the most popular of all theater forms in America, a genre that in our lifetimes has advanced from an emphasis solely on comedy to treatments of the most serious and significant social concerns. The unique section on plays by Afro-Americans, specially written on request by Darwin T. Turner, provides a selective, representative list of plays written by black Americans, including dramas specifically designed for presentation to audiences in black communities.

In addition to author and title indexes, the third edition includes an index arranged according to the number and sex of the players required in each play, and a topical index. Anthony Roy Mangione graciously brought his knowledge of ethnic literature to bear in the categorization of plays having ethnic interest for itemization in the topical index. His work is especially of value in a time when greater attention is paid to the contributions of the various ethnic and national groups of our American culture.

Nearly 850 plays are described, over 100 more than the second edition. To lend some structure to an otherwise formless list, these have been arranged according to playwright. The bibliography of anthologies and collections, generously provided by Christian H. Moe and Jay E. Raphael, lists over 400 volumes containing plays described in this guide. Although this represents a smaller number of works than were found in the second edition, greater attention has been paid to the selection of in-print, frequently paperbound editions. Morris Schreiber contributed to the final updating of the *Guide* by amplifying the section on television plays.

Of the NCTE Committee on Playlist who prepared the second edition of the *Guide to Play Selection* in 1958, Francis Griffith, Marcus Konick, and M. Jerry Weiss consented to serve on the liaison committee to prepare the third, signifying their interest and devotion to the theater. To the original committee there were many additions, including Richard L. Loughlin, Robert R. Buseick, William E. Schlosser, and Julian R. Hughes, but Professor Hughes had to resign because of heavy commitments elsewhere. However, when the bulk of the proposed work became apparent and it became clear that the *Guide* would have to be shortened, the Editorial Board recommended concentration on modern drama (roughly 1870—present) to effect the least painful excisions of material. Regretfully, the splendid sections prepared by Professor Griffith on ancient, Asiatic, medieval, and Renaissance drama, the excellent section on plays from 1650–1870 prepared by Richard Loughlin, and the section on guidance plays by Professor Weiss all had to be omitted. To all I wish to express my personal gratitude for their hard work which could not be rewarded but which I hope will see publication in some other form.

As the *Guide to Play Selection,* third edition, finally sees the light, I wish to thank all members and associate members of our committee for their devotion to the cause, their tireless efforts, and their good-humored patience with all kinds of delays; to the executive secretaries of the three sponsoring organizations who were always ready to assist us in every way; and to Paul O'Dea, NCTE director of publications, and Duncan Streeter, staff editor, who took many a burden off the shoulders of the members of our committee. I am, of course, human and prejudiced. But I believe that what we have here is the best reference book of its kind, not only because representatives of three professional organizations participated, but because *das Ding an sich* is so good. It will assist countless students of the theater to find plays for reading and production; it will help directors of high school, college, and community theater groups to find plays that are suitable for their particular audience; it will inspire lovers of the theater arts to read more in the field; it should lend a helping hand to the ever-present revival of that Fabulous Invalid, the Living Theater. *Ave atque vale,* my fine and loyal committee, and may you rejoice in the reception of your splendid work. And may the three sponsoring organizations cooperate on many similar projects in harmony and peace at a time when such words have almost become obsolete in so many fields.

                              Joseph Mersand,
                              Chairman, NCTE Liaison Committee
                              with the SCA and the ATA

York College of the
City University of New York

A Guide to Play Production

Play production may be defined as a process that brings the playwright's words to life through the performance of the actors; the response and reaction to those words in movements devised by the director; the sense of time, place, and mood established by the sets, lights, and costumes; and, for a comparatively short time, the dramatization of a facet of life before a live audience. Play production is theater. It is an all-inclusive experience with a cast that includes the playwright, the producer, the actors, the director, the designers, the technicians, the accountant, the investors, and the theatergoers. It is not limited, as some think, to the work of the designers and technicians. Rather, play production is a collaborative process that demands cooperation from all the theater's practitioners for the purpose of entertaining and enlightening an audience.

Selecting the Play

Methods for selecting the play vary. In the commercial theater, the producer selects the play. The selection may represent a play chosen from several recommended by professional play-readers hired by the producer. In the regional theater, the artistic director submits a list of plays to the board of directors for approval. The list usually recommends various combinations for a season of plays. In a community theater, a committee of play-readers make recommendations to an executive board that, in turn, offers a choice of one or more plays to a director-member. In the university theater, a theater department member indicates a choice within the framework of departmental policy and approval. In the secondary school theater, the teacher-director makes the choice, generally with the tacit approval of the chairperson and principal, and sometimes in conjunction with a student play-reading committee. Play selection is an exacting task and responsibility because a good percentage of the success of the venture depends on finding a play that will provide a meaningful play production and play-going experience. In selecting a play, therefore, consideration should be given to the play's dramatic values, artistic challenge, cast availability, production costs, and audience appeal.

Dramatic Values

An examination of a play's dramatic values necessitates evaluating the relative theatrical worth and strength of the dramatic elements that constitute a play. To begin, a play is a story meant to be performed by actors in front of an audience. Similar to a story, a play has a theme, plot, locale, and characters. Dialogue is the chief means by which the theme is developed, the plot advanced, and the characters explored. The theme is the idea of the play, the reason for its existence. It is the playwright's statement of his view of the world in which he lives. Thus, the theme is the heart of the drama that unfolds. All else is but additional dramatization of it. Consequently, a strong theme—and certainly in the case of farce and melodrama, a plausible one—is a plus factor in choosing a play because a strong idea will immediately catch and hold the interest and attention of the audience. The plot of the play consists of a number of related incidents and events that provide a course of action for developing the theme and exploring the characters. A weak plot may endanger the development of a strong theme because the story line may lead nowhere, whereas a strong plot may enhance a weak theme for the very reason that a good story can be enjoyed even when the basic premise is inconsequential. Characters personify the theme and are the prime movers in instigating what happens in the play. Carefully delineated characters provide portraits that reveal insight into human needs and behavior. Too, characters in pursuit of a course of action invariably conflict with those who feel and think otherwise. The result is a recognizable contest of wills, a display of emotion, a gasp of surprise, a moment of suspense, a question of outcome. Although all plays contain the same dramatic elements—theme, plot, characters, dialogue, conflict, action, emotion, surprise, suspense—not all plays are equally strong in the theatrical value of each element. When all the dramatic values are equally strong theatrically, the play is a likely masterpiece. When the elements are balanced in theatrical strengths and weaknesses, chances are that the play is at least stageworthy. In any case, analyzing and evaluating the dramatic values of a play can help one make the most of a play's strengths and suggest ways to minimize the weaknesses when directing, performing, and producing it.

Artistic Challenge

A play should challenge the creativity of the actors, the director, and the designers. Too, a play should challenge the cultural sights of the community. The actor is the human instrument that brings the character to life on stage. The actor's body gives the character form and shape. The actor's speech mechanism gives the character a voice to speak his thoughts and exclaim his emotions. The actor's intellect permits the character to think and respond. The actor's imagination creates a world on stage within which the character can function. The director is the interpreter of the words written by the playwright. He must translate those words into movements devised for, and characterizations extracted from, the actor. He must convey his interpretation through a directorial concept to the designers. The director must orchestrate the flow of events and the exploration of character to focus attention on the theme. The designers visualize the concept and the interpretation through sets, lights, and costumes. If the actors, and the director, and the designers are to mature as creative theater artists, then the selected play must challenge their respective talents. If the actors, and the director, and the designers are to develop range as creative theater artists, then a variety of plays must be selected to challenge their respective talents. Similarly, if a community aims to raise its cultural horizons, then the selected play should stimulate community imagination and awaken support of theater in the community. Challenge is an important factor in play selection because it recharges the creativity and the imagination of the theater's practitioners. Moreover, challenge encourages growth through experimentation with the new and different, development through trial and error, and maturity through experience and evaluation.

Production Costs

Once a play begins to receive serious consideration for production, there is a need to determine whether or not an adequate budget is available to absorb the costs of royalty, set construction, lighting equipment, and costume rental. Unless specified otherwise, a playwright is entitled to a royalty. He is protected by law from a production of his play that has been mounted without prior arrangements with the play-leasing company that controls the performance rights. The royalty scale is often a graduated one, decreasing each night if there is more than one performance. Sometimes there is a flat fee for an extended run. Play copies must be purchased from the play-leasing company. Copies cannot be reproduced, and a notice of the permission granted must be printed in the program. Usually, the royalty cost for a musical is higher than that for a legitimate play. The popularity of the musical at the box office accounts for the difference in royalty cost. If there is any question about the condition under which the play is being performed with respect to royalty payment, the play-leasing company should be contacted immediately. The Dramatic Publishing Company makes the following distinction in the payment of royalty when a play is being rehearsed or performed in the classroom:

> When a play is used in a regularly scheduled class where *no one* is present other than the students and the instructor, no performance takes place. The moment you invite anyone in to watch, you have an audience, and therefore a performance. The only way we know of for differentiating a rehearsal from a performance is by the presence of an audience. If the person invited in is the principal, the superintendent, or some other school official, no royalty is due. If, however, parents, other students, or any other member of the public witness the performance, whether they pay admission or not, then a royalty fee must be paid. A performance given without prior arrangements is a violation of the law. . . .

Set construction is a costly item for many reasons. Construction materials are expensive. The play may have more than one set, and it may be that a stock of flats does not exist. New flats, therefore, must be constructed rather than old ones rebuilt. Lighting equipment is expensive, and invariably there always appears to be a need to either purchase or rent the needed equipment. Each play is in its own way a period play. Consequently, costuming a play can be costly. If the play is a modern one, some of the cost can be offset by using the actor's wardrobe, if it is appropriate, or by purchasing clothing from thrift shops. If the period of the play is removed from the present, however, there is the need to rent costumes, especially if the organization does not employ a professional costumer. Costumes are expensive to rent, and the cost increases when the cast is a large one and when there are several costume changes. Additional production costs include the making or renting of special props, advertising and publicity costs, and payment for custodial assistance. Too, if the organization does not have its own theater, there is the cost of renting an auditorium. Producing a play is a costly venture. No play should be undertaken without an adequate budget.

Audience Appeal

A play should be analyzed for its appeal to an audience. Factors of audience appeal include identification with theme, plot, and characters; participation in the action; and response to the reputation of the play and the playwright. Audience interest is aroused and audience identification with the theme occurs when the idea of the play is explicated from a common experience or universal truth. An audience identifies with the theme of Arthur Miller's *The Crucible* because the rights of the individual and the freedom to believe and worship as one chooses in the society of which one is a part are universal rights and beliefs recognized and practiced in a free society. An audience identifies with the plot of a play when the plot or the course of action follows a recognizable pattern or ritual that parallels life. The course of action of Thornton Wilder's *Our Town,* for example, follows a life cycle that includes daily living, love and marriage, and death. An audience identifies with the *dramatis personae* when the characters possess human strengths and weaknesses. An audience identifies with the tortured characters in Eugene O'Neill's *Long Day's Journey into Night* because the human frailties of the Tyrone family are the human frailties of humanity.

An audience responds favorably to a play when it is permitted to participate in the action. Ayn Rand's *The Night of January 16th,* for example, draws a jury from the audience at the beginning of the play. The jury sits on stage throughout the play, is locked up during intermission, and passes judgment on the prisoner at the end. *Our Town* makes the theatergoer a member rather than a spectator of the wedding by bringing the wedding procession down the aisles of the auditorium. Plays that contain monologues, asides, and soliloquies invite participation. The character speaks to us directly, tells us his thoughts, thus involving us as his confidantes in the action that follows.

The reputation of the play is a strong audience appeal that should not be overlooked when selecting a play. The sweet smell of success spreads fast, and theatergoers are attracted to the box office because the play has proved a commercial success elsewhere. People want to see what others have seen and enjoyed, with or without the original cast. Similarly, the reputation of the playwright is an appeal factor. There is no denying that the plays of Arthur Miller, Tennessee Williams, Edward Albee, and Neil Simon arouse and stimulate theatergoing. Of course, the danger of always selecting the popular box-office play is limited play production and theatergoing experience.

In summary, the play is the foundation on which the theatrical experience rests. It is the catalyst that sets the dynamics of the theater in motion. Therefore, if the play production experience is to prove a rewarding and successful one, it is important to select a play that justifies the time and energy of the actors, director, and designers. It is equally important to select a play that will motivate an audience to give its time and its energy, as well as its money, to enjoy the playgoing experience.

Producing the Play

The producer initiates the production by choosing the play. His choice may be based on his belief in the stageworthiness of the play. He may be moved and inspired by its literary and artistic merits. His longtime association with the playwright may be another reason for choosing the script. Too, his friendship with a star may result in selecting a particular play for production. His commitment to the theater may lead him to select a play by an unknown playwright which has a pertinent theme but which may prove unpopular at the box office. Or, he may identify his choice as a certain success. The producer in today's theater continues to fill the responsibility of the actor-manager of the nineteenth century acting company, the patentee of the Restoration acting company, the manager of the Elizabethan acting company, and the Archon in the Greek theater.

The producer in the commercial theater is responsible for raising money to finance the cost of the production. Part of the financing may come from the producer's personal funds while the remainder is solicited from friends or "angels." In regional and community theaters, financing is generally obtained from theatergoers who either purchase tickets for a single attraction or who advance the cost of a subscription series. It is not unusual for an organization to receive a government grant or subsidy. In the university theater, a drama department is generally alloted a production budget by the university. In the secondary school theater, the activity is either self-supporting through ticket sales or financed all or in part through general organizational funds. The expenditures of money require an administrative and business staff that includes lawyers to handle necessary contracts and

accountants to verify the payment of salaries, the purchase of equipment
and materials, and the cost of advertising and publicity.

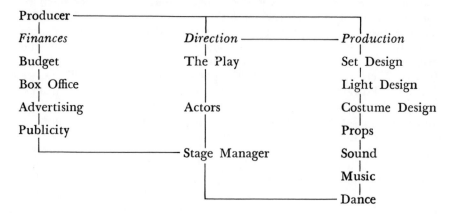

Fig. 1. Theater Organization

Generally, the producer is only indirectly involved with the
artistic interpretation and performance of the play. He usually selects
a director whose interpretative concept agrees with his own. He hires
designers whose visual concepts represent an extension of the directorial concept. Unless he is obliged to exercise his prerogative to take
issue with concepts and interpretations, or unless there is a need for him
to reconcile differences in artistic concept, the producer remains in the
background, keeping a watchful eye on financial expenditures and the
artistic development of the play.

Directing the Play

The director reads, studies, and analyzes the play assiduously.
He reads the play many times to crystalize his understanding of the
theme and how it is organized and developed by the playwright
through the plot and the characters. The director studies the play to
determine its structure, carefully noting the initial incident that propels
the action forward, observing how situations occur and how scenes
develop as the action approaches the climax. The director examines the
resolution to the play, pondering its relationship to the characters
and earlier scenes in the play. He studies the episodic structure of
another kind of play, contemplating the probable impact its cumulative
effect will have upon the audience. He explores the play to determine
its style in production and performance. He analyzes the characters
to discover inner feelings that motivate outer actions and behavior.
He thinks of the characters in terms of people he has known, friends
he has observed, actors who can flesh out the silhouettes created by the
playwright. The first phase of directing the play finds the director

steeping himself in the work of the playwright in order to cast the play, plot and block the movement, rehearse the actors, confer and plan with the designers.

Directorial Concept

Early on, the director develops a directorial and production concept as a result of studying and analyzing the play. The directorial concept is derived from the director's understanding and interpretation of the play as he envisions it in terms of the dynamics of the theater. The directorial concept becomes the basis for staging the play as well as the director's frame of reference when motivating the actors and when conferring with the designers. The director communicates his directorial and production concept to the designers in terms that are neither too general to mislead nor too specific to stifle the creativity of each designer. Accordingly, the director describes how he visualizes the environment of the play without encroaching upon the artistry of the scene designer. He depicts how he sees the characters costumed without obtruding upon the creativity of the costume designer. He outlines the feeling of the dominant mood and its variations without imposing upon the skill of the light designer. In time, the set designer furnishes the director with a ground plan and either a perspective sketch or model set; the costume designer submits sketches and a costume chart for the director's approval; the light designer provides a lighting plot for his consideration. Through discussion and conference during the rehearsal period, the director and the designers exchange ideas and resolve problems in order to mount a production that reflects a collaborative effort to the audience.

Casting

Properly casting actors whose talents can best serve the needs of the play is a difficult and complex procedure because it demands spending a relatively short period of time on a crucial element of play production. In the commercial theater, the problem is resolved by hiring professional actors with established reputations and by auditioning actors recommended by agents. In regional and summer theaters, casting is by assignment. Generally, the actor knows the roles he will play and contracts to join the company because of the experience some roles offer. In the university, community, and secondary school theater, open casting is the general procedure in order to provide everyone interested with an opportunity and to avoid accusations of prejudice in casting. The first call may be a reading or discussion of the play. At another time, actors may read for specific parts in specific scenes with other actors. Some directors employ a personal interview with each candidate because this method provides an opportunity to establish a working relationship if the actor is cast and because it provides the director with an opportunity to discuss the role and the play under conditions that are relatively pleasant for the actor. Other directors test the imaginative powers of the actor by asking him to perform a pantomimic improvisation that may or may not be related to the role. Too, in casting the play, directors take into consideration the actor's physical appearance, age, voice, diction, and sense of movement. Casting is an unenviable directorial task because the pressure of beginning rehearsals in order to meet a performance date and keep to a production schedule necessitates quick decisions that are sometimes regretted.

Plotting the Movement

In addition to reading the play to determine its theme, studying the play to discover its structure, and analyzing the play to understand its characters, the director scrutinizes the play to discover its pattern of movement. In the development of the plot, the director finds the natural coming and going of characters as one incident ends and another begins or as one character enters and another leaves. In what the characters say and feel, he perceives a motivation for behavioral movement. In what the characters do, he detects an underlying ritual that prompts movement. In shifting interests and alliances, he beholds a change in focus that actuates movement. Out of his experience with the ritual of everyday living, the director invents movement or business that is appropriate to the scene and the characters involved. When he can picture the movement of the play in his mind's eye, the director is ready to write down his directions. In the margin of his working script, the director records his directions to the actors in stage shorthand: "L xdc sofa," meaning, "Lily, cross down center to the sofa." Frequently, the director draws a rough sketch of the ground plan and marks the placement of characters who are arranged in group positions. At rehearsal, each actor writes the directions in his script. The stage manager or his assistant inscribes the directions in the production book copy. Plotting the movement finds the director alone in his most creative moment, a moment when the imaginative stirrings in his mind find their way to paper. Blocking the play finds the director testing his imagination by having the actors physically perform the created movements.

Rehearsing the Play

Rehearsing the play includes blocking the movement, motivating and coaching the actors. Blocking the movement is the physical working out of the planned movement written by the director in the margin of his script. Blocking the movement puts the play on its feet through the physical actions of the actors as they make their entrances and exits and as they engage in physical actions that emanate from the characters' behavior. Blocking the movement requires patience from the director and the actor because the director must stage the play at a time when the actor must absorb the movement as part of his characterization and, simultaneously, struggle to learn lines and identify with the personality of the role he is playing. Novice directors are cautioned to analyze printed directions. These printed directions represent patterns of movement devised by the original director and recorded by the stage manager. Sometimes the recording is neither complete nor accurate. If the directions are not analyzed and understood for concept, the novice director may find that his staging is without focus and meaning.

Motivating the actor finds the director collaborating with the actor in creating a character without stifling the actor's imagination and creativity. The actor should conceive the character. He searches into the character's past to determine what previous experiences contributed to his present behavior. He examines his relationship to the other characters in the play to determine what his response to them should be. He imagines a private life and a private world for his character and selects from both that which he can use in building a stage world for the role he plays. The director cultivates the character conceived by the actor, stimulating the actor through exercises that challenge and titillate the actor's imagination and creativity. The character that emerges is the child of the actor; its development is the work of the director. Rehearsing the play begins with the words of the playwright as printed symbols. It ends with the words of the playwright spoken by actors and performed before an audience.

The Director Today

The director in the twentieth century theater is a creative and interpretive artist who is mainly responsible for bringing life to the words and thoughts of the playwright. His eminence in our theater is the result of the realization that play production is a collaborative process, that the mounted play must reflect an integration of skills and talents, and that one person must have the authority and ability to both interpret the play and synthesize the talents and skills of the actors and designers. Although the counterpart of the director may be found in the playwright, the prompter, the actor-manager, and the stage manager in other eras of the theater, the director did not gain recognition as a skilled and imaginative craftsman apart from other theater practitioners until the latter part of the nineteenth century. Then the exemplary and esthetically exciting productions mounted by George II, Duke of Saxe-Meiningen, brought into sharp focus the wisdom of making one person responsible for planning all phases of a production and, further, justified his having the authority to execute the plan by overseeing and coordinating the skills of the actors and the designers to achieve a unified production. André Antoine in France, Otto Brahm in Germany, Harley Granville-Barker in England, Konstantin Stanislavski in Russia, and David Belasco in the United States followed the Duke's example and contributed to the identification of the function of the director. The highly creative and imaginative directorial accomplishments of Max Reinhardt established the director as an interpretive artist in the theater.

Designing the Set

The set designer first reads the play to learn what it is about and what it has to offer in the way of a theatergoing experience. He then reads and studies the play in depth in order to evolve a design that visualizes the environment in which the action takes place. From information supplied by the playwright, the designer learns the hour of the day, the season of the year, the century in which the play occurs, and the locale of the action. Such information foretells mood, atmosphere, decor, and style. If the playwright has included a detailed description of the set, the set designer has little difficulty determining the size and shape of the playing area, the location of architectural features such as doors, windows, archways, and the placement of furniture, platforms, and stairways. Sir Arthur Wing Pinero, George Bernard Shaw, and David Belasco wrote detailed set descriptions to guide the set designer. If the playwright has provided only a one-line description of the set—"the palace of Oedipus," "another part of the forest," "the scene is Paris"—the set designer must scrutinize and analyze the script to find a basis for his design. In the coming and going of characters he must discover the location of exits and entrances. In the dialogue and imagined behavior of the characters within a scene, he must recognize the need for and the placement of furniture. Whether or not a detailed description of the set has been provided by the playwright, the set designer must create an architectural environment that both visualizes and reflects the personalities of the characters that inhabit it.

The set designer prepares a ground or floor plan of the set after he has analyzed and discussed the play with the director. The plan outlines the physical boundaries of the set, thus giving shape to the acting area. It includes the location of windows, doors, stairways, and the placement of furniture. It is generally drawn to scale. The ground plan must have the approval of the director because the director uses the plan in plotting the action. His thinking and that of the designer must be in accord if the director is to effectively use the acting area provided by the designer and if the movement is to appear logically motivated when it is performed within the constructed design. A copy of the ground plan is furnished to the lighting designer for his use in placing lighting instruments and in planning a light design. After the director has approved the ground plan, the set designer draws a sketch that depicts his design in terms of architecture, furniture, decor, and color. The figure of one or more characters is generally included to show the relationship between an actor's height and the size of the set. Frequently, when the play is one that has many scene shifts, the set designer will construct a model set. The model set helps demonstrate how scenery changes will be made and what plans are necessary to assure efficient changes by a crew. Too, a model set is helpful in realistically depicting the set design to the director and producer. Finally, the submission of the ground plan, the sketch, and the model set at various phases of production assures continuing collaboration between the director and designer and prevents negative feelings when changes occur without notification by either party.

The set designer in the professional theater holds a membership in the United Scenic Artists Union, Local 829, Brotherhood of Painters, Decorators, and Paperhangers of America. Membership is through examination that requires a demonstration of skill in costuming and lighting. In addition to designing the set and providing drawings from which the set can be constructed, the set designer is responsible for the procuring and designing of properties that are related to dressing the set but which are not related to the costumes of the actors. The latter props are the responsibility of the costumer. The set designer in some theatrical organizations assumes the duties of the technical director when there is limited personnel.

Lighting the Play

The lighting designer comes to the director's conference prepared to explain how his lighting concept of the play can contribute to its visual effectiveness. He exchanges observations with the director and the designers. The lighting designer discusses how he intends to employ color and intensity to support the mood and movement created by the director. He points out how his lighting concept will enhance the physical environment devised by the set designer. He speculates on the general effectiveness his color choices will have on materials selected by the costume designer. He expects and makes changes that will assure the collaborative nature of the undertaking. His concept is subject to the approval of the director.

The lighting designer uses the ground plan to make his concept a reality. In locating his lighting instruments on the plan, the lighting designer keeps certain lighting principles in mind. The first principle is to make the actor and the action visible to the audience. The second principle requires use of a logical light source. Two such sources are (1) natural, or light from a source that suggests time of day, weather, and season; and, (2) artificial, or light from a source that is controlled by a switch or hand-operated device. The third principle demands application of the qualities of light—intensity, color, distribution, movement—to the mood, atmosphere, and stage picture.

A basic method of lighting the six acting areas of the stage assures visibility of the actor and the action. Cross spotlighting of each acting area reveals the contour of the actor's body and washes out a general flatness of the physical environment. Other instruments are used to highlight within the main acting areas and to provide a contrast in lightness and darkness as it applies to lighting the dramatic composition of the stage picture. An instrument schedule lists the number, kind, placement, and purpose of each instrument. The schedule is used when the instruments are physically hung and when attempting to locate the source of any mishap during the performance. A lighting cue

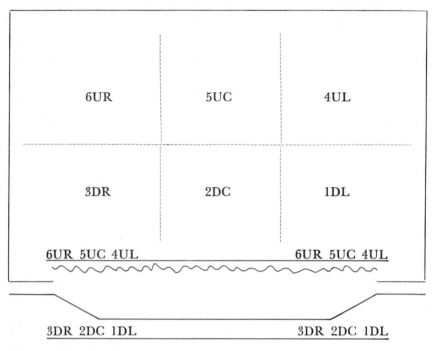

Fig. 2. Cross Spotlighting Layout

sheet is the work of both the stage manager and the lighting designer
and represents a list of the various light changes that occur during the
performance of the play.

Similar to the set designer, the lighting designer in the legitimate theater is a union member. Frequently, his responsibilities are
assumed by the technical director in some theatrical organizations.

Costuming the Play

A costume is scenery worn by an actor and built by the costume
designer. It tells us many things about the character who wears it without the character speaking a word. It reveals personality through choice
of style, color, fabric, and accessories. Its fit and the manner in which
it is worn suggests an emotional frame of mind. It announces a profession through use of uniform or established dress. A costume reflects
social status through identification of dress with different levels of society. It points up a relationship between characters through identical
trimmings, intermingling of colors, and similarity of line. A costume
relates to the environment in which the play occurs, and it establishes
a period through fabric and silhouette. It visually dramatizes the
dramatis personae through the use of line and fabric. In conference
with the director, set and lighting designers, the costume designer ex-
plains how his costuming concept contributes to visualizing the play.

Once his costume interpretation has received the director's approval, the costume designer proceeds to make his concept concrete. After he has researched the background of the period during which the action occurs, particularly the fashion of the time, the costume designer prepares a costume plot which contains a list of costumes worn by each character in the play, scene by scene, act by act. Next, a costume plate or sketch is drawn for each costume worn. The plate is usually in color with notations of fabrics, trimmings, and accessories. Frequently, swatches of materials are included. Canes, luggage, umbrellas, fans, and other props that seemingly relate to dress worn by the character are hand props that are the responsibility of the costume designer. Additionally, a costume chart is drawn by the designer. It includes all costumes in silhouette and color in order to view the overall effect and to check for unity in concept and design. A costume parade during the dress rehearsal phase of producing the play reveals any need for adjustment in fit or design.

A costume may be built or dismantled and rebuilt when a trained and experienced costume designer is a member of the organization. Research will reveal the fashion style of the period, and with imagination, the costume designer will adapt the silhouette to the visual needs of the production. Too, a costume may be built or dismantled and rebuilt when a person who has a talent with needle, thread, and scissors is a member of the organization. Costume books will give instructions in pattern cutting. Materials need not be expensive or rich in texture; cost has nothing to do with effectiveness on stage, and frequently richly textured fabrics do not show up well under stage lighting. Moreover, curtains, drapes, bedspreads, tablecloths, and rugs make good costume fabrics, and discarded clothing can be rebuilt into effective costumes. Although costume rental can be costly, costume houses are reliable and cooperative in filling orders. It is important to give all the measurements required because rented costumes cannot be altered or tailored, and the measurements provide the costume house with a physical profile of the wearer. When costumes can neither be rented or built, then the wardrobe of the actor can be borrowed, providing that it meets the costume needs of the production.

Stage Managing the Play

The stage manager is a key person in backstage organization, both because of his many responsibilities during the rehearsal period and performance and because of his working relationship with members of the company. He is generally selected when the director is assigned or hired. More often than not, he represents the director's choice because he closely assists the director throughout the rehearsal period, assuming responsibility for running the performance and for keeping the director's interpretation of the play intact after the director has completed his work. The stage manager compiles and organizes a play production prompt book that includes a copy of the play with a recording of the

Costume Plot   Act:_____ or Scene:_____

Play: _____

Playwright: _____

Performance Dates: _____

Costume Designer: _____

Wardrobe Manager: _____

Dresser: _____

Character	Actor	Garment	Accessories
1.			
2.			
3.			
4.			
5.			
6.			
7.			
8.			
9.			
10.			
11.			
12.			

Changes and Notes:

director's plotting; ground plan and set design or sketch drawn by the set designer; light design plan and light instrument placement list devised by the lighting designer; costume plot, chart, and sketches submitted by the costume designer; music, sound, light, and curtain cues; and a summary sheet that includes the starting and ending times of each performance, weather conditions at each performance, and a notation of any untoward event that may have occurred during the performance of the play. The purpose of the play production prompt book is to provide guidance for running the performance if the stage manager is indisposed and to provide a history of the production when the run of the play has concluded.

The stage manager functions as an assistant to the director, counselor to the actors, and coordinator to the designers. The stage manager assists the director in numerous ways. He posts all notices relevant to auditions and rehearsals. He makes the play available to the actors for study before auditions. He schedules the actor for his reading with the director. He manages the audition procedure, announcing the actor, and timing his presentation according to prior instructions from the director. He arranges for callbacks. In the absence of the director, the stage manager begins the rehearsal; in the absence of an actor, the stage manager walks the scene. On occasion, he is asked to coach the actor or rehearse a scene. To the actor, the stage manager is a counselor who files his personal data with the business staff, encourages him in developing his characterization, listens to his problems, and acts as intermediary in his association with the director and the producer. The stage manager serves as the director's liaison with the designers, advising them of changes in directorial concept, calling them to production conferences, seeking from them information that relates to progress in achieving visual objectives. Similarly, the stage manager acts as the designers' liaison with the director, informing him of production problems and decisions. The stage manager coordinates all backstage activity during the last weeks of rehearsal and during the dress rehearsal period. He records all light cues, sound cues, music cues, and curtain cues in the play production prompt book. He times all scene changes. He checks all props. He sets up a stage manager's desk from which he can see the performance and from which he can order and relay all cues. He runs the dress rehearsal as though it were a performance. He maintains quiet backstage, enforces no smoking and no visitors rules, runs the curtain call, and signals for house lights when he believes the audience has sufficiently rewarded the actors and the production with applause.

A person charged with such multifarious responsibilities and surrounded by such a variety of personalities and talents needs to be selected with care and consideration. He must appreciate the intricacies of play production. He must know backstage organization. He must relate to people. He must have leadership qualities. He must be con-

tent to be an unsung hero who is indeed the one who makes the show
go on. His is the role of the catalyst who organizes the creative efforts
of all and who releases those efforts when the lights dim and the performance begins.

Evaluating the Production

The theatergoing experience is incomplete without an evaluation of the play, the performance, and the production. Inasmuch as it
is within the nature of man to be discriminating, passing judgment on
that which he sees and hears, accepting that with which he agrees, and
rejecting that with which he disagrees, the theatergoer need not be a
skilled critic in order to state his response to the play and the performance. Although he may not know or appreciate the fine points of
playwriting, the theatergoer is tuned into life and is capable of commenting on the playwright's theme because the theme is a viewpoint
of life with which the theatergoer is likely to be familiar. Similarly,
the theatergoer is aware of both human behavior and emotions; he is,
therefore, capable of commenting on an actor's performance because
the performance is a characterization of a human being with whom the
theatergoer is likely to be acquainted or with whom he can personally
identify. However, the art and craft of both the director and the
designer is specialized and unlikely to be within the occupational experience of the theatergoer. Because criticism of the production
elements therefore tends to be cursory, the following questions are
proposed as guidelines when discussing the contributions of both the
director and the designers:

On Directing

a. Did the director's interpretation reinforce the theme and
plot of the play?
b. Did the director develop arresting stage pictures and group-
ings to visualize theme, conflict, and character relationship?
c. Did the director evoke a mood appropriate to the emotional
content of the play?
d. Did the director invent or make use of identifiable patterns
of movement to underscore plot development, character behavior and growth?
e. Did the characterizations and the performances by the actors
indicate a cast well chosen and assigned by the director?
f. Did the performance by the company reveal ensemble playing encouraged and generated by the director?

On Set Design

a. Did the set establish the locale, time, period, and mood of
the play?
b. Did the set provide a credible habitat for the characters?
c. Did the set decorations and properties reveal inner feelings
of the characters or relate to the meaning of the play?

d. Did the set allow for imaginative use of space by the director?
e. Did the set contribute to the general effectiveness of the production, or did it stand out as a design that distracted the attention of the viewers?

On Light Design
a. Did the light design illuminate the stage and the performers?
b. Did the light design establish the locale, time, period, and mood of the play?
c. Did the light design include "light pictures" that enhanced stage pictures created by the director?
d. Did the light design include imaginative special effects that were technically realized in performance?
e. Did the light design include numerous and complicated light cues that worked smoothly?

On Costume Design
a. Did the costumes establish the locale, time, period, and mood of the play?
b. Did each costume appear to be apparel chosen by each character?
c. Did the costumes tell you something about the characters?
d. Did the costumes collectively contribute to the general effectiveness of the production or did any one costume stand out as a distinctive silhouette that distracted attention from the play?

On Play Production Elements
a. Did the entire production indicate a successful collaborative undertaking by the producer, director, actors, designers, and technicians?

Bibliography

Directing the Production

Albright, H. D. *Working Up a Part.* Boston: Houghton Mifflin Co., 1947.

Canfield, Curtis. *The Craft of Play Directing.* New York: Holt, Rinehart and Winston, 1963.

Chilver, Peter. *Staging a School Play.* New York: Harper and Row, 1967.

Dean, Alexander. *Fundamentals of Play Directing.* Revised by Lawrence Carra. New York: Holt, Rinehart and Winston, 1965.

Sievers, David W. *Directing for the Theatre.* Dubuque: Wm. C. Brown Co., Publishers, 1965.

Spolin, Viola. *Improvisation for the Theater.* Evanston: Northwestern University Press, 1963.

Welker, David. *Theatrical Direction: The Basic Techniques.* Boston: Allyn and Bacon, 1971.

Designing the Production

Burris-Meyer, Harold, and Cole, Edward C. *Scenery for the Theatre.* Rev. ed. Boston: Little, Brown and Co., 1971.

Corson, Richard. *Stage Make-up.* 4th ed. New York: Appleton-Century-Crofts, 1967.

Gillette, A. S. *An Introduction to Scenic Design.* New York: Harper and Row, 1967.

————. *Stage Scenery: Its Construction and Rigging.* New York: Harper and Row, 1959.

Parker, W. Oren, and Smith, Harvey K. *Scene Design and Stage Lighting.* 2nd ed. New York: Holt, Rinehart and Winston, 1968.

Payne, Blanche. *History of Costume.* New York: Harper & Row, 1965.

Prisk, Bernice. *Stage Costuming Handbook.* New York: Harper and Row, 1966.

Welker, David. *Theatrical Set Design: The Basic Techniques.* Boston: Allyn and Bacon, 1969.

Play Production

Beck, Roy A., et al. *Play Production in the High School.* Skokie, Ill.: National Textbook Co., 1968.

Clifford, John E. *Educational Theatre Management.* Skokie, Ill.: National Textbook Co., 1972.

Dolman, John Jr., and Knaub, Richard K. *The Art of Play Production.* Rev. ed. New York: Harper and Row, 1973.

Engel, Lehman. *The Musical Show.* Rev. ed. New York: Crown Publishers, 1966.

Gassner, John. *Producing the Play.* New York: Dryden Press, 1941.

Gruver, Elbert. *The Stage Manager's Handbook.* New York: Harper and Row, 1953.

Nelms, Henning. *Play Production.* New York: Barnes and Noble, 1950.

Ommanney, Katherine A. *The Stage and the School.* 3rd ed. New York: McGraw-Hill Book Co., 1960.

Smith, Milton. *Play Production.* New York: Appleton-Century-Crofts, 1948.

Theater Appreciation

Brockett, Oscar G. *The Theatre: An Introduction.* 2nd ed. New York: Holt, Rinehart and Winston, 1969.

Cullman, Marguerite. *Occupation: Angel.* New York: W. W. Norton and Co., 1963.

Hughes, Glenn. *The Story of the Theater.* New York: French, 1928.

Kaufman, Julian M. *Appreciating the Theater: Cues for Theatergoers.* New York: David McKay Co., 1971.

Roberts, Vera Mowry. *On Stage: A History of Theatre.* Rev. ed. New York: Harper and Row, 1974.

Yurka, Blanche. *Dear Audience.* Englewood Cliffs, N.J.: Prentice-Hall, 1959.

Guide to Play Selection

Guide to Entries

Sample Entry

A.   B.   C.

Genet, Jean. *The Blacks: A Clown Show.* (1957) Translated by

                          D.   E.   F.

Bernard Frechtman. Drama. Interior. Symbolic costumes, masks.

G.   H.   I.   J.

9m. 5w. French $1.95. Restricted. Royalty $35–$25.

A. Playwright's name. Plays are entered alphabetically according to the author's last name. Musical plays are entered according to the author of the libretto. Translations and adaptations into English are listed according to the original author. Dramatic adaptations of prose or poetical works are listed according to the playwright's name. Spanish playwrights having two surnames are entered according to the first surname.

B. Title of play; date of first performance or publication.

C. Any additional information: name of translator or adaptor; names of composers of music or lyrics; or the source of material—e.g., a novel, story, poem, play, or other work from which the play is derived.

D. General classification, e.g., drama, melodrama, tragedy, comedy, fantasy, farce, verse play, morality play, documentary. The number of acts or scenes, or in the case of short plays, the approximate playing time, is sometimes noted.

E. Information about set requirements.

F. Information about costumes.

G. Number and sex of the players: m = men, w = women. Children, extras, animals, chorus, bit parts, possibility of doubling, as noted.

H. Distributor (s) of published playscript and price of book. Most entries list the playscript published or distributed by the firm issuing licenses for amateur productions and to whom royalties or performance fees must be paid. More than one publisher/distributor is sometimes listed. If the playscript contains other plays besides the one described, the words "in volume" or the title of the volume is given in parentheses. If no published playscript is available, the location of the play in a trade edition or in an anthology is noted (for information on the availability of plays in volume, see the title index to this guide, which is cross-referenced with the bibliography of anthologies and collections found in the appendix). Plays marked "manuscript" are available from the publisher/distributor in manuscript form. Consult the publisher's catalog for regulations pertaining to the rental of materials in manuscript, whether for previewing or performance purposes. For purposes of studying or previewing a play, a more inexpensive edition than the playscript listed may occasionally be available from another source; consult *Books in Print* or *Paperbound Books in Print,* published by the R. R. Bowker Company, New York.

I. Restrictions and other information. Because some plays may not have reached the end of their professional run, they may be available for amateur performances only in restricted territory. Other stipulations may pertain to admission fees, unsegregated audiences, or amateur performances.

J. Royalty (performance fee). All royalties quoted are for amateur performances and must be paid for each performance, whether or not an admission fee is charged. (Consult the publisher of the play for their definition of "performance.") Where two figures are given, the first is for the first performance, and the second is for each subsequent performance of the same production. Unless otherwise noted, royalty fees are payable to the publisher/distributor of the playscript listed. "No royalty," in general, refers to strictly amateur performances and does not necessarily apply outside the United States and/or Canada, nor to radio broadcasting or television productions. Permission must be obtained before planning any production of any play. *In all cases,* consult the publisher or agency in control of the play. For addresses, see the directory of play publishers and agents found in the appendix. Addresses of authors representing their own works, if known, are also listed in this directory.

Note: It is an infringement of copyright to copy all or part of any published play or unpublished play available in manuscript, by any means, including mimeograph, ditto, xerography, or any means of reproduction. Book prices and royalty fees noted are those found in publishers' catalogs and supplements of 1974–1975 and are subject to change without notice.

Short Plays

The one-act play, the most common short play, is designed to give a single unified impression, tending to emphasize primarily either character, or plot, or atmosphere. It usually deals with a single incident and contains one small group of characters.

The one-act play is as old or older than the longer form. The Greek tragedies are really one-act plays. So are early miracle plays. Even after the longer form had become dominant, many hundreds of one-act plays were written and played in the theaters of England and continental Europe. In the nineteenth century, it was the custom to produce a short play, called a "curtain raiser," as a preliminary to a longer one.

One-act plays are ideally suitable for amateurs. A bill of one-act plays usually gives a greater variety of characters, and a greater number of characters, than a single full-length play. They often furnish many more interesting problems in stagecraft. As a rule, insofar as the acting is concerned, they are apt to be easier to play effectively with inexperienced actors, for it is much easier to sustain a role effectively for thirty or forty minutes than it is to sustain one for an entire evening. They are more quickly prepared too, and do not demand so many rehearsals from the same group of people. Finally, there is not the competition and the inevitable comparison with the professional stage. One-act plays can be novelties in a city or town with one or two stock companies and several theaters which offer Broadway plays. Even though most American audiences prefer the full evening play, it is decidedly worthwhile for schools, colleges, and little theaters to help make the one-act play more popular with an occasional bill.

One of the most serious problems of presenting a bill of one-act plays is that of stage setting. The backgrounds must therefore be kept simple; a cyclorama will do, with a few simple props, or, better still, an arena theater.

In preparing a bill of one-act plays, a certain balanced variety must be kept in mind. The plays must not be all of the same type or of the same mood. Three plays are usually enough for a full evening's entertainment, or four, at the most, if they are short. Three longer one-act plays are usually better than five or six shorter ones. Or, if one very short one is used, a longer one will balance the bill. If there is a heavy play—a grim tragedy, for example—it is customary to have it come in the middle of the bill. The lightest, funniest play is usually placed at the end. For example, good bills would be a fantasy, a tragedy, a farce; or a melodrama, a drama, a light comedy. Often it is a good idea to group a bill of one-act plays about some idea or center. It might be possible to do three plays of the sea, or three plays of rural life. Especially if the atmosphere is similar, care must be taken to see that there is variety in plot and action.

Summaries of Plays

Albee, Edward. *The American Dream*. (1961) Interior. 2m. 3w. Dramatists Play Service $1.75 (in volume with "The Death of Bessie Smith"
and "Fam and Yam"). Royalty $25. Restricted to amateur performances
before unsegregated audiences.

Mommy and Daddy, seated on identical armchairs, make small talk.
Grandma appears, full of an old woman's complaints. Mrs. Barker, a
club lady, arrives and takes off her dress. At last the Young Man comes
in, a specimen of physical wholesomeness. The play attacks the sentimental ideals of family life, togetherness, physical fitness, faith in the
national mission, and the bourgeois assumptions and attitudes encouraged by euphemistic language and unwillingness to face the ultimate facts of the human condition in America.

————. *The Death of Bessie Smith*. (1960) Drama. Unit set. 5m. 2w.
Dramatists Play Service $1.75 (in volume with "The American Dream"
and "Fam and Yam"). Royalty $25. Restricted to amateur performances
before unsegregated audiences.

An excursion into grimly realistic social criticism; a re-creation of the
end of blues singer Bessie Smith in Memphis in 1937. She died after an
auto accident because hospitals reserved for whites refused to admit her.
Attention centers on the hospital receptionist, an intensely arrogant
daughter of the crumbling Southern aristocracy.

————. *The Sandbox*. (1960) Bare stage, minimum of props. 3m. 2w.
Dramatists Play Service $1.75 (in volume with "The Zoo Story").
Royalty $15. Restricted to amateur performances before unsegregated
audiences.

A look at contemporary life from an absurd point of view. While a man
in swimming trunks exercises on the beach, a couple arrives carrying the
woman's aging mother and dumps her in a sandbox. A clarinetist plays
on stage as the old woman recounts her history, covering herself with
sand in order to die. The athlete turns out to have a relationship to
her after all.

Alvarez Quintero, Serafín, and Alvarez Quintero, Joaquín. *A Sunny
Morning*. (1905) Translated by Lucretia Xavier Floyd. Comedy. 15
minutes. Simple exterior. Modern or early 20th century Spanish costumes. 2m. 2w. Baker $.85. French $.85. Royalty $10.

An aged couple meet on a bench in a public park and fall into conversation, only to discover that years before they had been in love. For a
moment the passions of youth become a flame rekindled. A tender
comedy of subdued irony.

Apstein, Theodore. *Wetback Run*. (1960) Drama. 2 exteriors, 1 interior.

15m. 1w. In *Eight American Ethnic Plays,* ed. by Francis Griffith and Joseph Mersand. Royalty to author.

Homesick for his family in Mexico and tired of evading United States immigration authorities, Jacinto Sandoval surrenders to the border police. The racketeer Torres, to whom Jacinto has been paying protection money, does not understand this action, but Ramirez, the sympathetic grower, does. To him Jacinto is a "man who holds his head up." For all groups. Ethnic interest: Mexican-American.

Atkinson, M. E. *Can the Leopard?* Farce-comedy. 30 minutes. Interior. Modern costumes. 6w. Baker $.85. Royalty $5.

To make their up-to-date niece feel at home, Minnie and Georgina exchange their sober attire for gaily colored playsuits and practice the arts of makeup and cigarette smoking. The niece, in order to make her aunts feel at ease, has changed into a demure Quaker gown and eliminated all makeup.

Baker, George M. *The Christmas Carol.* Based on the story by Charles Dickens. Comedy. 40 minutes. Interior. 19th century English costumes. 6m. 3w. 2 children. Baker $.85. No royalty.

The well-known story of the little cripple, Tiny Tim, and the conversion of hard-hearted Scrooge. Simply staged; may be arranged with music and tableaus.

Barrie, James M. *The Old Lady Shows Her Medals.* (1917) Interior. Costumes of 1914–1918. 2m. 4w. Baker $.85. French $.85. Royalty $10.

Mrs. Dowey is entertaining three other charwomen at tea. They are all proud of their sons in the army, but Mrs. Dowey has no son and so "adopts" from the newspaper a Kenneth Dowey, private in the army, and mothers him while he is on leave. She becomes highly attached to him. He doesn't return.

————. *Seven Women.* (1917) Comedy. 30 minutes. Interior. Modern and Navy costumes. 2m. 3w. French $.85. Royalty $10.

Captain Rattray, a bachelor, is told by his host that there will be seven women as guests for dinner. Rattray is pleased and thinks he will be in his glory, but the first woman to arrive baffles him completely. He can't seem to classify her, and soon he is completely taken by her charms. Then he learns that she is the only other guest; she is all seven women in one.

————. *Shall We Join the Ladies?* (1921) Mystery. 30 minutes. Interior. Modern costumes. 8m. 8w. Baker $.85. French $.85. Royalty $10.

Thirteen well-to-do people attend a dinner party at which their host unmasks them and implicates them in the murder of his brother at Monte

Carlo several years before. He is cool, patient, and witty as they stumble
into the traps he has carefully laid in his speech.

————. *The Twelve-Pound Look.* (1910) Comedy. 30 minutes. Interior. Modern costumes. 2m. 2w. Baker $.85. French $.85. Royalty
$10.
The typist whom Sir Harry Simms hires to answer congratulatory
messages on his knighthood turns out to be his former wife Kate. Oppressed by his grandeur and pettiness, she had learned to type, leaving
him when she had earned £12, the price of a typewriter. Her fearless-
ness and humor contrast with the cowed and joyless Lady Simms who,
when Kate has left, asks how much a typewriter costs.

————. *The Will.* (1913) Comedy in 3 scenes. 35 minutes. Interior.
1915 and modern costumes. 6m. 1w. French $.85. Royalty $10.
Mr. and Mrs. Ross, poor newlyweds, arrive at the law office to make
their tiny bequests. In later years, Mr. Ross the magnate disagrees with
his imperious wife over changes in the new will. In the last scene, Sir
Philip Ross, wealthy but bereft of heirs, comes to the law office alone,
realizing too late what his greed has cost.

Beach, Lewis. *The Clod.* (1914) Drama. 40 minutes. Interior. Civil
War costumes. 4m. 1w. French $.85. Royalty $10.
An uneducated country woman, a "clod," refuses to take sides in the
Civil War. A Northern soldier seeks refuge in her household, and the
two Confederate soldiers hunting for him insult and threaten her until
she can endure their abuse no longer. In a dramatic outburst, .she ex-
plains her hatred of both sides. An actable thriller, but needs a capable
actress.

Beckett, Samuel. *Krapp's Last Tape.* (1958) Comedy. 1 hour. 1m.
French $1.95 (in *Krapp's Last Tape and Other Dramatic Pieces*).
Restricted. Royalty $20—$15.
The portrait of an aging man who lives a lonely and shabby existence
in a darkened room. At year's end he takes out a bottle of wine, a
banana, and his tape recorder, and listens as his own voice of times past
recounts the glories and hopes of his more youthful years.

Benét, Stephen Vincent. *The Devil and Daniel Webster.* Comedy.
Interior. 19th century New England costumes. 6m. (12 jurymen) 1w.
extras. Dramatists Play Service $.75. Royalty $15.
Daniel Webster, lawyer and orator extraordinaire, defends Jabez Stone,
who has sold his soul to the Devil. The Devil out-argues Webster, who,
realizing that the Devil can better him on technical grounds, appeals to
the ghostly jury and wins a verdict of not guilty.

Box, Muriel, and Box, Sydney. *Anti-Clockwise*. Drama. 30 minutes. Interior. Modern costumes. 4w. French $.85. Royalty $5.

A woman is found dead, and her niece is accused of murdering her for the money she would inherit. The doctor proves that she is innocent. However, a flashback reveals that the niece had tried to suffocate the aunt and had failed, and that the woman had died of a heart attack as a result of her rage.

Broughton, James. *The Last Word*. Drama. 25 minutes. Interior. 1m. 1w. Baker $.85. Royalty $10.

Rusty and Dusty Augenblick, a sophisticated couple in their middle years, wait in a bar for the bombs that will end the world at any moment. Confronting one another as persons for the first time, husband and wife find themselves in a desperate last-minute search for the meaning of their existence. Uses jokes, songs, litanies.

Campton, David. *Out of the Flying Pan*. Bare stage. 2m. Dramatists Play Service $1.75 (in volume with "Little Brother, Little Sister"). Royalty $15.

Two diplomats meet for a bout of outlandish doubletalk, which ends in their angrily tearing apart the treaty they have signed. Sirens wail, guns rattle; after a cosmic-size explosion and the ensuing silence, the two return, shake hands, and launch into another round of pretentious gibberish.

Carlino, Lewis John. *The Brick and the Rose*. (1959) Dramatic reading. No scenery. 7m. 3w. Dramatists Play Service $.95. Royalty $25.

A kaleidoscopic drama of the life of a young man of the slums. Tommy turns to narcotics to escape from the gnawing awareness of the meaninglessness around him. He meets Alice, the rose behind the hard brick city. He knows that he has only touched this beauty for an instant, that it is moving farther away from him. As a final escape from the squalor around him, he takes an overdose, ending his search.

————. *Epiphany*. (1963) Drama. Interior. 1m. 1w. Dramatists Play Service $1.75 (in volume with "Snowangel"). Royalty $25—$15.

A man has failed so miserably as a man that he decides to become a rooster. His domineering wife, a successful advertising executive, taunts him with memories of a homosexual incident in his past. Just as he begins his metamorphosis, perched on a roost from which he may rule, he lays an egg. The play ends as the wife tears off his coxcomb and accepts him as her "henny-penny."

————. *Junk Yard*. Interior. 4m. 1w. Dramatists Play Service $.75. Royalty $10.

Simon Peterson and his daughter, who run a junkyard, feel that a junkyard is a place where things come to keep from becoming junk, things that can be useful again. A wounded young man who has just attempted a holdup forces Simon at gunpoint to hide him from the police. Instantly Simon realizes the challenge: here is a most valuable piece of human junk! But the only thing that can save the man is the sort of love that only a woman—only Simon's daughter—can give.

————. *Objective Case.* Interior. 2m. 2w. Dramatists Play Service $1.75 (in volume with "Mr. Flannery's Ocean"). Royalty $15.
A man and woman, desperately and pathetically in love, each has a defect: he likes to pull his ear and scratch his teeth; she likes to blink her eyes and droop her lip. These defects become the focal points for their ambivalent feelings of hate. The play builds to a love scene in which, unable to bare themselves, they take refuge behind mannequins. When they can no longer stand each other and leave, the mannequins continue the love scene.

————. *Sarah and the Sax.* Drama. Exterior. 1m. 1w. Dramatists Play Service $1.75 (in volume with "High Sign"). Royalty $15.
A study of two completely dissimilar people. Sarah, a plump middle-aged Jewish woman, represents everything conventional and detestable in society to a hostile black saxophone player whom she meets by chance in a deserted park. Sarah talks on, and the man answers her by playing passages on his saxophone. When she reveals that all that she has told him are lies concealing her loneliness, he plays for her.

————. *Snowangel.* (1963) Drama. Interior. 1m. 1w. Dramatists Play Service $1.75 (in volume with "Epiphany"). Royalty $25—$15.
A study of a prostitute and her unsettling customer, who attempts to transform her into the girl he lost. The play probes beneath the apparent tawdriness of their encounter to illuminate the inner reaches of their desperate lives. In the end he realizes that to get he must give, that he cannot erase another human's identity to suit his own needs. Advanced cast needed.

Chekhov, Anton. *The Marriage Proposal.* Translated by Baukhage and Clark. Farce. 30 minutes. Interior. Modern or Russian costumes. 2m. 1w. Baker $.85. French $.85. No royalty.
A nervous and excitable man starts to propose to an attractive young woman, but gets into a tremendous quarrel over a boundary line. This popular farce is one of the funniest ever written.

Conkle, E. P. *Minnie Field.* (1928) Drama. 20 min. Interior. Modern costumes. 5m. French $.85. Royalty $5.
The life history in miniature of a poor Midwestern farm woman who lies dead in the next room. The best known of Conkle's "Crick Bottom Plays."

————. *Sparkin'*. (1928) Folk comedy. 25 minutes. Interior. Modern costumes. 1m. 3w. Baker $.85. French $.85. Royalty $5.

Orry, a timid young man, comes to a farm kitchen to woo Lillie, but his shyness almost defeats him. He is unable to come to the point but, after many hilarious episodes, Granny intercedes for him and teaches him how to be a man.

Coppée, François. *The Lord's Prayer*. Translated by Mary Aldis. Drama. 15 minutes. Interior. French Revolution costumes. 3m. 3w. soldiers. Baker $.85. Royalty $3.

Rose's brother, an abbé, was killed by a soldier. Thinking of her love for her brother, she shelters and saves a soldier who is being sought.

Cottman, H. Stuart, and Shaw, LeVergne. *Submerged*. Tragedy. 25 minutes. Interior. 6m. Baker $.85. French $.85. Royalty $5.

An officer and five men are trapped at the bottom of the ocean in a submarine, and one man must sacrifice his life to attract the notice of searching parties. The manner in which the choice is made and the events immediately following the selection create a tense and gripping drama.

Coward, Noel. *The Astonished Heart*. 40 minutes. Interior. 4m. 3w. French $.85. Royalty $15—$10.

Christian Faber lies on his deathbed; in the drawing room his weeping wife Barbara and his sad assistants await Leonora's arrival. Four successive flashbacks tell the story of Leonora's visit to Barbara, her capture of her friend's husband, her rejection of Christian because of his jealousy, and his jumping out the window. Leonora arrives and enters his room, returning shortly to announce that he has died. His last words were tender ones to his wife, for whom he mistook Leonora.

————. *Fumed Oak*. Comedy. 40 minutes. Interior. Modern costumes. 1m. 3w. Baker $.85. French $.85. Royalty $15—$10.

Through Henry Gow's fumed-oak drawing room passes most of the family life—his shrew wife, whining daughter, and complaining mother-in-law. But Henry is a changed man when he gets enough money and courage to escape, and he jauntily leaves them, slamming the door in their faces.

————. *Hands across the Sea*. Comedy. 40 minutes. Interior. Modern costumes. 6m. 3w. Baker $.85. French $.85. Royalty $15—$10.

A London social butterfly is so busy with social duties and tidbits of gossip that she gets two Far-Eastern friends mixed up with some other Far-Eastern friends. After the guests are stumbled over, spilled upon, and completely ignored, the mistake is discovered, and the whole affair is straightened out.

————. *Ways and Means.* Comedy. 40 minutes. Interior. Modern costumes. 5m. 4w. French $.85. Royalty $15—$10.

Heiress Stella Cartwright and her gambling husband Tony are broke; their prolonged stay at the fabulous Villa Zephyre is becoming embarrassing as debts pile up. When a chauffeur comes in the night to rob them, they have nothing worth stealing, but they reveal the location of another guest's winnings (which he steals), and they split the take. The chauffeur, in turn, robs them of their share, thus saving their honor.

Davies, Mary Carolyn. *The Slave with Two Faces.* (1918) Fantasy-allegory. 30 minutes. Exterior. Modern and fantastic costumes. 3m. 4w. French $.85. Royalty $5.

On either side of a path through a wood stand two girls, expecting to meet Life. Life has two faces, one girl tells us; he can appear either beautiful or ugly. Life is a slave who will do your bidding if you are not afraid, but who becomes a cruel tyrant to all who show fear. One of the girls becomes a slave to Life, the other becomes his master.

de la Torre, Lillian. *Good-Bye Miss Lizzie Borden.* Drama. 35 minutes. Interior. 19th century costumes. 4w. 1 girl. Baker $.85. Royalty $5.

A sinister play about the famous Borden murder case and what happened to Lizzie, tried and acquitted, and Emma, who testified in her defense and later disappeared. What made it impossible for these two sisters to look each other in the face? A thrilling one-acter.

De León, Nephtalí. *The Death of Ernesto Nerios.* (1972) Drama. 2 interiors, 1 exterior. Modern costumes. 2m. 2w. voices, extras. In *Five Plays,* by Nephtalí De León. Royalty to Trucha Publications.

The fictionalized account of the brutal murder of a young man by police in the streets of Lubbock, Texas, in 1971. Depicts the suddenness and the intensity with which injustice and misfortune pursue Chicanos in the barrio. Not for the squeamish. Ethnic interest: Mexican-American.

DiDonato, Pietro. *The Love of Annunziata.* (1941) Comedy-drama. Interior. 8m. 7w. In *Best One-Act Plays of 1941,* ed. by Margaret Mayorga. Royalty: contact Dodd, Mead & Co.

A short play, done in a light vein, based on the lives of the characters in DiDonato's *Christ in Concrete,* an autobiographical novel that recounts the story of Geremio, an Italian-American construction worker who is fatally injured one Good Friday by a collapsing building made unsafe by the greed of men. For all groups. Ethnic interest: Italian-American.

Dizenzo, Charles. *The Drapes Come.* Interior. 2w. Dramatists Play Service $.95. Royalty $15.

Absurdist in style, this play examines the relationship between a mother and her teenage daughter, with lightning changes in their personalities as first one character dominates and then the other. Barbara has some caustic comments to make while mother patiently awaits the arrival of the living room drapes, and mother berates daughter for not being more aggressive. The drapes do arrive, and with them the realization that alienation is made of such petty obsessions as these.

Down, Oliphant. *The Maker of Dreams.* Fantastic comedy. 45 minutes. Cottage room. Modern and Pierrot costumes. 2m. 1w. French $.85, vocal score $1.75. Royalty $8.

Pierrot is always seeking his ideal love. With the aid of Cupid, the Maker of Dreams, he finds her in Pierette, who has long loved him secretly but whose affection and care he had spurned for the flattery of young ladies who praised his songs. Requires lightness of presentation. Pierrot needs a good singing voice.

Duffield, Brainerd. *The Lottery.* Based on the story by Shirley Jackson. Drama. Exterior. 8m. 5w. extras. Dramatic Publishing Co. $.85. Royalty $20.

The play starts gaily as people assemble for the lottery. Which family will it be this time? Which member? Only gradually do we begin to suspect the nature of the lottery, the fate of the person chosen, and the reason for the event as the play builds swiftly to a climax.

Dunsany, Lord. *A Night at an Inn.* Melodrama. 30 minutes. Interior. Modern costumes. 8m. Baker $.85. French $.85. Royalty $10.

An Eastern idol visits retribution on a set of thieves who have stolen his ruby eye. Tense.

Eastman, Fred. *Bread.* Drama. 30 minutes. Interior. Modern costumes. 2m. 4w. Baker $.85. French $.85. Royalty $5.

A human play portraying the struggle of a modern farm family for economic independence and culture.

Eaton, Walter Prichard. *The Purple Doorknob.* Comedy. 25 minutes. Simple interior (bedroom). Modern costumes. 3w. French $.85. Royalty $5.

A charming young actress succeeds in getting an old, bedridden woman to sell her an antique by performing for her in her chamber and, to the old woman's great delight, by inducing her to play one of the characters.

Feiffer, Jules. *Crawling Arnold.* Comedy. Exterior. 2m. 3w. Dramatists Play Service $.95. Royalty $15.

A young man in his thirties has regressed to crawling on all fours in order to be more conspicuous, and this leads to a relationship with Miss Sympathy, a young psychiatric social worker, who finds him overpoweringly attractive. The play pokes fun both at the maladjustments of our times and the fumbling hopefulness with which we so often try to cope with them.

Field, Rachel. *Cinderella Married*. Comedy. 40 minutes. Interior. Fantastic costumes. 2m. 4w. French $.85. Royalty $5.
Cinderella and Prince Charming are now married, but the fact that Cinderella has outgrown her glass slippers is just the beginning of their domestic problems. Cinderella's renewed acquaintance with her old suitor, the milkman, her unhappiness with her spiteful ladies-in-waiting, and the manner in which the newlyweds solve the problems of living "happily ever after" make a humorous, stylized satire.

————. *The Fifteenth Candle*. Drama. 25 minutes. Interior (kitchen-dining-living room). Modern costumes. 2m. 3w. French $.85. Royalty $5.
An Italian immigrant girl battles her father's greed so that her younger sister may continue her training in art school. For all groups. Ethnic interest: Italian-American.

Flanagan, Hallie. *The Curtain*. Drama. 30 minutes. Interior. Modern costumes. 4m. 2w. French $.85. Royalty $5.
A fugitive from justice shows his daughter how, through a series of lies, he has wrecked his life. He makes her promise always to tell the truth. Her faith is tested when the police come to search for her father.

Fletcher, Lucille. *Sorry, Wrong Number*. Drama. 30 minutes. Interior. Modern costumes. 3m. 4w. extras, voices. Dramatists Play Service $1.75 (includes stage and radio play versions). Royalty $15.
A mystery thriller about a neurotic invalid whose only contact with the outside world is her telephone. Because of crossed wires, she hears plans for a murder, which turns out to be her own. A full character portrait of the woman emerges from her frantic efforts to enlist help and her growing terror. A star performance for a capable actress.

Foster, Paul. *The Hessian Corporal*. Drama. Small set pieces. 6m. 9w. O'Neill Memorial Theater Center.
A young soldier faces his first battle on Christmas night alone and afraid. He contemplates certain death and the irony that he has no idea what he is dying for.

France, Anatole. *The Man Who Married a Dumb Wife*. (1912) Translated by Curtis Page. Based on a passage from Rabelais. Farce in 2 acts. 75 minutes. Interior. Medieval French costumes. 7m. 3w. extras. Baker $1.50. French $1.50. Royalty $25.
A lawyer, Judge Leonard Botal, marries a young and charming wife who is dumb. After he has her cured by the learned doctors, he finds her constant chatter drives him mad. As a final resort, he permits

himself to be made deaf to correct his error. A famous farce, full of satire and humor.

Fry, Christopher. *The Boy with a Cart.* (1951) 1 hour. Pastoral setting. 7m. 6w. Baker $1.25. Royalty $20.
The story of Saint Cuthman is little known outside Sussex, but few legends have more charm, humanity, and humor mingled with deep religious truth. Written for the village of Coleman's Hatch, Sussex, but since played by various drama societies in England.

Gale, Zona. *The Neighbors.* (1914) Comedy. 1 hour. Interior. Modern costumes. 2m. 6w. Baker $.85. Royalty $10. French $.85. Royalty $5.
A friendless child is cared for by "The Neighbors" in a small town.

Gilford, C. B. *Guest for Breakfast.* Drama. 30 minutes. Interior. 2m. 1w. Baker $.85. Royalty $10.
The relationship between Eve and Jordan Ross has deteriorated into a state of latent hostility. Tempers flare at breakfast and their marriage is threatened. Into this domestic crisis comes gunman Chester Lacey, a fugitive killer from a prison break, armed and very dangerous. A significant comment on modern marriage as well as a taut suspense drama.

Giraudoux, Jean. *The Apollo of Bellac.* Adapted by Maurice Valency. Comedy. Interior. 9m. 3w. Baker $.85. French $.85. Royalty $25.
A shy girl comes for a job. She is ignored until a nondescript little man demonstrates that she can have her way with any man if she will compare him to the statue of the Apollo of Bellac (nonexistent). She begins hesitantly with the clerk, working up most successfully to the chairman of the board. The play is alive with wry observations of the comical attitudes that people assume in life.

Glaspell, Susan. *Trifles.* (1916) Drama. 40 minutes. Kitchen. Rural costumes. 3m. 2w. Baker $.85. Royalty $10.
The wife of a strangled farmer is under arrest on suspicion. While officers and neighbors are searching the old farmhouse for evidence, two women friends discover a slain canary and a broken cage, evidence of the husband's unremitting cruelty and clues by which the wife can be proven guilty. They do not reveal her secret. Good parts for two actresses. Very popular.

Glaspell, Susan, with Cook, George C. *Suppressed Desires.* (1914) Satire. 40 minutes. Interior. Modern costumes. 1m. 2w. Baker $.85. Royalty $10.
Henrietta's obsession with psychoanalysis leads to a weird interpretation of a dream, and nearly to a divorce before the absurdity is realized. An amusing and effective travesty on misapplied Freudian psychology.

Goodman, Kenneth Sawyer. *The Dust of the Road.* (1913) Drama. 25 minutes. Living room in farmhouse. Modern costumes. 3m. 1w. Baker $.85. French $.85. Royalty $10 with admission, $5 without.

A mysterious tramplike character who is wandering in expiation of a crime committed long ago prevents a farmer from selling his soul for "thirty pieces of silver." Especially suited for Christmas.

————. *The Game of Chess.* (1913) Melodrama. 25 minutes. Room in a palace. 19th century Russian costumes. 4m. Baker $.85. French $.85. Royalty $10 with admission, $5 without.

The aging but quick-witted governor of a Russian state tricks a would-be assassin as though he were an opponent in a game of chess, and so saves his own life.

Green, Paul. *The Last of the Lowries.* (1920) Tragedy. 30 minutes. Kitchen. Rural costumes (1874). 1m. 3w. French $.85. Royalty $5.

The patient mother of the Lowries (Croatan outlaws in the mountains of North Carolina), who has seen her husband and four sons killed by the sheriff, suffers the death of her youngest son, who kills himself to escape capture. Effective; not too difficult except for the dialect.

————. *The Lord's Will.* (1921) Tragedy. 30 minutes. Interior. Modern costumes. 1m. 2w. French $.85. Royalty $5.

A ruthless study of a traveling preacher who by his narrow-mindedness and bigoted conception of religion brings about a tragedy in his own household. For advanced amateurs.

————. *The Man Who Died at Twelve O'Clock.* (1925) Folk comedy. 30 minutes. Interior. Modern costumes. 2m. 1w. French $.85. Royalty $5.

A young couple dress up and make the woman's old guardian believe he has seen the devil. After this he is forced to give up the money he has been unjustly holding, allowing the young couple to get married.

Green, Paul, and Green, Erma. *Fixin's.* Drama. 30 minutes. Room in a cabin. Farm costumes. 2m. 1w. French $.85. Royalty $5.

A young farm woman, whose ambitious but hard and dull husband cannot understand her desire for a little of the beauty of life, for "fixin's," realizes the hopelessness of the situation and leaves him. For advanced amateurs.

Gregory, Lady. *The Rising of the Moon.* (1907) Comedy. 20 minutes. Exterior. Irish costumes. 4m. Baker $.85. French $.85. No royalty in U.S.; $5 in Canada.

A homeless individual, disguised as a ballad-singer, is running from the law when he falls in with a police sergeant who is on the lookout for him. The individual gains the other man's sympathies to such an extent that he is assisted in escaping from the law, in spite of the £100 reward for his detection.

————. *Spreading the News.* (1904) Comedy. 30 minutes. Exterior. Irish peasant costumes. 7m. 3w. Baker $.85. French $.85. No royalty in U.S.; $5 in Canada.
Two men have an argument at the outskirts of a fair. When it is noticed that one of them is missing and that the other followed him with a hayfork, the story grows into one of murder and infidelity. When the "murdered" man appears, the gossips are confounded.

Guare, John. *Muzeeka.* (1967) Unit set. 5m. (3 are stagehands) 2w. Dramatists Play Service $.95. Royalty $25.
About a middle-class man who has "made" Muzeeka, a piped-in-music company that inflicts its bland music on all America, and who tries to assuage his conscience through hypocritical verbiage. Combines humor, social comment, and unique theatricality in its satirical depiction of a modern Everyman exterminated by the very system to which he sells out.

Hackett, Walter. *Air Tight Alibi.* Thriller. Interior. 2m. 1w. 3 extras. Baker $.85. Royalty $5.
Abby Cosgrove lives a miserable life on a remote New England farm. On a lonely winter night Abby murders her husband. Her alibi is perfect. As Abby is about to take leave of her lifeless husband, she is confronted by an intruder. The audience not only participates in the play but is one jump ahead of the cast—a surprise to both.

Hall, Holworthy, and Middlemass, Robert. *The Valiant.* Drama. 25 minutes. Interior. Modern costumes. 5m. 1w. Baker $1.25. David McKay $1.25. Royalty $15.
A young murderer conceals his identity, even from his long-unseen sister who has come to see if he is her brother, and goes bravely to his death, allowing his family to think he died nobly in France.

Halman, Doris F. *Will o' the Wisp.* Fantasy. 30 minutes. Kitchen. 4w. Baker $.85. Royalty $5.
A waif is befriended by a country woman who used to house a poet in the summer. The poet's wife, a worldly woman, comes for a stay. When she reveals that she has prevented her husband from writing, the waif leads her to her death in the sea.

Hamlin, Mary P. *He Came Seeing.* Biblical drama. 40 minutes. Interior. Biblical costumes. 3m. 2w. French $.85. Royalty $5.
After a young man comes under the personal influence of Christ, he casts off his earlier belief in order to embrace Christianity.

Hanley, William. *Mrs. Dally Has a Lover.* Interior. 1m. 1w. Dramatists
Play Service $1.75 (in volume with "Whisper into My Good Ear")
Royalty $25—$15. Restricted to amateur performances before unseg-
regated audiences.
A portrait of a woman in love, knowing that her love cannot last.
Married to a man she despises, Mrs. Dally carries on an affair with the
neighbor's teenage son. Her attempts to instill love for the sake of beauty
are a sensitive blend of humor and pathos. Not sordid.

Harrity, Richard. *Home Life of a Buffalo.* Comedy. Interior. 3m. 2w.
Dramatists Play Service $1.75 (in volume with "Hope Is the Thing
with Feathers" and "Gone Tomorrow"). Royalty $5.
Eddie, his wife, and young son Joey are a vaudeville team who have
reached what looks like the end of their futile career. At last, realizing
that the future holds nothing for them, Eddie prepares an elaborate
suicide by turning on the gas. While making plans for this last exit,
he gets a marvelous inspiration for a new act. He wakes his wife and
son, and the three go into a mad rehearsal, ready to face the future with
confidence.

————. *Hope Is the Thing with Feathers.* Comedy. Exterior. 9m.
Dramatists Play Service $1.75 (in volume with "Home Life of a Buffalo"
and "Gone Tomorrow"). Royalty $5.
The plot revolves about the ridiculous and tragic efforts of a group of
tramps and other down-and-outs to catch a duck on a lake in Central
Park and cook it. The efforts which the various derelicts make to
achieve their petty ends are presented in masterly comic fashion. Beneath the external contrast between the misfits and the ridiculous game
they pursue runs a savage and ironic commentary on mankind.

Hartman, Jan. *Flatboatman.* Unit set. 6m. 2w. 1 boy. Many bits for
men and women. Dramatists Play Service $.95. Royalty $15.
Details the New Salem years of young Abe Lincoln, the crucial years
which transformed him from a raw-boned riverboatman into a forceful
statesman. Portrays his romance with Ann Rutledge, her death, his
unsuccessful first candidacy for the state legislature, and his final victory.

Hayes, Joseph. *Christmas at Home.* Sentimental domestic comedy. 30
minutes. Interior. Modern costumes. 3m. 4w. Baker $.85. French $.85.
Royalty $5.
This is the first year the Burgess family will not be together for Christmas. Johnny is in Chicago and Grandpa died the preceding summer.
But the Burgesses do not feel sorry for themselves. We see sixteen-year-
old Julie falling in love for the first time, eighteen-year-old Emily re-
ceiving a proposal of marriage, twelve-year-old Janet learning the real
meaning of Christmas, and behind it all, the real Christmas spirit.

Helburn, Theresa. *Enter the Hero.* Comedy. 40 minutes. Living room. Modern costumes. 1m. 3w. French $.85. Royalty $10.

A sentimental girl invents a romance between herself and a boy who has been away for several years. When he returns, he has difficulty in extricating himself.

Horovitz, Israel. *The Indian Wants the Bronx.* (1968) 70 minutes. Open stage with props. 3m. Dramatists Play Service $.95. Royalty $25—$15.

A study of the mindless cruelty of two teenage toughs toward an East Indian man who cannot speak English and who they find waiting at a lonely bus stop. The play brings a shocking awareness of how close beneath the surface lurks the primitive impulse to hurt those who are helpless.

————. *It's Called the Sugar Plum.* (1968) 1 hour. Abstracted interior. 1m. 1w. Dramatists Play Service $.95. Royalty $25—$15.

Details the progressively more cordial relationship which develops between a college girl, whose fiancé has been accidently run down and killed, and the young man who was driving the car and whom she visits to confront with his guilt. The chilling speed with which their instinctive self-concern replaces the grief of one and the guilt of the other is both amusing and disturbing.

————. *Morning.* (1968) Part one of *Morning, Noon, and Night,* a trilogy of one-act plays; part two by Terrence McNally, part three by Leonard Melfi. 80 minutes. Abstract set (door frame, window frame, oversize bed). 3m. 2w. French $1.75 (in volume). Royalty $20—$10.

A fantasy in which we meet a black family the morning after they have taken the pill that will make them white. An irate white father enters looking for the black boy who got his daughter with child. But there are no black folks in the house, and the white father turns out to be "basic black" himself. For adult audiences only.

Houghton, Stanley. *The Dear Departed.* Based on a story by Guy de Maupassant. Satirical comedy. 30 minutes. Interior. Modern costumes. 3m. 3w. Baker $.85. French $.85. Royalty $5.

A family meets at the death of the grandfather and proceeds to divide up his few possessions. But the man has only pretended to be dead in order to see what his family thinks about him, and appears on the scene.

Hughes, Babette. *If the Shoe Pinches.* (1937) Comedy. Interior. Modern costumes. 4w. Dramatists Play Service, manuscript only. Royalty $5.

Mrs. Pell, a silly divorcée, is trying on various pairs of shoes for size. Her sister Laura, a businesswoman, is more sensible. Complications that cause a postponement of their contemplated European trip may lead to the marriage of Mrs. Pell and the shoe salesman.

Hughes, Glenn. *Red Carnations*. Comedy. 25 minutes. Exterior (bench in park). Modern costumes. 2m. 1w. Baker $.85. French $.85. Royalty $5.

She had met "him" at a masked ball, where they had arranged to meet again in the park, he wearing an identifying red carnation. Her father comes to chaperone, also wearing a red carnation. The ensuing complications end happily. Simple and entertaining.

Ionesco, Eugene. *The Chairs*. Translated by Donald M. Allen. Comedy. Interior. 2m. 1w. extras. Baker $1.95. French $1.95 (in *Four Plays*, by Eugene Ionesco). Royalty $15—$10.

Ionesco has defined its basic preoccupation: "The subject of the play is not the message, not the failure of life, not the moral disaster of the two old people, but the chairs themselves; that is to say, the absence of people, the absence of the emperor, the absence of God, the absence of matter, the unreality of the world, metaphysical emptiness. The theme of the play is nothingness. . . ." A challenging play for advanced amateurs.

———. *The Lesson*. Translated by Donald M. Allen. Comedy. Interior. 1m. 2w. Baker $1.95. French $1.95 (in *Four Plays*, by Eugene Ionesco). Royalty $15—$10.

This play concerns an elderly professor and his young female student. The professor undertakes to give a lesson to his pupil, and this must certainly be the most remarkable and bizarre lesson in the history of pedagogy. It ends with the professor murdering the pupil.

Jacobs, W. W., and Parker, Louis N. *The Monkey's Paw*. Based on the story by W. W. Jacobs. Melodrama. 40 minutes. Interior. Modern costumes. 4m. 1w. Baker $.85. French $.85. Royalty $10.

The Whites are given a monkey's paw, said to confer three wishes on its possessor. Mr. White wishes for £200, and news arrives that his son has been killed at work; his employer is sending £200. He wishes that his son may be returned to life, and there is a knock at the door. While the distraught mother tries to open the door, White asks that his son be returned to his grave. The door is opened, but no one is there. A suspenseful thriller.

Julian, Joseph. *Ups and Downs and Evens*. (1966) Comedy. Interior. 1m. 1w. O'Neill Memorial Theater Center.

A famous middle-aged artist, tormented by failing creativity, brings a pretty young girl to his studio intending to seduce her, hoping to renew himself with her innocence. The girl, who consumes large amounts of tranquilizers, tries to convince him to do the same, but he rejects the pills. She slips some in his drink, and the seducer is seduced. Or is he?

Kass, Jerome. *Make like a Dog.* Interior. 1m. 1w. Dramatists Play Service $1.75 (in volume). Royalty $15. Restricted to amateur performances before unsegregated audiences.

Whimsical and bizarre in mood, this play deals with a childless suburban couple who take turns making believe they are the dog which the husband wants but which the wife won't allow in their compulsively clean house. Behind their antics are hints of resentments and frustrations and threats of ugliness and disorder, so the game is abandoned for their former, normal behavior, where boredom leads only to talk.

————. *Princess Rebecca Birnbaum.* Interior. 1m. 4w. Dramatists Play Service $1.75 (in volume). Royalty $15. Restricted to amateur performances before unsegrated audiences.

The plight of a young girl about to attend her first prom. Though Rebecca wishes to dress simply, deploring elaborate makeup, her mother, sister, and piano teacher insist on makeup, colored sash, artificial flowers, wig, and mink stole. When her escort arrives, it appears he has suffered the same ordeal—pink tuxedo jacket, plaid cummerbund, patent leather shoes, and red roses sprayed white for the occasion.

Kaufman, George S. *If Men Played Cards as Women Do.* Satirical comedy. 30 minutes. Interior. Modern costumes. 4m. Baker $.85. French $.85. Royalty $5.

A group of men around a bridge table speak, behave, and think after the manner in which women are supposed to conduct their game.

————. *The Still Alarm.* (1930) Satirical comedy. 15 minutes. Interior. Modern and firemen costumes. 5m. Baker $.85. French $.85. Royalty $5.

When a fire breaks out in the hotel, two actors are trapped in their room. They ignore it in the best drawing-room manner and go placidly about their work. Two firemen enter, one with a violin case. The musical firefighter cannot find any time to practice and so takes this opportunity. While the hotel burns, he calmly goes into "Keep the Home Fires Burning."

Kelly, George. *Finders Keepers.* Comedy. 40 minutes. Living room. Modern costumes. 1m. 2w. Baker $.85. French $.85. Royalty $10.

A woman who has found a purse containing $400 makes little effort to trace the owner, but she reacts in a different manner when she finds out it has been stolen from her, and has cost her the respect of her husband. Effective and interesting; not difficult.

————. *The Flattering Word.* Satiric comedy. 30 minutes. Living room. Modern costumes. 2m. 3w. Baker $.85. French $.85. Royalty $10.

A famous actor would like a friend to see his performance in a play, but his friend is convinced that her pompous husband, a pastor, would never consent to take her. The actor succeeds in breaking down the man's prejudice against the stage by flattering him into thinking he can act. For advanced amateurs.

————. *Poor Aubrey.* Comedy. 30 minutes. Sitting room. Modern costumes. 1m. 3w. Baker $.85. French $.85. Royalty $10.

When Amy Piper receives a visit from an old girlfriend, her husband, Aubrey, tries desperately to impress the visitor. This is his usual vein. He tells impressive tales of his wealth, his home, his car, only to have his mother-in-law burst his balloon in comic fashion. The friend compliments his masculine beauty, but not until she has gone does he realize that he has lost his toupee during the conversation. Needs capable actor.

————. *The Weak Spot.* Satirical comedy. 25 minutes. Interior. Modern costumes. 1m. 2w. French $.85. Royalty $10.

As a husband and wife are quarreling, she spills salt and predicts bad news. He laughs it off. When a peddlar woman tells the wife's fortune, she predicts news of the husband's death from heart trouble. A message comes from the hospital saying that a friend who borrowed Mr. West's raincoat has died. Mr. West is won over to superstition, and when he spills the salt, he dashes it over his left shoulder.

Kennedy, Charles Rann. *The Terrible Meek.* (1912) Religious drama. 50 minutes. Exterior. Roman and Oriental costumes. Played in darkness. 2m. 1w. Baker $.85. French $.85. No royalty.

The effect of the Crucifixion on a Roman captain, a soldier, and an unknown woman.

Kirkpatrick, John. *The Castle of Mr. Simpson.* Farce. 30 minutes. Interior. Modern costumes. 4m. 4w. French $.85. Royalty $5.

A man's home is his castle, and Lil undertakes to have her father spend a quiet evening at home, making elaborate plans to get rid of her sister's boyfriends. Then she discovers a boyfriend for herself.

————. *Married at Sunrise.* Comedy. 35 minutes. Interior. Modern costumes. 2m. 4w. French $.85. Royalty $5.

A young soldier and his sweetheart decide to get married at dawn after he lies and tells her that his leave has been cancelled. She awakens her family at 2 a.m. to tell them the news, which is met with considerable apprehension and excitement. The young man confesses his lie, but in the meantime his furlough *is* cancelled.

————. *Sleeping Dogs.* (1940) Comedy. 30 minutes. Interior. Modern costumes. 2m. 3w. French $.85. Royalty $5.

When a magazine editor takes a nationwide poll on the question, "Are you happy with your husband?" she gets into trouble with her next-door neighbors.

————. *The Strangest Feeling.* (1942) Comedy. 35 minutes. Interior. Modern costumes. 2m. 4w. French $.85. Royalty $5.
Ethel can't quite explain to Father why she doesn't want to go to the lecture with Johnny, and there is a great deal said about "intuition." So Johnny takes little sister Naomi instead. But Johnny meets an old flame, a dancing teacher, who wants to take Naomi as a pupil, and Johnny invests $1000 in the dancing school and becomes business manager. Little sister, using her intuition, finds her way out of a dilemma.

————. *The Tea-Pot on the Rocks.* Comedy. 40 minutes. Interior. Modern costumes. 3m. 3w. French $.85. Royalty $5.
A young woman puts her career of running a tearoom ahead of marriage, thus making her boyfriend hope and pray for the tearoom to fail. He has his chance to make it fail, but his good sportsmanship saves the day.

————. *A Wedding.* Comedy. 35 minutes. Interior. Modern costumes. 4m. 3w. Baker $.85. French $.85. Royalty $5.
While the bridegroom is looking for his collar button, the best man complains because the bride's aunt is trying to run things. Mishaps and misunderstandings occur and almost ruin the wedding, but the bride and groom are reconciled in time.

Larkin, Margaret. *El Cristo.* (1926) Drama. 20 minutes. Interior. Mexican costumes. 4m. 2w. French $.85. Royalty $10.
A colorful drama about a universal human struggle. The scene is the Mexican border, and the action has to do with the strange and interesting customs of a secret religious sect. For advanced amateurs.

Latham, Jean Lee. *Gray Bread.* Drama. 25 minutes. Interior of peasant cottage. Modern costumes. 4w. Baker $.85. French $.85. Royalty $5.
An old wise woman imparts some of her wisdom about living to one of her daughters. Out of years of experience she tells things as they happened before, as they will happen again. In three generations of women we see the choices they have made.

Logan, John. *Of Poems, Youth, and Spring.* Comedy in 4 scenes. No scenery. 1m. 1w. 3 voices, 4 chorus members. Baker $.85. French $.85. Royalty $5.
The play's four scenes correspond with the seasons of the year, and each season represents a stage in the first romance of a boy and girl in high school. Each season is introduced by two small choruses which, in a mood of light humor and fantasy, tease, scold, and provide contrast to the light drama of the romance. They also act incidental roles in the story and perform stagehand duties.

MacLeish, Archibald. *The Fall of the City*. (1937) Poetic drama. Exterior. 7m. 1w. chorus of voices. Dramatists Play Service $1.75 (in *Three Short Plays*, by Archibald MacLeish) . Royalty $5.

A poetic drama, originally written for radio, depicting the terror of the inhabitants of a city expecting an invading dictator momentarily. An exacting mood piece.

Maher, Ramona. *When the Fire Dies*. Morality play. Interior. 1m. 4w. Baker $.85. French $.85. Royalty $5.

An educated young Indian girl returning home from a government school has trouble adapting to traditional customs. Initially critical of her parents' ways, she refuses to accompany her parents to the deathbed ceremony for an old brave. An ancient Indian woman helps her to understand her mission: to lead her people out of confusion and mis-understanding, not to change their ways. For all groups. Ethnic interest: American Indian.

Mankowitz, Wolf. *It Should Happen to a Dog*. Based on the Book of Jonah. Religious comedy. 2m. Baker $1.75, French $1.75 (in *Five One-Act Plays,* by Wolf Mankowitz) . Royalty $10. Not available in Canada.

A humorous change-of-pace story about Jonah, who is put out at the Lord for ordering him to sea to deliver a jeremiad. Jonah's sacrifice to the Lord is tossed back by the sea, and Jonah himself tossed in. Jonah is a very human, unsaintly character who just can't get used to the devious ways of the Lord.

Martens, Anne Coulter. *Patterns*. Based on the poem by Amy Lowell. 2m. 2w. Dramatic Publishing Co. $.85. Royalty $10.

Up and down the patterned garden paths walks the lovely Lady Isabel, waiting for her lover to return from the wars. With her powdered hair and jeweled fan, Lady Isabel herself makes a pattern of beauty. Even now a rider may be on his way to bring her word, but as she tells all this to pretty young Dulcie, a cold finger of fear touches her heart. When the messenger comes, she scarcely needs to ask.

May, Elaine. *Adaptation*. Comedy. Open stage with lectern. 3m. 1w. Dramatists Play Service $.95. Royalty $25.

A funny and satiric play which examines and dissects the shortcomings of modern society. A man is a contestant in a television game show, a contest in which the players advance or are set back through the seven ages of man, from "mewling infant" to "second childness and mere oblivion." An incisive parody for advanced actors.

McNeely, Jerry. *The Staring Match*. Comedy-fantasy. Unit set. 6m. 2w. 1 girl, extras. Dramatists Play Service $.95. Royalty $25.

Suffering from drought, the community holds a large meeting to pray for rain. There is a knock on the door and in comes a man dressed completely in white, who greets them all by name. Can Mr. White be an angel of the Lord? The townspeople are convinced. A second man enters, dressed completely in black, who announces that he too has been sent to help the community. It's quite apparent that only one of these two is an angel, and to solve the dilemma a "staring match" is decided upon, with Mr. White and Mr. Black as contestants. The real angel is revealed, and water is discovered. Ideal for all groups.

Medcraft, Russell. *The First Dress Suit.* Comedy. 30 minutes. Interior. Modern costumes. 2m. 2w. Baker $.85. French $.85. Royalty $10.
The trials and tribulations of a young man ordering and wearing his first dress suit.

Millay, Edna St. Vincent. *Aria da Capo.* Poetic fantasy. 30 minutes. Interior. 4m. 1w. Baker $.85. French $.85. Royalty $15.
Under the prompting of Cothurnus, the muse of tragedy, two shepherds interrupt a harlequinade, innocently kill each other, and are again superseded by the harlequin. Requires skillful setting, directing, and acting.

————. *The Princess Marries the Page.* (1932) Music by Deems Taylor. Verse play. 40 minutes. Interior (tower room). Imaginative costumes. 6m. 1w. Baker $.85. Royalty $10.
A princess sits in her tower; suddenly a young page breaks in on her privacy. There follows a war of words, accompanied by soft looks. An alarm is sounded. Soldiers march to the tower. The page is not a page at all, but the son of a neighboring ruler.

Milne, A. A. *The Man in the Bowler Hat.* (1923) Burlesque melodrama. 30 minutes. Living room. Modern costumes. 4m. 2w. Baker $.85. French $.85. Royalty $10.
John and Mary find themselves in the midst of an exciting adventure with thieves and detectives while the "man in the bowler hat" sits quietly in the corner. It turns out that he is the stage manager, and the whole thing is a rehearsal. Good travesty, easy to play.

————. *The Ugly Duckling.* Comedy. 30 minutes. Interior. Costumes variable. 4m. 3w. Baker $.85. French $.85. Royalty $5.
Arrangements have been made for the marriage of Prince Simon and Princess Camilla. Because the latter is plain, the King and Queen decide to have a beautiful maid impersonate her. Hearing of the princess's great beauty, Simon decides he is too plain for her, and so has handsome Carlo, his man, impersonate him. Simon and Camilla meet by chance and fall in love. Each looks quite beautiful to the other, and they live happily ever after.

Monkhouse, Allan. *The Grand Cham's Diamond.* Comedy-mystery. 30

minutes. Simple interior. Modern costumes. 3m. 2w. Baker $.85. Royalty $5.

Mrs. Perkins' humdrum existence promises to be broken when a diamond comes hurtling through her window, and she romantically plans a trip to South America. However, she reluctantly yields to honesty and to her prospective son-in-law.

Mosel, Tad. *Impromptu.* Interior. 2m. 2w. Dramatists Play Service $.75. Royalty $15.

Four actors sit on a darkened stage, awaiting the arrival of the stage manager. Their own personalities seem unformed and shallow next to the full-blooded figures they are used to playing. Suddenly aware of the audience, they decide to improvise. Ernest, the "leading man," assumes command, assigning roles to himself and his colleagues. The "drama" that unfolds brings an awareness of the real people behind their theatrical facades.

Motter, Vail. *The Birthday of the Infanta.* Dramatization of the story by Oscar Wilde. 35 minutes. Palace room overlooking a garden. 6m. 2w. David McKay $1.50. Royalty $10.

The birthday surprise that most pleases the Infanta of Spain is a little hunchback who comes to dance for her. The princess throws the dwarf a rose, and he falls in love with her. By chance he sees himself in a palace mirror, realizes that it is his ugliness that has amused people, and dies of a broken heart. The finest dramatization of a favorite story.

Niggli, Josephina. *Sunday Costs Five Pesos.* Comedy. 30 minutes. Exterior. Mexican costumes. 1m. 4w. Baker $.85. French $.85. Royalty $5.

A young girl, through jealousy, breaks off her engagement. Repentant, she tries to win back her man with the aid of some well-meaning friends, who only manage to involve her in further difficulties.

Nusbaum, N. Richard. *So Wonderful (in White).* Drama. 25 minutes. Hospital interior. Hospital costumes. 9w. Baker $.85. French $.85. Royalty $5.

Margaret Shipman, a nurse in training, brings bright hope and idealism to her calling. The necessity of sacrificing personal love, the rigidity and mercilessness of her superintendent, the tragedy of suicide, the loneliness of a narcotic addict—all begin to cloud her idealism. But there emerges new clarity, new hope.

O'Neill, Eugene. *Before Breakfast.* (1916) Drama. Interior. 1w. Dramatists Play Service $1.95 (in volume). Royalty $10.

A woman, while preparing breakfast for her husband, complains of her struggles to make ends meet. The husband, once considered a desirable catch, has steadily degenerated until he is no longer good for anything. When his wife has said everything hateful and bitter that is in her, she subsides into silence. A moment later we know that the desperate man in the next room has just cut his throat. A monologue for an experienced actress.

————. *Bound East for Cardiff.* (1914) Drama. 25 minutes. Interior. 11m. Dramatists Play Service $1.95 (in volume). Royalty $10.
Yank and Driscoll, two rough sailors, make plans on their homeward voyage to leave the sea and settle down on a farm. While the other sailors exchange yarns and reminiscences, Yank, who is very ill, quietly rambles on, wishing he had never gone to sea. Then he dies. A fine ironic play for advanced amateurs.

————. *The Dreamy Kid.* (1918) Drama. Interior. Modern costumes of the South. 1m. 3w. Dramatists Play Service $1.95 (in volume). Royalty $10.
A murderer, pursued by the police, goes to see his dying mother and is captured.

————. *'Ile.* (1917) Tragedy. 25 minutes. Cabin of a ship. 5m. 1w. Dramatists Play Service $1.95 (in volume). Royalty $10.
Captain Keeney, a New England whaler, has only a small part of his quota at the end of the two-year period his crew have signed up for. The crew are mutinous, and his wife, driven almost mad by her loneliness, persuades her husband to start home without "'ile." But a whale is sighted and he breaks his promise, determined not to go home until he is successful. This drives her to madness. A strong play with difficult roles.

————. *In the Zone.* (1917) Drama. Interior. Sailor costumes. 9m. Dramatists Play Service $1.95 (in volume). Royalty $10.
Smitty, a sailor, is behaving suspiciously, and the others believe he is a spy. They lash him to his bunk, force open the box he had been safeguarding, and read aloud the letters inside. They are love letters from a girl who had broken her engagement to Smitty because of his dissipated habits, forcing him to go to sea. The sailors are ashamed and release Smitty.

————. *The Long Voyage Home.* (1912) Drama. Interior. Sailor costumes. 6m. 3w. 2 extra m. Dramatists Play Service $1.95 (in volume). Royalty $10.
A group of sailors on shore leave carouse in a waterfront dive. The crew have just been paid off, but Olson, who has always squandered his savings, refuses to drink in order to be able to go home. Induced to take a soft drink—which is drugged—he is robbed and put on a ship bound on a long voyage. A fine ironic play.

————. *The Moon of the Caribbees*. (1919) Drama. Ship's deck. Sailor costumes. 17m. 4w. Dramatists Play Service $1.95 (in volume). Royalty $10.

A dramatic episode in the life of a group of sailors as their ship docks in a Caribbean port. The harbor women bring their wares on board, smuggling liquor so that the men may have a party.

————. *Where the Cross Is Made*. (1918) Drama. 40 minutes. Interior. Modern costumes. 6m. 1w. Dramatists Play Service $1.95 (in volume). Royalty $10.

An old sea captain, who years before committed a crime in connection with a treasure hunt, is seen going mad when shadows from the past come to haunt him.

Parker, Louis N. *A Minuet*. Verse drama. 25 minutes. Gaoler's living room. Costumes of French Revolution. 2m. 1w. Baker $.85. French $.85. Royalty $10.

A marquis and marquise, long separated and estranged, meet in prison on the eve of their executions. Reunited, they go bravely out together to the guillotine.

Pertwee, Roland. *Evening Dress Indispensable*. Comedy. 25 minutes. Interior. Modern costumes. 2m. 3w. French $.85. Royalty $10.

A faithful suitor calls one evening, but Sheila is rude. Her mother, however, tells the caller that if Sheila will not go out with him, she will. The young man's enthusiasm arouses jealousy in Sheila, who disappears to discard her arty, mod clothes and put on her prettiest dress, and together they go out. Mother is left home with her own friend, who hopes to be her second husband.

Pillot, Eugene. *Two Crooks and a Lady*. Melodrama. 30 minutes. Interior. Modern costumes. 3m. 3w. French $.85. Royalty $10.

A crippled old lady, unable to move from her chair, outwits two crooks, one of whom is her maid, and saves her pearls.

Pinero, Arthur Wing. *Playgoers*. (1913) Satirical comedy. 25 minutes. Interior. Modern costumes. 2m. 6w. French $.85. Royalty $5.

The young mistress of a London household decides to favor her servants with a visit to the theater. The maid insists on a seat for her fiancé, while the cook stipulates that her nephew be accommodated. Which play to select proves the insurmountable obstacle, and the dispute that ensues results in all the domestics giving notice.

Pinter, Harold. *The Collection*. (1961) Divided interior. 3m. 1w. Dramatists Play Service $1.95. Royalty $25—$15.

Harry and Bill receive an anonymous phone call, followed by a visit from a young man. The visitor is James, whose wife has confessed a one-night affair with Bill and who is obsessed with a desire to meet the man who has cuckolded him. When he does, a weird attraction-repulsion arises between the two young men. Harry discovers what is going on and, casting doubt on whether the affair ever took place, reestablishes an uneasy status quo.

————. *The Dumb Waiter.* (1960) Interior. 2m. Dramatists Play Service $1.75. Royalty $25—$15.

Two hired killers nervously await their next assignment in the basement of a long-abandoned restaurant. Barred from daylight and public contact by the nature of their work, they expend their waiting time in bickering. Ben rereads a newspaper and exclaims in disbelief over the news items. Gus fusses with the stove and plumbing off-stage. Ben bludgeons Gus into silence if he as much as mentions their work. Gus worries that someone has slept in his bed. When the ancient dumb-waiter comes to life, the suspense becomes almost unbearable.

————. *The Dwarfs.* (1960) Divided interior. 3m. Dramatists Play Service $1.75 (in volume). Royalty $25—$15.

The play concerns three young men—Len, Pete, and Mark. Sometimes all three come together, sometimes only two, and often Len is on stage alone. Conversations and soliloquies are filled with brilliant convolutions of thoughts and range in mood from calm introspection to explosive outpouring. There emerges a sense of horror and alienation, of our impenetrable insularity, our aloneness. Requires an advanced cast.

————. *The Lover.* (1963) Interior. 2m. 1w. Dramatists Play Service $.95. Royalty $25—$15.

A man's wife will be entertaining her lover in the afternoon, and so as not to return home before six, he will visit his mistress. When the wife's lover arrives, he is her husband. Their relationship as master and mistress provides the necessary titillation and release of hostility, but there is a problem—the lover is weary of his mistress. The woman is still disturbed when he returns home in the evening as husband. She realizes she must seduce him now as wife, not as mistress, and she does.

————. *A Night Out.* (1960) 3 acts. Multiple set. 10m. 5w. Dramatists Play Service $1.95. Royalty $25—$15.

A meek, retiring young man who lives with his domineering mother is falsely accused of pinching a girl at the office party, and the resulting furor is more than he can cope with. Home early, he is confronted with a maternal diatribe, and in a rage he rushes out and finds a pick-up. In her room, she rambles on about what a lady she is, and he turns on her vindictively, annihilating her pathetic pretensions. When he returns home there is a difference in him, sensed by his mother, who now fears him.

————. *The Room*. (1960) Interior. 4m. 2w. Dramatists Play Service $1.75. Royalty $25—$15.

Rose worries aloud to her silent husband about the mysterious tenant who occupies the damp, windowless room in the basement of their tumble-down rooming house. Neither her husband nor the landlord do anything to allay her nameless fears, and the more she hears of this strange room, the more she is filled with apprehension. The tenant, a blind Negro, insists on meeting her. He has a message for Rose—her father wants her to come home. Rose is deeply moved, but her husband, returning home, silently and brutally murders him before her eyes.

Powers, Verne. *High Window*. Melodrama. 28 minutes. Interior. Modern costumes. 2m. 3w. Baker $.85. French $.85. Royalty $5.

A high window overlooking a street holds Walter Hodge in mental torment: it is the center of an enigma involving the recent death of his uncle, who fell from that window. His autocratic aunt, with whom he lives, taunts him about his weakness and the awful secret they seem to share. A newspaperwoman, spurred by curiosity, frees the nephew from his torment and solves the mystery of the high window.

Rattigan, Terence. *The Browning Version*. (1948) Drama. 70 minutes. Interior. Modern costumes. 5m. 2w. Baker $.85. French $.85. Royalty $20

An unfortunate professor at a boys' school is much maligned: to his wife he is an academic fool, to his colleagues he is dull and stodgy, and his students think him ridiculous. He is none of these things, really, but he has been so often abused that he has withdrawn into a thick shell. His wife plays around with younger instructors, and the headmaster passes him by at commencement, but the cruelest blow is being tricked into sympathy by a student and then mocked and laughed to tears.

Reach, James. *Good Neighbors*. Comedy. 30 minutes. Interior. Modern costumes. 9w. extras if desired. French $.85. Royalty $5.

A women's literary and civic club meets to hear a speech by a South American lady. Before the lecture, there is a business meeting at which is debated the momentous question of what flowers to plant on the club grounds. The señora finds herself involved, and draws an apt moral.

Rees, Phoebe M. *Idols*. Drama. 30 minutes. Interior. 18th century French costumes. 6w. Baker $.85. Royalty $5.

During the Reign of Terror in France, a mother maliciously attempts to denounce a daughter-in-law to the Tribunal. But her beloved son walks into the ingenious trap laid for his wife.

Rogers, Howard Emmett. *Yes Means No*. Added dialogue by Helen Leary and Nolan Leary. Farce. Interior. Modern costumes. 3m. 2w. Dramatists Play Service $.75. Royalty $5.

Ted Lawson tells Dad he wants to marry Edith and needs cash for honey-moon expenses. Dad hits the ceiling. To teach him to be less easy with giving credit to customers, Dad promises Ted $100 every time he says "No" during lunch hour. In his overeagerness to say "No," Ted nearly ruins Dad's business, but all ends well and the young couple are ready for their honeymoon with plenty of Dad's money to their credit.

Rostand, Edmond. *The Romancers*. (1894) English version by Barrett H. Clark. Romantic comedy (act 1 of the original 3-act play). 40 minutes. Exterior. Fantastic costumes. 5m. 1w. French $.85. No royalty.

Two sentimental youngsters rebel against their parents' wishes for them to marry. Both their fathers pretend a mortal enmity, which brings the young people together, but only after they have run away from home and returned disillusioned.

Ryerson, Florence. *A Cup of Tea*. Farce. 30 minutes. Interior. Modern costumes. 2m. 2w. French $.85. Royalty $5.

Wilford, a poet, sends some sonnets to Azalea, a young married woman. Azalea's husband discovers the poems and comes to shoot Wilford, and Azalea comes to prevent him. But Jane, Wilford's wife, straightens out the complications while serving tea.

Ryerson, Florence, and Clements, Colin. *Angels Don't Marry*. Comedy. 35 minutes. Interior. Modern costumes. 1m. 2w. Baker $.85. French $.85. Royalty $5.

A train wreck near a small Midwestern town results in the unexpected meeting of a young couple who had once been married. They are re-united, then quarrel, but the old, philosophical hotel-keeper helps them to realize that they will be more miserable apart than together.

————. *Sugar and Spice*. Based on a scene from Ryerson's novel *Mild Oats*. Comedy. 40 minutes. Interior. Modern costumes. 2m. 3w. Baker $.85. French $.85. Royalty $5.

Jane's girlfriend returns from Paris with a boy-complex and some in-furiating mannerisms. When the friend steals Jane's boyfriend, Jane is roused to a realization of his worth, and learns that more flies are caught with honey than with vinegar.

Saroyan, William. *Hello, Out There*. (1941) Drama. 30 minutes. In-terior (prison). Modern costumes. 3m. 2w. Baker $.85. French $.85. Royalty $10.

Photo Finish, an itinerant gambler, is arrested, charged with rape, and jailed in a small Texas town. The charge is a lie, but the only one who hears Photo's call for justice and understanding is Ethel, a young girl who cooks for the prisoners. Photo gives all his money to Ethel before a mob breaks into the jail and the lying woman's husband shoots him.

————. *The Hungerers.* (1939) Drama. Simple interior. Modern costumes. 3m. 2w. French $.85. Royalty $10.
In this symbolic fantasy, a writer dreams up four lonely people who hunger for spiritual as well as physical nourishment. It is a hunger for immortality. They reveal that the answer to death is immortality which "comes about when human beings rid themselves of all world-imposed absurdities and know the foolishness of pride. . . . When they know there can be no death if there is love." (from the author's preface)

————. *Subway Circus.* (1940) Fantasy. 45 minutes. Simple sets. Modern costumes. Flexible cast of men and women. French $.85. Royalty $10.
The dreams of ordinary people riding on a subway train, shown in a series of sketches unified in mood.

Schaefer, Lee. *The Little Flaw of Ernesto Lippi.* (1954) Domestic comedy. Interior. 3m. 6w. In *Best Short Plays of 1953–1954,* ed. by Margaret Mayorga. Royalty: contact Dodd, Mead & Co.
Set in Brooklyn. A five-scene play in which the little flaw of Ernesto Lippi is exposed for what it is—no flaw at all. For all groups. Ethnic interest: Italian-American.

Schisgal, Murray. *The Chinese.* Comedy. Interior. 2m. 3w. Dramatists Play Service $1.75 (in volume with "Dr. Fish"). Royalty $25.
The scene is a Chinese laundry, which is also home for the Lee family. Humorous misunderstandings prevent Chester, and the audience, from knowing whether his ancestry is Chinese or otherwise. Chester, who is usually taken to be Jewish, wants to marry a nice Jewish girl, but his family, indignant at his reluctance to *be* Chinese, have other plans. Eventually Chester's identity is unearthed, but the mystery remains: Who are his parents? Requires sensitive handling by teacher or director, since ethnic stereotypes persist. Advanced cast needed. Ethnic interest: Chinese-American, Jewish-American.

————. *Dr. Fish.* Comedy. Interior. 2m. 2w. Dramatists Play Service $1.75 (in volume with "The Chinese"). Royalty $25.
Anxious to make their sex life more "meaningful," a middle-aged couple consult the eminent Dr. Fish, a sex expert whose doctorate happens to be in American history. The wife and the doctor get along well once she has overcome her reluctance to say certain forbidden words, but the husband, a down-to-earth type, remains unconvinced. The one who finally wins over the husband is Dr. Fish's slightly dotty grandmother, who keeps bustling in with unwanted advice and steaming bowls of homemade lentil soup.

Shaffer, Peter. *Black Comedy.* (1965) Farce. Interior. 5m. 3w. Baker

$1.75, French $1.75 (in volume with "White Liars"). Royalty $50—
$25.

Opens on a dark stage—which is light to the characters. A blown fuse
throws them all in the dark—which is light to the audience—and this
is what we see in the "dark." A girl brings her wealthy father to meet
her fiancé, an improvident sculptor. To impress him, the sculptor has
invited a wealthy art patron and has stolen the fine furniture from the
apartment next door for his bare pad. The neighbor returns home too
soon, and the art patron is mistaken for an electrician. For little theater
and college.

Shannon, Martha B. *The Promised One.* 30 minutes. Biblical costumes.
6m. 3w. 2 children, angels, shepherds, choir, travelers. Baker $.85. No
royalty if 8 copies are purchased.

A pageant of the first Christmas, for production in church auditoriums,
with Bible readings, processional singing, street scenes in Bethlehem,
and the tableau of adoration.

Shaw, George Bernard. *The Dark Lady of the Sonnets.* (1910) Comedy.
20 minutes. Terrace of palace. Elizabethan costumes. 2m. 2w. French
$1.65. Royalty $10.

Shakespeare, coming to meet the Dark Lady to whom he addressed his
sonnets, meets Queen Elizabeth, and seizes the opportunity to talk with
her and to appeal to her for help for the theater. He does not notice
the approach of the Dark Lady, who is furiously jealous and berates them
both. Clever and effective.

Shaw, Irwin. *Bury the Dead.* (1936) Unit set. 20m. 8w. Dramatists
Play Service $.95. Royalty $25.

In "the second year of the war that is to begin tomorrow night," a
military burial detail goes about its sad duties. The chaplains arrive to
say prayers for the dead—but a groan is heard from the newly dug
graves, and then another. Slowly the dead soldiers rise up, pleading not
to be buried, asking to be allowed to rejoin the living. Word of their
insurrection spreads rapidly—to the soldiers in the field, the generals,
and the news media—with alarming effect. In a series of touching
scenes the dead men talk with their loved ones of the days of living,
now lost forever. But must the dead yield so easily? As the play ends,
the corpses rise and move away, as a shaken general stands by helpless
to stop them.

Simms, Willard. *The Acting Lesson.* Part of a trilogy entitled *Variations
on an Untitled Theme.* Simple interior. 3m. 1w. Dramatists Play
Service $.95. Royalty $15.

Beginning with rudimentary exercises in self-expression, the teacher has
his three students become plants opening forth to the sun, then various

trees with their characteristic natures. From this they go on to depict children playing with imaginary toys, then young lovers proposing marriage. The last lesson is the most difficult: they are to play themselves. Two of the three fail.

Staadt, Edward. *Cabbages.* Comedy. 1 hour. Interior. Modern costumes. 3m. 4w. French $.85. Royalty $5.

The Grossmeiers, erstwhile farmers, have struck oil, but they do not know what to do with their newly acquired wealth. He wants a new car, but she forbids, driving all car dealers from the door. She has sent to Chicago to have her husband's family tree established, and the genealogist arrives, along with a newspaperman. The genealogy is so startling that Grossmeier must pay more to keep the listeners from exposing it than he did to obtain it. When the next car dealer arrives, he is admitted with no remarks.

Swan, Jon. *Fireworks for a Hot Fourth.* (1968) Interior. 4m 3w. O'Neill Memorial Theater Center.

Chronicles the crisscross progress of a variety of passions during the course of a Fourth-of-July cocktail party. Passions flare, ranging from an old local's urge to get away from it all, a developer's passion to build more of the same, and a young man's desire for the unattainable woman, to the older woman's lust for the joys of destruction. Stylized action and speech; sardonic.

―――――. *Football.* Drama. Stylized locker room. 5m. 1w. O'Neill Memorial Theater Center.

Reporters at a press conference try to discover who actually won an increasingly mysterious game of what seems to be football. The coach responds evasively, and as the pressure mounts, the conference turns into a frenzied cheerleading rally. A somber play-by-play recount of the actual game reveals a savage sport: the two teams play completely different games and butcher each other. The innocent spectators, caught in the cross fire, are wiped out to a man.

Synge, John Millington. *Riders to the Sea.* (1904) Drama. 20 minutes. Interior. Irish peasant costumes. 1m. 3w. extras. Baker $.85. French $.85. Royalty $10.

In a cottage off the west of Ireland an old fisherman's widow mourns the loss of her five sons, drowned at sea. Now the sixth and last is about to ride down to the sea. She prophesies his death. Later his body is carried into the cottage on a stretcher. The most impressive of the Synge one-acters.

Tarkington, Booth. *The Travelers.* Farce. 40 minutes. Hotel bedroom. Modern costumes. 6m. 5w. French $.85. Royalty $10.

An American family, traveling in Sicily, spends a terrifying night in an apparently mysterious hotel. Morning brings the logical explanation that sinister remarks were only Sicilian pleasantries.

————. *The Trysting Place.* Comedy. 45 minutes. Interior. Modern costumes. 4m. 3w. Baker $.85. French $.85. Royalty $10.
Four couples meet simultaneously for a rendezvous in the same hotel lounge, and the situation is humorously complicated before each man meets his proper partner.

Tompkins, Frank G. *Sham.* Satire. 25 minutes. Living room. Modern costumes. 3m. 1w. Baker $.85. Royalty $5.
A young couple find a burglar in their home and have the usual reactions. However, the burglar forestalls them by showing that, because of the man's reputation as a connoisseur, if he does *not* take anything, the neighbors will realize that everything in the apartment is imitation. Excellent plot and characterizations.

Totheroh, Dan. *Pearls.* Comedy. 40 minutes. Interior. Modern costumes. 2m. 2w. French $.85. Royalty $5.
Tad, accused of stealing a valuable string of pearls from the store in which he works, gives his sister Polly a string of pearls for her birthday. Although suspicion and suspense develop quickly, Tad is exonerated.

Valdez, Luis, y El Theatro Campesino. *Actos.* (1971) Satire and comedy. Cucaracha Publications $3.00. Royalty to author.
Nine short plays or skits for street theater dealing with the subjects of strikes, unionization, and the problems of the farm worker. Plays use humor against a background of oppression and exploitation. The workers theater demonstrates the politics of survival and that it takes comedy to make sense of tragedy. Written for a bilingual theater company created in 1965 to teach and organize Chicano farm workers. Ethnic interest: Mexican-American.

Valency, Maurice. *Feathertop.* Based on a story by Nathaniel Hawthorne. Unit set. Colonial New England costumes. 7m. 3w. Dramatists Play Service $.75. Royalty $15.
Mother Rigby, a witch, fashions a scarecrow, christens him Lord Feathertop, and sends him to the house of Judge Gookin, who has claimed that no suitor in town is worthy of his daughter. Gookin is very impressed by this refined and noble young gentleman, but Polly, already in love with another, is less impressed. She glimpses in a mirror the scarecrow he really is. Feathertop, struck by the sham of his existence, forces the others to look, and then returns to Mother Rigby, sad and dismayed.

van Itallie, Jean-Claude. *Interview.* Part one of the trilogy *America Hurrah.* Open stage with props. 4m. 4w. Dramatists Play Service $1.75

(in volume with "TV" and "Motel"). Royalty $25. Royalty $50—$25 for all three plays on a single bill.

Four masked, smiling interviewers interview a scrub woman, a house painter, a banker, and a lady's maid. All is commonplace and familiar enough except that suddenly the most innocent statements are foreboding. Abruptly the scene shifts—a street, a psychiatrist's office, a confessional—but the compelling involvement continues. In the vicious intensity of the interviewers' assault on personal dignity and the clients' struggle to preserve their self-respect, we see what has happened to us. A satirical, stylized, mordantly comic play.

————. *Motel.* Part three of the trilogy *American Hurrah.* Stylized interior. "Doll" masks and bodies. 3 actors (m. or w.), off-stage voice. Dramatists Play Service $1.75 (in volume with "Interview" and "TV"). Royalty $25. Royalty $50—$25 for all three plays on a single bill.

A guy and a blonde—giant, stylized dolls with actors inside—take a room at a modern, antiseptically stark motel. While the landlady—also a doll—gives her fifteen-minute spiel on the hooked rugs, self-flushing toilets, and other features of their lodgings, guy and blonde crawl around, scribble on walls and doors, rip and smash everything in sight. Underscores the irony of our aching emptiness amidst the "advantages" which affluence and technology have brought.

Wefer, Marion. *The Best There Is.* Drama. 25 minutes. Hospital interior. 3m. 4w. extras. Baker $.85. Royalty $5.

Tessie's father is critically ill in a ward. She remembers Mom and Jimmy, who died in a ward, and is sure that if Pop had a private room, he'd recover—she would work the rest of her life to pay for it. Wealthy Petersham has a private room, nurses, flowers, and gifts—but no one cares. His only daughter is going on a cruise without visiting him. So he gives up his own room to Pop. In the morning, Pop is going to get well, but Petersham's chart reads death. Not knowing this, Tessie tries to express her gratitude.

Wilde, Percival. *The Enchanted Christmas Tree.* Fantastic comedy. 45 minutes. Living room. Modern costumes. 2m. 1w. 19 or more children. Baker $.85. Royalty $10.

Ella and Josiah Benton, a self-centered couple who believe that children should be seen and not heard, order some "no trespassing" signs to be placed about their property. But the expressman brings a Christmas tree by mistake. It turns out to be a magic tree, and in a dream the couple are tried by children. All their selfishness is charged against them, but the children discover that the two are very kind-hearted, each being grouchy to please the other, and win them over. Opportunity for Christmas music.

————. *The Finger of God*. Drama. 30 minutes. Interior. Modern costumes. 2m. 1w. Baker $.85. French $.85. Royalty $10.

Strickland has filled his pockets with money belonging to the firm which he heads. He is on the point of leaving when one of the stenographers comes in, revealing she knows his secret plans and past history. He decides to stay and "face the music," turning the tables on the treacherous valet who, unknown to him, is waiting at the station with the police.

————. *Hour of Truth*. (1916) Formerly entitled *Confessional*. Drama. 30 minutes. Cottage parlor. Modern costumes. 3m. 2w. Baker $.85. Royalty $10.

Robert Baldwin, an honest bank cashier, is offered a large bribe by the dishonest president of the bank. Although his family urges him to accept, he refuses. His honesty brings him due reward. Requires skillful acting.

Wilder, Thornton. *The Happy Journey (to Trenton and Camden)*. Comedy. 30 minutes. No scenery except 4 chairs and cot. 3m. 3w. Baker $.85. French $.85. Royalty $10.

Pa, Ma, and the two children journey from Newark in the family car to visit their daughter in Camden. The American scene, the American home dramatically drawn while the figure of the mother stands out as a brilliant piece of portraiture representing the backbone of the nation.

————. *The Long Christmas Dinner*. 30 minutes. Interior. 5m. 7w. Baker $.85. French $.85. Royalty $10.

This play traverses ninety years and represents ninety Christmas dinners in the Bayard home. The development of the countryside, the changes in customs and manners, the growth of the Bayard family and their accumulation of property, sum up vividly a wide aspect of American life.

————. *Queens of France*. Satiric comedy. 30 minutes. Interior. 1m. 3w. Baker $.85. French $.85. Royalty $10.

Under the cover of his profession, Monsieur Cahusac, a greedy lawyer, extorts money from credulous women by convincing them that they are the rightful heirs to the throne of France through relationship to the lost Dauphin. Set in New Orleans in 1869. Requires expert acting.

Williams, Emlyn. *Pepper and Sand*. Comedy. 20 minutes. Interior. 1m. 1w. Baker $.85. Royalty $5.

An imaginary interview given by the distinguished French author George Sand—romantically associated with the poet de Musset and the composer Chopin—and a small-town reporter out to make a scoop.

Williams, Tennessee. *The Case of the Crushed Petunias*. Lyrical fantasy. Interior. 2m. 2w. Dramatists Play Service $1.75 (in volume) . Royalty $10.

Miss Dorothy Simple, spinster of Primanproper, Massachusetts, serenely goes through the motions of her trivial existence behind the counter of her simple notion shop until the fateful morning she discovers her double row of petunias trampled into the mud by a size 11-D shoe. The culprit is a salesman of Life, Inc.; his bill of goods: living. The lure of this excitement is so strong that Miss Simple says goodbye—forever.

―――. *I Rise in Flame, Cried the Phoenix.* Interior or exterior. 1m. 2w. Dramatists Play Service $.75. Royalty $10.
A play about D. H. Lawrence. We see Lawrence at the very end of his career—in fact the very day he dies—and recognize him as the erratic, inspired, ill-tempered genius who was never able to come to terms with life. Yet he stands revealed here as the man who, in Williams' words, "felt the mystery and power of sex as the primal life urge, and was the lifelong adversary of those who wanted to keep the subject locked away in the cellars of prudery."

―――. *The Lady of Larkspur Lotion.* (1941) Interior. 1m. 2w. Dramatists Play Service $1.95 (in volume). Royalty $10.
A powerful play about two derelicts who struggle to make life worthwhile with their dreams and fancies and who live in a world of pitiful fiction. As one of the characters relates, "there are no lies but the lies that are stuffed in the mouth by the hard-knuckled hand of need, the cold iron fist of necessity."

―――. *The Last of My Solid Gold Watches.* (1942) Interior. Modern costumes. 3m. Dramatists Play Service $1.95 (in volume). Royalty $10.
Pockets filled with watches from his company, Charlie Colton, the top salesman with many years of service, reflects to a younger member of his profession that the times "have changed." No longer is quality the important consideration of a product. This legendary character of 78 is the last of the *solid* gold watches.

―――. *Moony's Kid Don't Cry.* (1940) 30 minutes. Interior. Modern costumes. 1m. 1w. Dramatists Play Service $1.75 (in volume). Royalty $10.
A timely play about a young husband and wife, married only a short time and already burdened with the responsibility of a one-month-old child, who dream of what might have been, want something more than what life ever gives, but finally become resolved to accept what "is."

Yeats, William Butler. *The Land of Heart's Desire.* (1894) Poetic drama. 30 minutes. Kitchen. Irish peasant costumes. 3m. 3w. Baker $.85. French $.85. Royalty $5.
On the eve of May Day, Maire Bruen gives away food and fire to the fairies. A fairy child comes into the home, bids them hide the crucifix, enchants the people, and entices Maire's soul away.

Yerby, Lorees. *Save Me a Place at Forest Lawn*. Comedy. Cafeteria interior. 2w. Dramatists Play Service $.75. Royalty $15.

Two elderly and lonely widows meet daily to have a meal, discuss grandchildren, recall their lives, and contemplate death. Their resignation is touched with wisdom and humor. When one reveals that she had an affair with the other's husband, her friend admits she had known, but it had seemed better to protect their friendship, which might relieve their final loneliness in old age.

Plays by Afro-Americans

The following annotated list is a selective but representative sampling of the kinds of plays created by black Americans from 1821, the year of production of the first play known to have been written by an Afro-American, to 1970. The list is limited partly by a dearth of published scripts which can be supplied to acting groups. Many blacks whose plays have been produced by community or college theatrical groups have been unable to publish the plays in books or in acting scripts. Until recently, publishers presumed a limited reading audience for plays about blacks; consequently, they rarely sought or accepted the work of black playwrights except when those plays were scheduled for production in the downtown theaters of New York or when the dramas already had earned national reputations. For this reason, many potentially useful plays exist only in manuscript form or in the pages of periodicals which are not widely known. Since this guide is intended primarily to assist acting groups, it seems useless to include plays which are not available in script form.

Conspicuously absent from the following list are pageants and musical dramas, which constitute an important contribution of black artists to the theater. The usual problems of publication seem to be compounded when musical scores and choreographic directions must be included. Hence, few pageants or musicals are available in print.

Despite these limitations, the list is representative. It includes dramas intended for audiences in black communities as well as plays designed for presentation to predominantly white audiences in the commercial theater; it includes one-act and full-length dramas; it includes dramas written in the 1920s and those of the 1960s.

It is important to observe that the protagonists of these dramas are black (African, Afro-American, Afro-Caribbean). Whereas many black authors have written novels and even radio, film, and television scripts about white protagonists, most black playwrights have chosen or have been compelled to restrict themselves to black protagonists. If a playwright has aimed for a commercial production, preferably on Broadway, he has considered the judgment of producers that the value of a black playwright is limited to exotic or sensational presentations of blacks. If the dramatist has written specifically for a black community group, he has recognized the absurdity of deliberately creating "white" roles for a cast of black actors and actresses when such roles are readily available in famous plays. Finally, some black playwrights have written dramas about black people primarily to educate or instill pride in the black community. Regardless of the reason, the general topic of the black playwright has been the black person.

One should not assume, however, that all dramas by blacks are severely restricted to one subject or one style. Dramatists have not limited themselves to issues unique to black Americans; they have also explored the kinds of problems common to people of various races and various nations. Black dramatists have created characters from the professional classes as well as slaves, peasants, and ghetto dwellers. They have written fantasy and farce as well as melodrama, social commentary, and problem plays. They have written for entertainment and for instruction. They have used experimental techniques of expressionism and constructivism as well as the more common techniques of realism.

Readers interested in a history of drama by Afro-Americans will find further information in the introduction to *Black Drama in America: An Anthology,* edited by Darwin T. Turner, and in the historical and critical books listed in the appended bibliography.

Bibliography

Abramson, Doris E. *Negro Playwrights in the American Theatre, 1925–1959.* New York: Columbia University Press, 1969.

Bond, Frederick W. *The Negro and the Drama: The Direct and Indirect Contribution Which the American Negro Has Made to Drama and the Legitimate Stage.* Washington: Associated Publishers, 1940.

Brown, Sterling A. *Negro Poetry and Drama.* Washington: Associates in Negro Folk Education, 1937.

Hatch, James V. *The Black Image on the American Stage, 1770–1970.* New York: Drama Book Specialists, 1970.

Hatch, James V., and Abdullah, Omanii Modiera, eds. *Black Drama: An Annotated Bibliography (1823–1975).* New York: Drama Book Specialists, 1976.

Hughes, Langston, and Meltzer, Milton. *Black Magic: A Pictorial History of the Negro in American Entertainment.* Englewood Cliffs, N.J.: Prentice-Hall, 1967.

Isaacs, Edith. *The Negro in the American Theatre.* New York: Theatre Arts, 1947.

Johnson, James Weldon. *Black Manhattan.* New York: Alfred A. Knopf, 1930.

Lawson, Hilda J. "The Negro in American Drama (Bibliography of Contemporary Negro Drama)." *Bulletin of Bibliography* 17 (1940) : 7–8, 27–30.

A List of Negro Plays. Washington: WPA Federal Theater Project, 1938.

Mitchell, Loften. *Black Drama: The Story of the American Negro in the Theater.* New York: Hawthorn Books, 1967.

Patterson, Lindsay, ed. *Anthology of the American Negro in the Theater.* International Library of Negro Life and History. Washington: Associated Publishers, 1967.

Turner, Darwin T. *Afro-American Writers.* Goldentree Bibliographies. New York: Appleton-Century-Crofts, 1970.

One-Act Plays

Baraka, Imamu Amiri (LeRoi Jones). *A Black Mass.* (1966) Drama. Interior. 4m. 3w. In *Four Black Revolutionary Plays,* by LeRoi Jones. Royalty to Ronald Hobbs Literary Agency.

Despite the warnings of his fellow black magicians, Jacoub, believing that knowledge cannot be evil, creates a soulless white monster, which destroys the magicians and runs loose in the world. A dramatic interpretation of the Black Muslim story of the creation of white men, it is intended primarily for a black audience.

―――. *The Death of Malcolm X.* (1969) Multiple set. Mixed cast. In *New Plays from the Black Theater,* ed. by Ed Bullins. Royalty to Ronald Hobbs Literary Agency.

White Klansmen, government officials, and bankers organize and train brainwashed Negroes to kill Malcolm X. Designed for black community theater.

―――. *Dutchman.* (1964) 1 hour. Subway car interior. 2m. 1w. extras. French $3.95 (in volume with "The Slave"). Royalty $35―$30.

A white woman boards a subway train, entices a young black man sexually, castigates him for imitating the ways of white men, then has him killed when he defends his way of life and demonstrates his understanding of white people. Winner of an off-Broadway award; a powerful presentation of the destructive attitudes of blacks and whites. Designed for community theater.

―――. *Great Goodness of Life: A Coon Show.* (1966) Multiple set. 8m. 1w. In *Four Black Revolutionary Plays,* by LeRoi Jones. Royalty to Ronald Hobbs Literary Agency.

Having spent his life trying to do the right thing according to white men's instructions, a Negro man is arrested, charged with harboring a murderer, killed in an alleged jailbreak, and, in a white heaven, is ordered to purify himself for return to earth by killing the murderer, who is his son. A sociofantasy castigating the manner in which white people manipulate Negroes to destroy their own potential. Intended for black community theater.

―――. *The Slave.* (1964) 1 hour. Interior. 2m. 1w. French $3.95 (in volume with "Dutchman") Royalty $35―$30.

In what the author describes as a fable, a black revolutionary confronts his former wife, a white woman, and kills their two children. A fable describing the need of a black revolutionary to rid himself of attitudes and standards developed by his education in a white system. Designed for community theater.

————. *The Toilet.* (1967) Interior. 11m. In *Baptism and The Toilet,*
by LeRoi Jones. Royalty to Sterling Lord Agency.

In an arranged confrontation, a popular black youth beats a white youth
who has offered homosexual advances, but in the absence of the others,
he returns to comfort the white youth. A symbolically suggestive exploration of the ambivalent reactions of black youth to the white world.

Bullins, Ed. *Clara's Ole Man.* (1968) Interior. 4m. 4w. French $4.95
(in *Five Plays,* by Ed Bullins). Royalty $15—$10.

A middle-class young black man who accepts a girl's invitation to visit
while her "old man" is at work learns that the "old man" is a woman.
The language and the theme of lesbianism require maturity in cast and
audience.

————. *The Electronic Nigger.* (1968) Interior. 4m. 3w. French $4.95
(in *Five Plays,* by Ed Bullins). Royalty $15—$10.

A black writer who has accepted a post as creative writing instructor in
evening classes of a junior college quits after the first evening because
the class has been dominated and divided by a pompous Negro who is
a "Sociological Data Research Analysis Technician Expert" in penology.
A satire about the ignorance of people who take courses in creative
writing and about Negroes whose thinking has been programmed. Possible for actors of high school age and beyond.

————. *A Son, Come Home.* (1968) Interior. 2m. 2w. French $4.95
(in *Five Plays,* by Ed Bullins). Royalty $15—$10.

Returning home after nine years' absence, a son recalls with his mother
memories and attitudes which continue to separate them. An interesting
use of actors to reveal the thoughts and memories that people will not
communicate to others. Can be played by high school groups and older.

Butcher, James W. *The Seer.* (late 1930s) Comedy. Interior. 4m. 1w.
In *The Negro Caravan,* ed. by Sterling A. Brown, et al. (New York:
Arno Press, 1969). Royalty to author.

Lucy Toles and her sweetheart, Willie Gordon, play upon her uncle's
superstition to persuade him to approve their marriage. Effective for
junior high school groups or older.

Caldwell, Ben. *Family Portrait (or My Son the Black Nationalist).*
(1967) Interior. 2m. 1w. In *New Plays from the Black Theater,* ed. by
Ed Bullins. Royalty to author.

Rejecting his father's admonitions to work hard and to prove to white
people that he is ready to live and work among them, a black youth,
insisting that such efforts are futile, declares his refusal to change himself
in order to conform to white standards. An indictment of discrimination
and an affirmation of the values of ethnic groups. Designed for a black

audience but has relevance for white audiences also. Can be played by mature cast.

Childress, Alice. *Florence.* (1950) 1 set. 2w. In *Masses and Mainstream* 3 (October 1950). Royalty to Flora Roberts, Inc.

After a conversation with a white "liberal" reveals that woman's ignorance of and subconscious contempt for black people, a black mother urges her daughter to remain in the North and to continue to try to realize her dream of becoming an actress. A satire which can be performed by high school groups or older.

Davidson, N. R., Jr. *El Hajj Malik.* (1967) Interior. 6m. 4w. In *New Plays from the Black Theater,* ed. by Ed Bullins. Royalty to author.

In a work designed for theater reading or full production, the performers, aided by music and dance, trace the life and thought of Malcolm X. Can be handled by performers of junior high school age or older.

Duncan, Thelma. *Sacrifice.* (1930) Interior. 2m. 2w. In *Plays and Pageants from the Life of the Negro,* ed. by Willis Richardson. Royalty: contact Associated Publishers.

A teenaged black youth takes the blame for having stolen an examination in order to protect the guilty one, a friend whose mother has struggled and sacrificed so that her son will receive an education. Sentimental but effective for junior high school.

Edmonds, Randolph. *Bad Man.* (1934) Drama. 1 set. In *Black Theater, USA,* ed. by James V. Hatch and Ted Shine. Royalty to author.

In order to avoid endangering the life of a girl who is visiting her sweetheart in a saw-mill camp, Thea Dugger, a "bad man" feared by all the workers, sacrifices himself to a lynch mob. On the familiar but still effective theme of a bad man with a golden heart, this play is distinguished from the others by the theme of protest against racial oppression.

————. *Bleeding Hearts.* (1934) Drama. 1 set. In *Six Plays for a Negro Theater,* by Randolph Edmonds. Royalty to author.

Embittered because his employer has refused to permit him to leave work to attend his dying wife, a black worker leaves the South. Melodramatic cry against racial oppression. Possible for high school groups or older.

————. *Breeders.* (1934) Drama. 1 set. In *Six Plays for a Negro Theater,* by Randolph Edmonds. Royalty to author.

A slave girl kills herself rather than mate with the plantation stud and breed new slaves. A dramatic refocusing on conditions and customs of slavery. Possible for high school groups or older.

————. *Gangsters over Harlem.* (1939) Melodrama. Interior. 4m. 1w. In *The Land of Cotton and Other Plays,* by Randolph Edmonds. Royalty to author.

A girl is killed while avenging her younger brother, who had been killed by gangsters. Typical gangster melodrama of the 1930s but still effective for high school or college groups who may find comedy in the too familiar sensationalism.

————. *Nat Turner.* (1934) Exterior. 10m. 1w. In *Six Plays for a Negro Theater,* by Randolph Edmonds. Royalty to author.

The story of Nat Turner's heroic effort to lead a rebellion of slaves in Virginia. Especially useful for high school and college groups interested in plays about the history of Afro-Americans.

————. *The New Window.* (1934) 1 set. In *Six Plays for a Negro Theater,* by Randolph Edmonds. Royalty to author.

The murder of a cruel bootlegger verifies his wife's prediction that bad luck will follow his having broken a new window. Melodramatic but satisfactory for junior and senior high school.

————. *Old Man Pete.* (1934) 1 interior, 1 exterior. In *Six Plays for a Negro Theater,* by Randolph Edmonds. Royalty to author.

Unable to change their rural habits and, consequently, unwanted by their sophisticated children, two elderly Afro-Americans decide to return to the South but freeze to death while trying to walk from Harlem to the downtown train station. Sentimental; popular among high school and college groups.

————. *Silas Brown.* (1927) 1 set. 4m. 2w. In *The Land of Cotton and Other Plays,* by Randolph Edmonds. Royalty to author.

When Silas Brown, disregarding his wife's pleas, loses all his money and the mortgage on the house in an unwise investment, his wife, who has remained through the years of abuse, finally decides to leave him. Suitable for high school or college.

————. *Yellow Death.* (1935) Interior. 9m. In *The Land of Cotton and Other Plays,* by Randolph Edmonds. Royalty to author.

Although 42 of 60 volunteers from black regiments have died in the experiments doctors are conducting in a desperate effort to find a cure for yellow fever, the regiments volunteer to the last man when the next call comes. A tribute to the heroic black soldiers who, during the Spanish-American War, gave their lives to save the lives of others and to earn respect for the courage and character of Afro-Americans. Suitable for high school groups or older.

Garrett, Jimmie. *And We Own the Night.* (1968) Exterior. 5m. 2w. In *The Drama Review* 12:4 (Summer 1968). Royalty to author.

A dying black revolutionary kills his mother because she represents the Negroes who may destroy the revolution by their determination to believe in God and white men. Designed for a black community theater.

Hughes, Langston. *Soul Gone Home.* (1937) Drama. Interior. 3m. 1w. In *Five Plays,* by Langston Hughes. Royalty to Harold Ober Associates.
When the spirit of her recently dead son accuses her of neglect, a black mother defends herself by arguing that prostitution was the only method she had to provide the money which they needed. Brief but dramatic confrontation suggesting problems of impoverished families. Suitable for college and community theaters.

Johnson, Georgia Douglas. *Frederick Douglass.* (1935) Drama. Interior. 3m. 1w. In *Negro History in Thirteen Plays,* ed. by Willis Richardson and May Miller. Royalty: contact Associated Publishers.
After he learns that his former master has demanded that he be returned to work in the fields, Frederick Douglass escapes from slavery. An historical drama about a famous Afro-American leader. Suitable for junior and senior high school.

————. *William and Ellen Craft.* (1935) Drama. Interior. 3m. 1w. In *Negro History in Thirteen Plays,* ed. by Willis Richardson and May Miller. Royalty: contact Associated Publishers.
To avoid being sold into a situation in which she will be sexually abused, Ellen Craft and her husband William begin their flight from slavery. A dramatic treatment of an historical episode. Suitable for junior and senior high school performers.

Jones, LeRoi. See Baraka, Imamu Amiri.

Kennedy, Adrienne. *Funnyhouse of a Negro.* (1964) Morality play. Drop and wing. 3m. 5w. French $.85. Royalty $20—$15.
An expressionistic presentation of the psychoses of a mulatto who, imagining herself variously to be Queen Victoria, Christ, Lumumba, or a duchess, hates her black father. Winner of an off-Broadway award; the sophisticated expressionism demands an experienced cast and a theatrically knowledgeable audience.

Miller, May. *Christophe's Daughters.* (1935) Interior. 3m. 4w. In *Negro History in Thirteen Plays,* ed. by Willis Richardson and May Miller. Royalty to author.
The daughters of King Henri Christophe of Haiti prepare to die bravely in the people's revolution against their father, who kills himself. Historical drama suitable for junior high and older.

————. *Harriet Tubman.* (1935) Drama. Exterior. 4m. 3w. In

Negro History in Thirteen Plays, ed. by Willis Richardson and May Miller. Royalty to author.

A slave girl helps Harriet Tubman evade a trap and lead black slaves to freedom. Historical drama about a famous black who repeatedly returned South to lead slaves to freedom. Suitable for junior high and older.

————. *Riding the Goat.* (1929) Interior. 2m. 2w. In *Plays and Pageants from the Life of the Negro,* ed. by Willis Richardson. Royalty to author.

Fearing that the black community will turn against her physician sweetheart unless he demonstrates his identity with the common people by marching in his lodge's parade, a black woman dons his uniform and takes his place, only to learn later that, having changed his mind, he would have marched. A still relevant exploration of the black population's suspicion that the black middle class may seek to escape identification with the common people. Designed for college and community production.

Milner, Ronald. *The Monster.* (1968) Drama. Interior. 5m. 1w. In *The Drama Review* 12:4 (Summer 1968). Royalty to author.

After failing to convert a Negro dean of students who worships whiteness, black revolutionary students hang him. But, in the awareness which comes moments before death, he urges blacks to work for their own people. Black revolutionary drama intended for black community theaters.

Muhajir, El (Marvin X). *Take Care of Business.* (1968) Interior. 5m. In *The Drama Review* 12:4 (Summer 1968). Royalty to author.

A black, college-educated youth who is alienated from his father attempts unsuccessfully to persuade his father to arrange his release from jail. Later, learning that his father has died of a heart attack while on the way to the jail, the youth vows not to become alienated from the children he will have in the future. A polemic against alienation; intended primarily for black community theaters.

Richardson, Willis. *Antonio Maceo.* (1935) Drama. Interior. 7m. 2w. In *Negro History in Thirteen Plays,* ed. by Willis Richardson and May Miller. Royalty to author.

A black patriot dedicated to the fight for Cuban freedom is assassinated by Spanish soldiers after he has been betrayed by his physician. Historical drama suitable for high school and above.

————. *Attucks, the Martyr.* (1935) Drama. Interior. 7m. In *Negro History in Thirteen Plays,* ed. by Willis Richardson and May Miller. Royalty to author.

Crispus Attucks, a fugitive slave who knows the value of freedom, leads colonists against British soldiers and thus inspires other colonists to fight for their freedom. Freely interpreted history of the first man to die in the Boston Massacre. Suitable for high school groups and older.

————. *The Broken Banjo.* (1925) Folk tragedy. Interior. 4m. 1w. In *Plays of Negro Life,* ed. by Alain Locke and Montgomery Gregory. Royalty to author.

A man who, in anger, has killed the man who had broken his banjo is turned over to the police by an angry brother-in-law who witnessed the murder. Suitable for junior or senior high school and older.

————. *The Chip Woman's Fortune.* (1923) Drama. 5m. 2w. In *Black Drama in America,* ed. by Darwin T. Turner. Royalty to author.

Suspecting that his elderly roomer will bring her son to live with her after his release from prison, a porter-landlord plans to evict her after he has borrowed money from her to make an installment payment on his Victrola. Although the woman refuses so that she can save the money for her son, her son offers enough to meet the payment. The first serious drama of an Afro-American author to be produced on Broadway. Somewhat dated but possible for junior and senior high school.

————. *The Dragon's Tooth.* Exterior. In *The King's Dilemma and Other Plays for Children* (Hicksville, N.Y.: Exposition Press, 1956). Royalty to Exposition Press.

To prove himself to those who doubt that the descendant of a slave is worthy to become a leader, a black youth, after passing the test of strength, passes the test of bravery by going to the dragon's lair and seizing the dragon's tooth, which has inscribed on it the message that young people can find happiness only if they love all men as their brothers. Sufficiently exciting and didactic to be excellent material for children's theater.

————. *The Elder Dumas.* (1935) Interior. 3m. 4w. In *Negro History in Thirteen Plays,* ed. by Willis Richardson and May Miller. Royalty to author.

A duel between Alexander Dumas, a writer and the greatest pistol shot in France, and a critic, who is the greatest swordsman in France, is prevented by the critic's wife, who castigates her husband for criticizing Dumas unfairly. Historical drama about a mysterious incident in the life of the famous author, whose grandmother was a black Haitian. Suitable for junior or senior high school.

————. *The Flight of the Natives.* (1927) Interior. 6m. 2w. In *Plays of Negro Life,* ed. by Alain Locke and Montgomery Gregory. Royalty to author.

Threatened with being separated from his wife and sold down the river, a slave escapes, leaving behind his wife who is too weak to travel but vowing to return for her. Suitable for high school.

———. *The House of Sham.* (1929) 1 set. 4m. 3w. In *Plays and Pageants from the Life of the Negro,* ed. by Willis Richardson. Royalty to author.

When her fiancé, a Negro physician, breaks their engagement because he has learned that her father is not as wealthy as he had supposed, a young woman, sick of the sham of her family's life, turns happily to a more honest man. Social satire for high school groups or older.

———. *The King's Dilemma.* (1929) Interior. 5m. 1w. extras. In *The King's Dilemma and Other Plays for Children,* by Willis Richardson (Hicksville, N.Y.: Exposition Press, 1956). Royalty to Exposition Press.

Unable to understand the depth of his twelve-year-old son's love for people, a king unsuccessfully tries to end his son's friendship with a black boy first by threatening to give the black boy half of the kingdom and later by threatening to turn the kingdom over to the people. Obvious moral but suitable for junior high.

———. *Near Calvary.* (1935) 5m. 4w. In *Negro History in Thirteen Plays,* ed. by Willis Richardson and May Miller. Royalty to author.

The brother of the black man who carried the cross for Jesus wins the respect of his children and his wife by bravely refusing to deny his belief in Jesus to the Roman soldiers who arrest him. Suitable for junior high.

Sanchez, Sonia. *The Bronx Is Next.* (1968) Drama. Exterior. 5m. 2w. In *The Drama Review* 12:4 (Summer 1968). Royalty to author.

While evacuating people to prepare for the burning of the ghetto of Harlem, black revolutionaries harass a black woman who takes white lovers and harass the white policeman-lover in the manner in which white police badger black youths in the ghetto. Black revolutionary drama designed for black community theaters.

Shine, Ted. *Contribution.* (1969) Simple interior. 1m. 2w. Dramatists Play Service $1.50 (in volume with "Plantation" and "Shoes"). Royalty $15.

Although her grandson, excited about his participation in sit-ins, believes that his grandmother is a female Uncle Tom because she never seems to complain and even cooks cornbread for the sheriff's breakfast, she has continuously worked in her own way to improve the lot of black people, as she reveals when she assists her grandson's cause by poisoning the sheriff. Focused on the generation gap and the struggle for civil rights; suitable for high school performers and older.

Ward, Douglas Turner. *Day of Absence.* (1965) Farce. Unit set. 8m. 6w. doubling possible. Dramatists Play Service $1.50 (in volume with "Happy Ending"). Royalty $15.

The departure of black people from a Southern community for a single day reveals how dependent the white community is on the presence of the blacks. Satirical farce which is entertaining for high school groups and older.

————. *Happy Ending.* (1965) Farce. Interior. 2m. 2w. Dramatists Play Service $1.50 (in volume with "Day of Absence"). Royalty $15. A black youth chastises his relatives for worrying about the possible marital breakup of their white employers. But, when he learns how much his standard of living depends upon those jobs, he too worries until the happy ending results when the employers become reconciled. Satirical farce which can be performed by high school groups and older.

Full-Length Plays

Baldwin, James. *The Amen Corner.* (1952) Comedy in 3 acts. Composite interior. 4m. 10w. French $4.50. Royalty $50—$25. An Afro-American woman who has sacrificed love in order to become the minister of a store-front church in Harlem loses both her church and her son, the church organist, when her dying jazz-musician husband returns. For all groups.

————. *Blues for Mr. Charlie.* (1964) Drama in 3 acts. Bare stage. 16m. 7w. extras. French $.75. Restricted. Royalty $50—$25. A black minister who has dedicated himself to peaceful means of improving race relations and helping his people in his Southern home decides that he may need to support the Bible with a gun after a jury acquits the white man who murdered his son. A powerful social drama of racial injustice. Language and thought restrict playing to twelfth grade, college, and community groups.

Bass, Kingsley B., Jr. *We Righteous Bombers.* (1968) 3 acts. Interior. 8m. 3w. In *Black Drama in America,* ed. by Darwin T. Turner. Royalty to author. A black revolutionary who believes that he has killed a black Grand Prefect in an effort to liberate his people learns that he has merely killed a double and that, in order to save his friends from torture and execution, he must become the new executioner. An absorbing study of the differing personalities and motives of individuals involved in a revolution. For a black cast in twelfth grade, college, or community.

Bullins, Ed. *Goin' a Buffalo.* (1968) Drama in 3 acts. 2 interiors. 4m. 2w. extras. French $4.95 (in *Five Plays,* by Ed Bullins). Royalty $50—$25. A black man who has been befriended by a former prison buddy destroys his friend's dreams, causes his return to prison, and steals his wife. An interesting presentation, in an underworld of hustlers, of traditional themes of dreams and the dangers of misplaced trust. The subjects of pimps, prostitutes, and drugs necessitate a cast and audience with maturity. Designed for community theater.

————. *In the Wine Time.* (1968) Drama in 3 acts. Exterior. 6m. 7w. French $4.95 (in *Five Plays*, by Ed Bullins). Royalty $50—$25.
After exciting his nephew-in-law with romantic tales about the Navy and encouraging him to drink, Cliff Dawson takes the blame for a murder which the boy may have committed in a drunken stupor. An occasionally lyric drama of problems of dreams and maturity amid the reality of the slum. Although the characters are teenagers, the language and actions seem to require presentation by a college or community group.

Davis, Ossie. *Purlie Victorious.* (1961) Farce in 3 acts. Exterior, 2 composites. 6m. 3w. French $1.75. Royalty $50—$25.
A self-proclaimed black minister returns to his Southern home and realizes his dream of establishing a church. A popular Broadway play and a delightful satirical attack on all the stereotypes and clichés traditional in interracial relations in America. Excellent for high school groups or older.

Dodson, Owen. *Bayou Legend.* (1946) Romantic fantasy in 2 acts. Several exteriors. 21m. 15w. extras. In *Black Drama in America,* ed. by Darwin T. Turner. Royalty to author.
After years of dreaming, telling tales, wooing and abandoning mortal and supernatural women, and questing for power, Reve Grant, in an effort to save himself from the toy molder who collects human rubbish, attempts to prove that he is sufficiently evil to be consigned to Hell. But all those whom he has betrayed agree that he is not actually evil. A lyric relocation of the Peer Gynt legend in the world of blacks of the bayou. Intended for college or community cast.

Edmonds, Randolph. *Earth and Stars.* (1961) Social drama in 3 acts. Interior. 9m. 3w. In *Black Drama in America,* ed. by Darwin T. Turner. Royalty to author.
Having incurred opposition from blacks because of his attempts to modernize his church and from whites because of his encouragement of attempts to organize unions and campaign for civil rights, Reverend Joshua Judson, horrified by brutal attacks on union organizers and freedom riders, wins converts after he is killed while practicing his determination to preach in the streets until Christianity comes to the South. A dramatic and timely indictment of oppression based on race or class. Highly popular among college groups.

————. *The Land of Cotton.* (1938) Social drama in 4 acts. 2 exteriors, 1 interior. 20m. 8w. extras. In *The Land of Cotton and Other Plays,* by Randolph Edmonds. Royalty to author.

Despite the efforts of landowners to destroy a union of sharecroppers by arresting the leaders, turning blacks against whites, and attacking them, the sharecroppers gain hope that the unity of black and white will end oppression. Somewhat dated in its concern for unions and its insistence upon unity, but focuses on an issue which continues unresolved. Written for college groups.

Elder, Lonne III. *Ceremonies in Dark Old Men.* (1969) Drama in 2 acts. Interior. 5m. 2w. French $1.75. Royalty $50—$25.

When his daughter refuses to kill herself supporting the family as her mother did, Russell Parker and his sons attempt to assume responsibility, but their efforts are abortive. A poignant domestic drama centered on an old man who has abandoned responsibility for a life of dreams that will not be realized. College level and above.

Gordone, Charles. *No Place to Be Somebody.* (1969) Melodrama in 3 acts. Interior. 11m. 5w. French $1.75. Restricted. Royalty $50—$35.

A black man who wishes to compete with white racketeers in New York is killed by a light-skinned friend who, despite his own failures to achieve success through integration, insists that blacks need not war with whites. Thought-provoking Pulitzer Prize drama designed for professional production but excellent for mature amateurs in community theater.

Hansberry, Lorraine. *A Raisin in the Sun.* (1959) Drama in 3 acts. Interior. 7m. 3w. 1 child. French $1.75. Royalty $50—$25.

Divided by conflicting personalities, interests, and attitudes, members of a black family in Chicago find unity in the pride which makes them determined to move into the home which they have purchased even though that home is located in a white neighborhood. Although frequently described as a comedy, the play is a perceptive presentation of the personalities and attitudes of black people, especially of the mother, who has been the bulwark, and of the son, who struggles to gain confidence in himself as a man. Popular in professional theater and as a motion picture but excellent also for college groups.

Hughes, Langston. *Emperor of Haiti.* (1938) 3 acts. 4 sets. 16m. 14w. extras. In *Black Drama in America,* ed. by Darwin T. Turner. Royalty to Harold Ober Associates.

After uniting black slaves and mulattoes and leading them to victory against the French rulers of Haiti, Jean Jacques Dessalines abandons his slave wife and declares himself emperor. But he is defeated by his own inefficiency as an administrator and by his excessive faith in mulattoes, especially his second wife, who hates him because he had been a slave. An excellent dramatic interpretation of an important episode in black history; also perceptively develops the familiar theme of the danger of a man's becoming excessively proud of his own glory. Excellent for college groups and community theaters.

―――. *Little Ham*. (1935) Farce in 3 acts. Several sets. In *Five Plays*, by Langston Hughes. Royalty to Harold Ober Associates.

Amidst the swirl of the numbers racket, tangled love affairs, and a Charleston contest, Little Ham, a sporty shoe-shiner, finds romance with huge Tiny. Somewhat dated by its topicality, the play still offers amusement for high school groups and older.

―――. *Mulatto*. (1931) 2 acts. Interior. 10m. 2w. extras. In *Five Plays*, by Langston Hughes. Royalty to Harold Ober Associates.

Continuing conflicts between a white Southerner and the mulatto youth who wants to be acknowledged as his son result in the son's killing his father and committing suicide rather than exposing himself to the lynch mob which seeks him. Very popular in professional theater at the time of its creation, but dated now by topical allusions and by subsequent treatments of a theme that was then new to American theater. Suitable for high school groups and older.

―――. *Simply Heavenly*. (1957) Based on Hughes' novel *Simple Takes a Wife*. Comedy in 2 acts. Music by David Martin. Unit set. 11m. 8w. Dramatists Play Service $1.50. Piano and vocal music at additional cost. Royalty $50.

A musical comedy about the troubles which befall Jesse B. Semple as he struggles to secure a divorce from one woman and to marry a second. Amusing, sometimes farcical. Suitable for college or community groups.

―――. *Tambourines to Glory*. (1949, 1962) Morality play in 2 acts. 6m. 9w. In *Five Plays*, by Langston Hughes. Royalty to Harold Ober Associates.

When the Devil assists two black women in their efforts to establish a street-front church, trouble accompanies success. One woman kills him in a jealous rage, but regains her soul when she confesses in order to prevent the imprisonment of her friend. A musical morality play on the old theme of good versus evil. Suitable for college or community theater but requires singing voices in cast.

Mitchell, Loften. *A Land beyond the River*. (1963) Multiple set. 9m. 5w. 2 boys. Pioneer Drama Service $1.75. Royalty $25.

After assisting black parents in their protests against inadequate educational facilities for their children, a black minister, who has defended himself from physical attack by whites, is forced to flee for his life. A moving drama based on actual incidents in one of the protests against segregated schools later brought to the Supreme Court in 1954; effective for college or community theater.

Patterson, Charles. *Legacy*. (1969) Drama in 2 acts. 2 exteriors, 1 interior. 5m. 4w. In *Nineteen Necromancers from Now*, ed. by Ishmael Reed (New York: Doubleday, 1970). Royalty to author.

Despite efforts by his daughter, her sweetheart, and his wife, a middle-class Negro cannot understand that instead of attempting to force his daughter to accept his standards and possessions, he must permit her to develop in her own way. Educational drama intended for black community theater; develops one of the most popular themes—the difference between older and younger Afro-Americans.

Peterson, Louis. *Take a Giant Step*. (1952) Drama in 6 scenes. 4 interiors. 9m. 7w. French $1.75. Royalty $50—$25.

When his white companions begin to exclude him from their parties and their homes as they reach the dating age, an Afro-American youth who has been reared in a predominantly white neighborhood searches unsuccessfully for companionship with members of his race and learns to develop sufficient pride and maturity to pretend indifference to his isolation. A perceptive presentation of the problems of an Afro-American youth whose rearing and environment isolate him in a world which bases critical decisions on skin color. Designed for professional production but effective for college or community theater.

Ward, Theodore. *Our Lan'*. (1941) Drama in 2 acts. 2 exteriors. 22m. 12w. In *Black Drama in America*, ed. by Darwin T. Turner. Royalty to Hatch-Billops Studio.

Although they have been promised land which formerly belonged to Southern rebels, blacks are driven off the land by soldiers when the government policy changes. Dramatic historical study of a bitter period in black history during the years following the Civil War. Suitable for college or community theater groups.

Full-Length Plays

Modern plays are as turbulent and transitory as the very times which are responsible for their creation. In an age when we find ourselves on the threshold of the limitless universe and yet incapable of living with our neighbor, the theater at once represents the grandeur and chaos that is our experience. In the search for understandable explanations for existence and acceptable guides for behavior, all human acts must be examined and put to the test. Just as every idea and every act, from the most noble to the most base, is presented on stage, so every form of theater—classical, romantic, realistic, symbolistic, fantastic, oriental—pure or in combination, is used. There is a never-ending search for new forms—the theater of the absurd, the theater of cruelty, happenings, guerrilla theater—any form a playwright can dream.

If the theater of our day has any outstanding characteristic, it is its diversity. Available to the public are spectacular musicals devoted to escapism; detailed re-creations on stage of the human condition which require the realistic portrayal of every human act; faithful reproductions of plays from past theatrical eras that are truly visits to a museum; intimate gatherings where the audience and actors unite to create the action as they proceed, either as a religious experience or as a demonstration of and defense against the dehumanization of our contemporary society. There are no schools, no trends. Each play stands alone, reflecting the clearly defined philosophy of the playwright or his complete lack of philosophy.

Serving this drama of diverse forms are theater plants of all physical configurations with stage machines of the utmost technical sophistication. In addition to the traditional proscenium form, there are arena theaters where the audience completely encircles the action; the apron stage extending forward so that the audience surrounds the action on three sides; and flexible spaces which allow for every imaginable shape of acting area and audience arrangement. Stages are equipped with wagons, turntables, elevators, and complicated winch-grid equipment. Powerful light sources have been developed and electronic lighting control systems perfected. Both the stage machine and the stage lighting are computer-controlled. Settings are no longer limited to traditional wood and canvas construction. Projected scenery on film, used alone or in combination with other elements, provide scenic backgrounds. There is no limit to the kind of theater or setting that can be provided.

To meet the demands of the modern theater, the actor must master a variety of styles. Actors may be called upon to perform in the classical style of the Greeks or the French, the robust action of the Elizabethans, the realism of the Moscow Art tradition, the alienation of Brecht, the absurdism of Beckett or Ionesco, or the stylization of the Kabuki. They must have voices of great range and be able to dance, fence, tumble, and box. They must possess stamina and durability of both mind and body.

To the producer and to the audience, this is a theater of confusion and challenge, frustration and gratification, but most of all, a theater that is vibrant and alive. In spite of high production costs and the competition of motion pictures and television, the theater remains one of the most important activities of our society and culture.

Bibliography

Artaud, Antonin. *The Theatre and Its Double.* New York: Grove Press, 1958.

Bentley, Eric. *Theatre of Commitment.* New York: Atheneum Publishers, 1967.

———. *Theatre of War: Modern Drama from Ibsen to Brecht.* New York: Viking Press, 1973.

Blum, Daniel. *A Pictorial History of the American Theatre, 1860–1970.* 3rd ed. Ed. John Willis. New York: Crown Publishers, 1969.

Bogard, Travis, and Oliver, William I., eds. *Modern Drama: Essays in Criticism.* New York: Oxford University Press, 1965.

Brustein, Robert. *The Theatre of Revolt: An Approach to the Modern Drama.* Boston: Little, Brown and Co., 1964.

Clark, Barrett H. *European Theories of Drama.* Rev. ed. Ed. Henry Popkin. New York: Crown Publishers, 1965.

Cunliffe, John W. *Modern English Playwrights.* New York: Harper and Bros., 1927. Reprinted by Kennikat Press, Port Washington, New York.

Esslin, Martin. *The Theatre of the Absurd.* New York: Doubleday and Co., Anchor Books, 1969.

Flexner, Eleanor. *American Playwrights, 1918–1938.* New York: Simon and Schuster, 1938. Reprinted by Books for Libraries, Plainview, New York.

Gagey, Edmond M. *Revolution in the American Drama.* New York: Columbia University Press, 1947. Reprinted by Books for Libraries, Plainview, New York.

Gassner, John. *Theatre at the Crossroads: Plays and Playwrights on the Mid-Century American Stage.* New York: Holt, Rinehart and Winston, 1960.

———. *Directions in Modern Theatre and Drama.* New York: Holt, Rinehart and Winston, 1965.

Grossvogel, David. *Twentieth Century French Drama.* New York: Columbia University Press, 1958.

Guicharnaud, Jacques, and Guicharnaud, June. *Modern French Theatre from Giraudoux to Genet.* Rev. ed. New Haven: Yale University Press, 1967.

Hudson, Lynton Alfred. *The English Stage, 1850–1950.* London: George

Harrap and Co., 1951. Reprinted by Greenwood Press, West-port, Connecticut.

Kirby, E. T., ed. *Total Theatre: A Critical Anthology.* New York: E. P. Dutton and Co., 1969.

Kirby, Michael, ed. *Happenings: An Illustrated Anthology.* New York: E. P. Dutton and Co., 1965.

Lumley, Frederick. *New Trends in Twentieth Century Drama: A Survey since Ibsen and Shaw.* 4th ed. New York: Oxford University Press, 1972.

Lesnick, Henry, ed. *Guerrilla Street Theater.* New York: Avon Books, 1973.

Nicoll, Allardyce. *A History of English Drama, Vol. 5: Late Nineteenth Century Drama, 1850–1900.* New York: Cambridge University Press, 1959.

———. *A History of English Drama: The Beginnings of the Modern Period, 1900–1930.* New York: Cambridge University Press, 1959.

Robinson, Lennox. *The Irish Theatre.* London: Macmillan Ltd., 1939. Reprinted by Haskell House Publishers, New York.

Schechner, Richard. *Environmental Theater.* New York: Hawthorn Books, 1973.

Simonson, Lee. *The Stage Is Set.* New York: Theatre Arts, 1962.

Taylor, John R. *Anger and After: A Guide to the New British Drama.* London: Methuen and Co., 1962.

Wellarth, George E. *Theatre of Protest and Paradox: Developments in Avant-Garde Drama.* 2nd ed. New York: New York University Press, 1970.

Summaries of Plays

Achard, Marcel. *A Shot in the Dark.* (1961) Adapted from the French by Harry Kurnitz. Comedy. Interior. Modern costumes. 5m. 3w. Baker $1.75. French $1.75. Royalty $50—$25.

A young girl is brought before the magistrate for the murder of her lover, who was found dead next to her. Her frankness during the investigation impresses the magistrate, who frees her and eventually uncovers the real murderer. Suitable for all groups.

Albee, Edward. *The Ballad of the Sad Cafe.* (1963) Based on the novel by Carson McCullers. Drama. Unit set. Modern Southern costumes. 14m. 6w. Dramatists Play Service $1.75. Royalty $55—$30. Restricted to amateur performances before unsegregated audiences.

A study of love and violence centering on three characters: a huge, mannish woman, the moody, tempestuous ex-convict whom she marries; and the dwarf who spurs on the violence which erupts between them. Advanced groups only.

————. *A Delicate Balance.* (1966) Morality play. Interior. Modern costumes. 2m. 4w. Baker $1.75. French $1.75. Royalty $50—$25.

A man and woman, whose marriage has drifted loose and who harbor the wife's alcoholic sister from the shocks of a bitter world, receive in one night their daughter, who has lost her fourth marriage, and friends fleeing from unknown fears. The result is the realization that their lives are a delicate balance between sanity and madness. Requires mature characterizations. For advanced groups only.

————. *Tiny Alice.* (1964) Drama. 2 interiors, 1 simple exterior. Modern costumes. 4m. 1w. Dramatists Play Service $1.75. Royalty $50—$25. Restricted to amateur performances before unsegregated audiences.

The interaction between a lawyer and a cardinal, former classmates, when the lawyer, representing Miss Alice, offers the church a gift, and a lay leader goes to Miss Alice's castle to work out the details. A confusing story for advanced groups only.

————. *Who's Afraid of Virginia Woolf?* (1962) Drama. Interior. Modern costumes. 2m. 2w. Dramatists Play Service $1.75. Royalty $50. Restricted to amateur performances before unsegregated audiences.

The lives of four people, two professors and their wives, are disclosed one drunken evening in the home of the established professor. Each character reveals without inhibitions the degrading mess he has made of his life. The language and action make this play unsuitable for high school production.

Alfred, William. *Hogan's Goat.* (1966) Tragedy in 3 acts. Composite interior-exterior. Costumes of 1890. 10m. 5w. 5 extras. Baker $1.75. French $1.75. Royalty $50—$25.

Matthew Stanton, ward leader, is caught up in a web of duplicity, adultery, and conspiracy that eventually undermines his marriage and his bid for the mayoralty of Brooklyn. Fear of being discovered as having been called Hogan's goat—the dupe of a lower class woman and the butt of community gossip—only seals his destruction. Advanced groups only. Ethnic interest: Irish-American.

Allen, Woody. *Play It Again, Sam.* (1969) Comedy. Interior. Modern costumes. 3m. 8w. Baker $1.75. French $1.75. Royalty $50—$35.

A homely little hero with a Humphrey Bogart fixation has his dream come true when Bogart enters his life to help him make it in the world. Unfortunately, the dream turns into a nightmare, and the hero bumbles through a series of misadventures which end in his accepting himself for what he is. Suitable for all groups.

Anderson, Maxwell. *Anne of the Thousand Days.* (1948) Romantic drama. 1 simple setting, minimum of props. 16th century English costumes. 11m. 5w. extras. Dramatists Play Service $1.75. Royalty $50—$25.

The story of Henry VIII and his second wife, Anne Boleyn, is played against the well-known historical background of the court of Henry. Requires mature actors.

————. *Both Your Houses.* (1933) Satire in 3 acts. 2 interiors. Modern costumes. 13m. 3w. French $1.75. Royalty $25—$20.

A young, idealistic congressman is pitted against a group of old-time politicians, all at work on a big appropriations bill. When he cannot get an honest bill, he makes the bill ridiculously dishonest. Ironically, the bill now passes through both houses. For advanced groups.

————. *Elizabeth the Queen.* (1930) Romantic drama in 3 acts. 4 interiors, 1 exterior. Elizabethan costumes. 16m. 7w. extras. French $1.75. Royalty $25—$20.

Elizabeth, an aging woman, delights in Essex as courtier and lover but sees him as a threat to her throne. Essex, though loving Elizabeth, longs for action, power, and glory and despises Elizabeth's crafty statesmanship. Summoned home from his expedition to Ireland, he returns with an army, determined to get his way. But Elizabeth will not give up the throne and Essex must die. Advanced groups only.

————. *The Eve of Saint Mark.* (1942) Drama in 2 acts. 1 set. World War II costumes. 13m. 8w. Dramatic Publishing Co. $1.50. Royalty $35.

Quizz, a GI in the Philippines, talks with Janet in her home on the eve of Saint Mark, the time when, according to legend, those who are about to die are able to talk with those they love. Suitable for all groups.

————. *Joan of Lorraine.* (1946) Romantic drama. Bare stage, suggestions of scenery. Joan of Arc in traditional costume, the rest modern. 18m. 5w. Dramatists Play Service $1.75. Royalty $50—$25.

A play within a play, the outer play showing a group of actors rehearsing a production of a play about Joan of Arc. Through the rehearsal, the actress playing Joan learns that each person has his own kind of faith and idealism. Requires sensitive acting; for advanced groups only.

————. *Mary of Scotland.* (1933) Drama in 3 acts. 4 interiors, 1 exterior. Elizabethan costumes. 22m. 5w. French $1.75. Royalty $25—$20.

The six years of Mary's life from her return to Scotland to rule as queen to her incarceration in Carlisle Castle. Mary and Elizabeth are contrasted: Mary, the romantic idealist, bewildered by the crafty young Elizabeth, who sees Mary as a threat to her crown. Within the range of high school groups.

————. *The Wingless Victory.* (1936) Tragedy. 2 interiors. Costumes,

1800. 8m. 8w. Dramatists Play Service, manuscript. Royalty $35—$25.
A Malay woman kills herself and her two children when she finds that
her husband will not stand by her against the prejudice of his hometown.
A deeply moving poetic tragedy. Advanced groups only.

————. *Winterset.* (1935) Verse drama in 3 acts. 1 interior, 1 exterior.
Modern costumes. 16m. 3w. bits and extras. Dramatists Play Service
$1.75. Royalty $35—$25.
The young Mio, believing his father was innocent of the crime for
which he was executed, comes to the tenements of New York seeking
proof of his father's innocence. He falls in love with Miriamne, and
both are silenced by the true killers. Obvious allusions to the Sacco-
Vanzetti case of the 1920s. Within the range of advanced high school
groups. Ethnic interest: Italian-American.

Anderson, Robert. *Tea and Sympathy.* (1953) Drama in 3 acts. Composite interior. Modern costumes. 9m. 2w. French $1.75. Royalty $50—
$25.
A forlorn and sensitive boy is ridiculed at boarding school for lack of
manliness, and what begins as kidding is augmented by rumor and
becomes persecution. Trying to prove himself, the youth goes out on
the town with the village strumpet. This attempt fails because of his
revulsion for her, and he is now no longer ridiculed, but shunned. It
is the schoolmaster's wife who restores his self-respect in a delicate final
scene. For advanced groups.

Anderson, Walt. *"Me, Candido!"* (1958) Comedy-drama in 2 acts.
Unit set. 8m. 6w. 1 boy, 2 girls. Dramatists Play Service $1.75. Royalty
$35—$25.
A Puerto Rican family, an alcoholic Irishman, and a lonely old woman
get into trouble with the law when they try to take care of a homeless
eleven-year-old Puerto Rican orphan. A tribute to love and brotherhood
in a troubled world. For all groups. Ethnic interest: Puerto-Rican
American.

Andreyev, Leonid. *He Who Gets Slapped.* (1921) Translated by
Gregory Zilboorg. Tragedy in 4 acts. Interior. Fantastic and modern
costumes. 20m. 13w. French $2.00. Royalty $25—$20.
To forget the theft of his wife and his literary work, a mysterious
gentleman seeks refuge as a clown in the circus, and there falls in love
with the beautiful Consuelo, a bareback rider. Theirs is a highly symbolic love, which her father plans to end by marrying her to a wealthy
and degenerate baron. Rather than accept this, Consuelo and the clown
take poison and die. Interesting variety of character roles, costumes, and
makeup. Demands a mature and experienced actor for the lead.

Anouilh, Jean. *Antigone.* (1944) Translated by Lewis Galantiere.

Tragedy. Interior. Modern costumes. 8m. 4w. Baker $1.75. French $1.75. Royalty $25—$20.

The struggle between Antigone and her uncle Creon over the burial of her brother results in her execution, the death of Creon's son Haemon, her lover, and doom to the entire family. This modern version of the Greek legend has political overtones, reflecting France torn by war and complicity, and presents the existential dilemma of choice between absolute principles and compromise with the social order and life's circumstances. Moving drama within the range of advanced high school groups.

————. *Becket.* (1959) Translated by Lucienne Hill. Tragedy. Various interiors and exteriors. 12th century English costumes. 15m. 3w. Baker $1.75. French $1.75. Royalty $50—$25.

The account of the tragic relationship between the primitive-minded King Henry II and the friend of his youth, Thomas à Becket. After Henry made him archbishop, Becket was forced to oppose him. The irony of their struggle is that Henry, for all his hostility toward his former friend, always continued to love him, while Becket, the man of saintliness, held no more than an affection for this savage and simple-hearted monarch. Requires mature, advanced actors.

————. *The Lark.* (1953) Translated by Lillian Hellman. Drama. Set of movable platforms, no scenery. Period costumes. 15m. 5w. Dramatists Play Service $1.75. Royalty $50—$25.

The story of Joan of Arc, the country girl who was inspired by unearthly voices to lead the armies of France and then was tried by the church. Is within the range of advanced high school groups.

————. *Poor Bitos.* (1965) Translated by Lucienne Hill. Drama. Interior. Modern and 18th century French costumes. 10m. 3w. 1 child. Baker $1.75. French $1.75. Royalty $50—$25.

A group of French patricians gather for a party in the vaulting room of an old chateau, where they recreate a scene from the French Revolution to humiliate Bitos, a prosecutor who has been likened to Robespierre. Advanced groups only.

————. *Ring round the Moon.* (1948) Translated by Christopher Fry. Comedy. 1 adjustable exterior. Modern costumes. 6m. (2 roles played by same actor) 7w. 2 extras. Dramatists Play Service $1.75. Royalty $50—$25.

A fable about twin brothers—Frederic, who is shy and sensitive, and Hugo, who is heartless and aggressive. To save Frederic from an unhappy marriage, Hugo invites a dancer to the family ball to masquerade as a mysterious person. She succeeds in breaking up all the cynical romances that have been going on before she arrived and loses her own heart as well.

————. *Time Remembered.* (1939) Translated by Patricia Moyes. Romantic comedy. 1 interior, 2 exteriors. Late 19th century costumes. 13m. 2w. French $1.75. Royalty $50—$25.

The handsome Prince Albert, aided and abetted by his aunt the Duchess, struggles to keep alive the memory of his love for the dead Leocadia. The Duchess prevails upon a young woman to impersonate the dead lady, but the plot is discovered by Albert. The resemblance is so strong, however, that his anger soon turns to fascination and, though he resists this treachery to his memories, the young lady succeeds in winning his heart. Suitable for all groups.

Archibald, William. *The Innocents.* (1950) Based on Henry James's *The Turn of the Screw.* Melodrama in 2 acts. Interior. 19th century costumes. 1m. 3w. 1 boy. 1 girl. Baker $1.75. French $1.75. Royalty $50—$25.

A young governess arrives at an English estate to assume charge of two precocious, orphaned youngsters. The governess, with the cook, are terrified by phantoms, shadows, and faces in moonlight, and the governess gradually learns that the two youngsters are possessed by the spirits of a former caretaker and maid, both of them evil and perverse, who have corrupted the souls of the innocents. A gripping story, suitable for all groups.

Ardrey, Robert. *Thunder Rock.* (1939) Drama. Interior. Modern costumes. 8m. 3w. Dramatists Play Service $1.75. Royalty $35—$25.

A disillusioned young man becomes a lighthouse keeper to escape from the world. He is visited by spirits of the past, who help to restore his faith in mankind and help him to reenter the world. Suitable for all groups.

Aurthur, Robert Alan. *A Very Special Baby.* (1957) Drama in 2 acts. Unit set. 5m. 1w. Dramatists Play Service $1.75. Royalty $35—$25.

Father Casale, self-made, rich, and self-centered, rules his immigrant family with an iron will. Because he is their father, Anna and Joey submit to his patriarchal ways until, one day, they realize the destructiveness of his tyranny. For advanced groups. Ethnic interest: Italian-American.

Axelrod, George. *The Seven Year Itch.* (1956) Comedy. Interior. Modern costumes. 6m. 5w. 1 boy. Dramatists Play Service $1.75. Royalty $50—$25.

After seven years of marriage the wife goes to the country for the summer. The husband realizes that life is slipping by and accepts an invitation to a fling, which results in one zany complication after another. A light divertissement for mature groups.

Ayckbourn, Alan. *How the Other Half Loves.* (1970) Farce. Split set.

Modern costumes. 3m. 3w. Baker $1.75. French $1.75. Royalty $50—$35.

A complicated farce concerning extra-marital activities. The charm of the production lies in the placement of two households on stage at the same time, weaving together the action taking place in each. Simple show, but requires skilled comic actors and sophisticated audiences.

Bagnold, Enid. *The Chalk Garden.* (1954) Drama. Interior. Modern costumes. 2m. 7w. Baker $1.75. French $1.75. Royalty $50—$25.

An English gentlewoman devotes her life to a garden in the arid soil and to advertising for and interviewing applicants for the position of governess for her granddaughter. She has no intention of hiring one, but one applicant is so excellent that she cannot be so easily overlooked. This governess possesses a strange power, and it is only when a famous jurist comes to dinner that the source is revealed. Requires strong characterizations. Suitable for all groups.

————. *The Chinese Prime Minister.* (1964) Comedy. Interior. Modern costumes. 5m. 3w. French $1.75. Royalty $50—$25.

An aging actress muses on the wisdom of age and the reverence given it in ancient China. She has a party, during which the issue is discussed and her marriage and the marriages of her two sons are enhanced.

Balderston, John L. *Berkeley Square.* (1926) Suggested by Henry James's story "A Sense of the Past." Fantasy in 3 acts. 2 interiors. Costumes, 1784 and modern. 7m. 8w. French $1.75. Royalty $25—$20.

Peter Standish changes places with an ancestor, taking the ancestor's body but retaining his 20th century soul. He becomes engaged to Kate, whom his ancestor married, and later falls in love with Kate's sister Helen. They love and have to part, for Peter and his ancestor must return to their places in time. Both are disillusioned men. Peter rejects the 20th century girl he was to marry to live alone with his memories. Requires sensitive characterizations and strong direction.

Barrie, James M. *The Admirable Crichton.* (1902) Fantasy in 4 acts. 2 interiors, 1 difficult exterior. Period or modern costumes. 13m. 12w. Baker $1.75. French $1.75. Royalty $35—$25.

The family of Lord Loam are shipwrecked on an island where it is Crichton, the butler, who takes command to save the family. He wins the affection of Lord Loam's daughter, Lady Mary, but they are rescued and return to civilization, where they return to their old social positions. Suitable for all groups. Excellent for high school.

————. *Alice Sit-by-the-Fire.* (1905) Comedy in 3 acts. 2 interiors. Modern or 1905 costumes. 3m. 6w. French $1.75. Royalty $35—$25.

Alice, who had been the center of social life, returns with her husband from India and must readapt herself to her home and family. Her imaginative teenage daughter Amy misunderstands Alice's coquettish remarks to a family friend and believes her mother is to have a rendezvous with him. In a grand gesture, Amy decides to meet the "lover" first. Alice finds her daughter's glove in her friend's apartment, and fears for her daughter. The misunderstanding is cleared up, and Alice accepts the fact that her place in the social whirl has changed. Suitable for all groups; excellent for high school.

————. *Dear Brutus.* (1917) Fantastic comedy in 3 acts. 1 interior, 1 exterior. Modern costumes. 4m. 6w. French $1.75. Royalty $35—$25.
It is Midsummer Eve and there are nine people gathered at an English country house. A magic woods appears, and the nine are given a second chance to live their lives. When the experience ends, they resume their lives, if not happier, at least wiser. Requires sensitive characterization; within the range of high school groups.

————. *Quality Street.* (1902) Comedy in 4 acts. 2 interiors. Costumes, about 1800. 6m. 9w. extras. French $1.75. Royalty $35—$25.
Phoebe, a plain but personable young woman, loves Valentine, who leaves for the Napoleonic wars without proposing. Phoebe is the butt of ridicule. After ten years, Valentine returns, but Phoebe's personality has changed so much that he mistakes her for a fictitious niece. He discovers his love for her and, fortunately, the deception as well. Suitable for all groups.

————. *What Every Woman Knows.* (1908) Comedy in 4 acts. 4 interiors. Costumes, about 1900. 7m. 4w. extras. French $1.75. Royalty $35—$25.
The Wylies offer to finance John's education if he will give their common-looking and heartsick sister Maggie the option of becoming his wife. He agrees. Later, she offers to release him, but he sticks to the bargain and marries her. John becomes infatuated with a beautiful countess and Maggie is heartbroken, but he discovers that Maggie, and not the countess, is the source and spirit of his success and that he cannot do without her. Suitable for all groups.

Barry, Philip. *The Animal Kingdom.* (1932) Comedy in 3 acts. 2 interiors. Modern costumes. 5m. 4w. French $1.75. Royalty $50—$25.
The story of a man with two marriages, one with the benefit of the clergy. Tom Collier, an unconscious artist and nonconformist at heart, finds it difficult to determine which of the two women in his life is wife and which is mistress. Sophisticated comedy for advanced groups.

————. *Heritage.* (1933) Folktale. Open stage, no scenery. 19th century costumes. 7m. 5w. extras. Baker $1.75. French $1.75. Royalty $25.

This is the story of the women behind Abraham Lincoln, from the time of his maternal grandmother, Lucy Hanks, through his marriage to Mary Todd and life in the White House. An exciting look at the personal history of Lincoln's life. Especially good for high school.

————. *Hotel Universe.* (1930) Morality play. Exterior. Modern costumes. 5m. 4w. French $2.00. Royalty $50—$25.

When a group of strangers are faced with the suicide of a young man, there starts a series of psychological revelations in each. They relive personal crises as they face the baffling problems of their lives. For advanced groups.

————. *The Philadelphia Story.* (1939) Comedy in 3 acts. 1 interior, 1 exterior (porch). Modern costumes. 9m. 6w. Baker $1.75. French $1.75. Royalty $50—$25.

In the midst of making arrangements for her second marriage, Tracy Lord, a spoiled Philadelphia socialite, finds herself growing interested in Connor, a reporter sent by a social gossip weekly to do a feature. There is champagne, a midnight dip in the pool, and a confrontation with Kittredge, her prospective husband. Connor offers to marry her, but she chooses to remarry her former husband, to the satisfaction of everyone. Requires a high degree of sophisticated acting. For all groups.

————. *Second Threshold.* (1951) Revised by Robert E. Sherwood. Drama. Interior. Modern costumes. 4m. 2w. Dramatists Play Service $1.75. Royalty $50—$25.

The dilemma of an eminent public official who has reached the heights of achievement through devoted service, only to realize that he has lost all human contact with his family. Advanced groups.

Batson, George. *Ramshackle Inn.* (1944) Melodramatic mystery-farce. Interior. Modern costumes. 9m. 6w. Dramatists Play Service $1.75. Royalty $35—$25.

An old maid librarian has saved her money for twenty years to buy a hotel where she can meet interesting people. She purchases a strange tumbledown place near the ocean, and she gets what she bargains for— plus a good deal more. Fun for all groups.

Beckett, Samuel. *Waiting for Godot.* (1953) Tragicomedy. Open stage. Modern costumes. 4m. 1 boy. Dramatists Play Service $1.95. Royalty $50—$25.

Two bums idle away their time waiting for the mysterious Godot. They are joined by a brutal man and his slave; later the same individuals return as a blind man led by a mute servant. It is a portrait of man's persistence in a world of no hope. Excellent for all groups. Requires mature audience.

Behan, Brendan. *The Hostage.* (1958) Comedy. Composite interior-exterior. Modern costumes. 11m. 7w. Baker $1.95. French $1.65. Royalty $50—$25.

An innocent British soldier is held by the IRA in a bawdy Irish bar as a hostage, to be shot if the British go through with the execution of an IRA youth. As we wait to see whether or not the British will comply, the lives of these people are revealed, and a tender romance develops between the soldier and one of the girls. A raucous play, it makes a statement against violence and injustice. Mature groups only.

Behrman, S. N. *Lord Pengo.* (1962) Comedy. 2 interiors. 1930s costumes. 7m. 4w. French $1.75. Royalty $50—$25.

Lord Pengo gulls many an uncultured millionaire, but at the same time he performs an inestimable service in bringing to America some of the greatest art treasures of all time. He even gets one client to establish a national gallery in Washington. It is difficult to determine if he is a villain or hero. Advanced groups.

————. *The Second Man.* (1927) Comedy in 3 acts. Interior. Modern costumes. 2m. 2w. French $1.75. Royalty $50—$25.

Clark Storey is a novelist with whom two women are in love. He is determined to marry the young romantic one, but in the end throws her over to marry the older, more practical woman, with whom he can be comfortable. Requires a high degree of sophisticated style.

Berns, Julie, and Elman, Irving. *Uncle Willie.* (1956) Farce in 3 acts. 1 interior, 1 exterior. 6m. 5w. 3 girls. French $1.75. Royalty $50—$25.

Immigrant life among the Irish and Jewish inhabitants of the Bronx early in the century. Uncle Willie is the general salesman of the neighborhood who will sell anybody anything. His generous heart finances a boardinghouse for his niece, arranges housing for an Irish policeman and his family, and negotiates a second marriage for the Irishman's widow after her husband is killed in a gun war. Uncle Willie sees to everything! For all groups. Ethnic interest: Jewish American.

Berrigan, Daniel. *The Trial of the Catonsville Nine.* (1970) Documentary drama. Interior. 9m. 2w. Baker $1.75. French $1.75. Royalty $50—$35.

The trial of the two priests, the Berrigan brothers, and their seven confederates who destroyed selective service records at Colmsville, Maryland, reveals the personal commitment of this group of protestors against the Vietnam War. Theirs is the cry of conscience in defiance of the strictures of law. Within the range of advanced high school groups.

Besier, Rudolf. *The Barretts of Wimpole Street.* (1930) Romantic comedy. Interior. 19th century costumes. 12m. 5w. Dramatists Play Service $1.75. Royalty $50—$25.

The love of Robert Browning rescues Elizabeth Barrett from her semi-invalid existence in the house of her domineering father. Suitable for all groups.

Betti, Ugo. *Corruption in the Palace of Justice.* (1949) Translated by Robert Corrigan. Melodrama. Interior. Modern costumes. 9m. 2w. French $2.25. Royalty $35—$25.

Following the suicide of a corruptor and rumors of bribery at court, an investigator is appointed to determine who among the judges is venal, who is the moral leper. The action is suspenseful and intriguing. Advanced groups only.

Bevan, Donald, and Trzcinski, Edmund. *Stalag 17.* (1951) Comedy-melodrama. Interior. World War II Army costumes. 21m. Dramatists Play Service $1.75. Royalty $50—$25.

A group of American prisoners in a German prison camp plot the escape of a new prisoner. There is a German spy among them. They suspect the wrong man, but the real traitor is unmasked, and the escape is successful. Requires a great number of proficient men; within the range of advanced high school groups.

Bolt, Robert. *A Man for All Seasons.* (1960) Tragedy. Unit set. 16th century English costumes. 11m. 3w. Baker $1.75. French $1.75. Royalty $50—$25.

Sir Thomas More, Lord Chancellor of England, is forced to oppose the wishes of Henry VIII. More must take stands which involve conflicting loyalties—country, church, family, and self. The play follows these decisions which result in his death. Excellent for advanced groups.

Bolton, Guy. *Anastasia.* (1953) Adapted from the play by Marcelle Maurette. Drama in 3 acts. Interior. Royal and peasant Russian costumes. 8m. 5w. Baker $1.75. French $1.75. Royalty $50—$25.

Russian Prince Beunine, now a Berlin taxi driver, discovers a young girl lost and confused by amnesia who claims to be the sole surviving member of the Russian royal family. To share in £10 million held in foreign banks for the children of the Tsar, Beunine conspires to train the girl to fulfill the role. But the Imperial grandmother is alive; her acceptance is essential. In a suspenseful scene the two women meet, one with half-awakened memories, the other fighting against opening old wounds. Tense story, suitable for all groups.

Bond, Nelson. *Animal Farm.* (1964) Based on the novel by George Orwell. Reading. Bare stage. 5m. 2w. Baker $1.75. French $1.75. Royalty $25—$20.

Beasts who emancipate themselves from the cruelty of their human masters find themselves subject to the oppressive rule of the greedy, cunning pigs. Suitable for advanced groups.

Boothe, Clare. *The Women.* (1936) Comedy. 11 interiors (several very simple). Modern costumes. 35w. Dramatists Play Service $1.75. Royalty $35—$25.

The story of one woman's fight to save a marriage in an artificial society that offers vain show, comedy, tragedy, hope, and disappointment to women. For mature groups only.

Boruff, John. *The Loud Red Patrick.* (1956) Based on the novel by Ruth McKenney. Romantic comedy in 3 acts. Interior. Costumes of 1912. 4m. 5w. French $1.75. Royalty $50—$25.

Patrick Flannigan, an Irish-American widower who runs his household of four daughters on the parliamentary principle, finds his system upset when the marriage plans of his eldest daughter are approved by the family council over his opposition. He scraps the council and the daughters declare war. A parallel plot involves a sour love affair between Patrick's old friend Finnegan, who has come to sponge off the Flannigans, and the housekeeper. Fresh, unsophisticated. For all groups. Ethnic interest: Irish-American.

Brecht, Bertolt. *Brecht on Brecht.* (1962) Arranged and translated by George Tabori. Revue. Modern costumes. 4m. 3w. Baker $1.75. French $1.75. Restricted. Royalty $50—$25.

Readings and enactments from the works of Brecht. The first half shows some of Brecht's philosophy and ideology while the second half consists of a song, a monologue, and excerpts from his plays. Advanced, mature groups only.

————. *The Caucasian Chalk Circle.* (1945) Suggested by the Yüan dynasty play *The Chalk Circle.* English version by Eric Bentley. Tragicomedy in 2 parts. 6 interiors, 4 exteriors, 1 composite interior-exterior. Modern or Chinese costumes. 39m. 14w. 4 children, chorus, extras. French $1.25. Restricted. Royalty $50—$25.

A prince deposes the governor and scatters his family, but a woman named Grusha saves the governor's child and protects it. She is captured and brought before Azkak, a scoundrel who has promoted himself to a judge during the civil strife. He must determine whether the child should be given to her or to the mother, who deserted it. Advanced, mature groups only.

————. *Mother Courage and Her Children.* (1939) English version by Eric Bentley. Morality play in 3 acts. Interior and 5 exteriors. 17th century costumes. 18m. 5w. extras. Baker $1.75. French $1.75. Restricted. Royalty $50—$25.

The life of Mother Courage and her family is viewed through twelve years of the Holy War of the early seventeenth century—through Sweden, Poland, Finland, Bavaria, and Italy. A sharp comment on the futility of war and on those who fail to oppose it. Extremely difficult to interpret and direct. Requires outstanding acting.

————. *The Private Life of the Master Race.* (1945) English version by Eric Bentley. Melodrama. Platform style, many characters. World War II costumes. French, manuscript. Royalty $50—$25.

A series of episodes showing the terror and dehumanization of the people in Germany as Nazism takes control of the land. Advanced groups; can be produced by high school students.

Brewer, George Jr., and Bloch, Bertram. *Dark Victory.* (1934) Drama. 2 interiors. Modern costumes. 7m. 7w. extras. Dramatists Play Service $1.75. Royalty $35—$25.

Judith, a spoiled, casual socialite, discovers that alcohol and random affairs cannot replace love and devotion, but only after submitting to an operation which gives her but a few months to live with her new-found love. Advanced groups only.

Bridie, James. *Tobias and the Angel.* (1930) Based on the Book of Tobit. Comedy in 3 acts. 1 interior, 3 exteriors. Biblical costumes. 8m. 8w. French $1.75. Royalty $25—$20.

Timid and diffident Tobias is sent by his father Tobit to a distant city to reclaim an old debt from Raguel, now a wealthy merchant. Accompanying Tobias is the archangel Raphael, who styles himself as hired hand and porter. In Raguel's garden, Tobias woos and wins the merchant's daughter Sara. Everything goes smoothly despite the fact that, possessed by the demon Asmodey, Sara has strangled seven previous bridegrooms on their wedding nights. Advanced groups.

Burrows, Abe. *The Cactus Flower.* (1966) Based on a play by Pierre Barillet and Jean P. Gredy. Comedy. 4 sets. Modern costumes. 7m. 4w. Baker $1.75. French $1.75. Royalty $50—$35.

A bachelor dentist has a sure gimmick to keep himself single: he simply tells his many girlfriends that he is married and has three children. But the device backfires when he falls in love with one particular girl and she wants to meet the family. Mature groups only.

Cannan, Denis, and Bost, Pierre. *The Power and the Glory.* (1959) Based on the novel by Graham Greene. Tragedy. Unit set. Mexican costumes, 1910. 28m. 9w. extras. French $1.75. Royalty $35—$25.

In the revolutionary days of Mexico a priest decides to stay in disguise with his people rather than escape. Wherever he goes, however, the police are close behind and execute those who harbor him. Humanly weak, with a past of many sins, he travels to another province and there falls into his old pleasures. At the moment of his escape, he chooses to attend a dying man, and is there ambushed and executed. Advanced groups, within the range of high school.

Čapek, Josef, and Čapek, Karel. *The World We Live In (The Insect Comedy).* (1921) Adapted and arranged by Owen Davis. Comedy in prelude, 3 acts, epilogue. Modern and fantastic costumes representing insects. 21m. 9w. extras. French $1.75. Royalty $25—$20.

A wanderer who is something of a philosopher falls asleep- after heavy drinking and in his dream observes the comedy and tragedy of the insect world, whose problems and affairs are uncomfortably like those of humans. Suitable for advanced groups.

Čapek, Karel. *R.U.R.* (1921) Translated by Paul Selver and Nigel Playfair. Fantastic melodrama in 3 acts and epilogue. 2 interiors (can be played in 1 set). Modern costumes. 13m. 4w. Baker $1.75. French $1.75. Royalty $25—$20.

The central office of the factory of Rossum's Universal Robots, on an island in our planet. The robots become humanized by a secret formula and overthrow mankind, until only one human is left. Finally, a man-robot and a woman-robot, with a bit of Adam and Eve in them, are about to start mankind afresh. Suitable for all groups.

Capote, Truman. *The Grass Harp.* (1954) Comedy-fantasy. 1 interior, 1 exterior. Modern costumes. 10m. 8w. Dramatists Play Service $1.75. Royalty $50—$25.

The pure in heart, like the meek, inherit the earth. A trio finds temporary refuge in a tree house from the selfishness and cant of the small town they live in. Demands sensitive acting. Advanced groups.

Carroll, Paul Vincent. *Shadow and Substance.* (1934) Drama. Interior. Modern costumes. 6m. 4w. Dramatists Play Service $1.75. Royalty $35—$25.

A study of the faith of the Irish in the Catholic Church, portrayed by a simple young girl serving as caretaker in the house of an aloof canon. Advanced groups.

Casella, Alberto. *Death Takes a Holiday.* (1929) American stage version by Walter Ferris. Drama in 3 acts. Interior. Modern costumes. 7m. 6w. Baker $2.00. French $2.00. Royalty $50—$25.

Death suspends all activities for three days. During this period he falls in love with a beautiful girl, and through her realizes why mortals fear him. A novel and optimistic philosophical consideration of the problems of love and death. Suitable for all groups.

Caspary, Vera, and Sklar, George. *Laura.* (1948) Based on the novel by Vera Caspary. Mystery. Interior. Modern costumes. 5m. 3w. Dramatists Play Service $1.75. Royalty $50—$25.

Mark McPherson first falls in love with a picture of Laura, whose murder he has come to investigate. When she appears, she becomes a prime suspect for the murder of the person originally thought to be her. Tense, exciting; for all groups.

Chase, Mary. *Bernardine.* (1953) Comedy. Simple, stylized scenery. Modern costumes. 13m. 6w. Dramatists Play Service $1.75. Royalty $50—$25.
Several prankish youths, "nice" Dead End kids, imagine themselves in the ideal town, where the relations between them and grownups are completely reversed, a teenage utopia featuring the ideal female. Suitable for all groups, especially mature high school.

————. *Harvey.* (1944) Comedy in 3 acts. 2 simple interiors. Modern costumes. 6m. 6w. Dramatists Play Service $1.75. Royalty $50—$25.
Harvey is a seven-foot white rabbit who accompanies the lovable hero Elwood. When Elwood is to be dispatched to a mental hospital for observation, his sane sister is committed instead. Hero must be strong character actor. Especially suited for advanced, mature groups.

————. *Mrs. McThing.* (1952) Comic fantasy. Interiors. Modern costumes. 9m. 10w. 1 boy, 1 girl. Dramatists Play Service $1.75. Royalty $50—$25.
A witch's tricks save a family by convincing the mother to accept her little boy on his own terms and not to look down on other people. Suited for all groups.

Chayefsky, Paddy. *Gideon.* (1962) Drama. Unit set. Biblical costumes. 18m. 6w. 1 boy. Dramatists Play Service $1.75. Royalty $50—$25.
Gideon is chosen by the Lord to save the people of Israel from the persecutions of the Midianites. At first he refuses and is rejected by his people, but he succeeds in the end. Requires actors capable of age. Suitable for all groups.

————. *Middle of the Night.* (1956) Drama. Interior. Modern costumes. 3m. 8w. Baker $1.75. French $1.75. Royalty $50—$25.
A 53-year-old widower meets a beautiful girl, nearly thirty years his junior, who is in turn lonely and adrift. They fit together; they belong together. But the disturbing question is whether or not he has any right to a woman so young. For mature groups.

————. *The Tenth Man.* (1959) Comedy in 3 acts. Composite interior. Modern costumes. 12m. 1w. French $1.75. Royalty $50—$25.
An old meeting room now used as a temple contains ten interesting persons. Among those gathered for prayer are an elderly man and his attractive granddaughter who, some believe, is possessed by a dybbuk, or evil spirit. During her more lucid moments, she and the agnostic lawyer are attracted to each other, which brings hope to the girl and a

capacity for love to the young skeptic. Requires mature character types; for advanced groups. Ethnic interest: Jewish-American.

Chekhov, Anton. *The Cherry Orchard.* (1903) Translated by Stark Young. Drama in 4 acts. 1 exterior, 2 interiors. Russian costumes of 1903. 10m. 5w. Baker $1.75. French $1.75. Royalty $25—$20.

An estate, its beautiful trees and grounds symbolic vestiges of the dying Russian aristocracy, is auctioned off to the son of a boorish peasant who has succeeded in industry. The family of Mrs. Ranevsky, once proud landowners, depart to take up their lives anew elsewhere under the solemn strokes of the woodsmen's axes, as the cherished trees make way for a project. For skilled actors only.

————. *The Sea Gull.* (1896) Translated by Stark Young. Drama in 4 acts. 2 interiors, 2 exteriors. Costumes, about 1896. 8m. 6w. French $1.75. Royalty $25—$20.

Nina is enchanted by the debonair Trigorin, a moderately popular author. She runs off with him to the great city where she bears him a child and becomes a common actress. Deserted by him, she returns home, where once again she rejects the advances of the melancholy and lovesick son of a middle-aged and fading actress. Whereupon, he kills himself. Skilled, mature actors only.

————. *The Three Sisters.* (1900) Translated by Stark Young. Drama in 4 acts. 2 interiors, 1 exterior. Costumes, about 1900. 9m. 5w. French $1.75. Royalty $25—$20.

Three sisters are stranded by their father's death in a provincial town and are longing to return to Moscow. Their efforts to escape are thwarted and they must settle for a life of boredom and disillusionment. Skilled, mature actors only.

Chin, Frank. *The Year of the Dragon.* (1974) Drama in 2 acts. Interior. 4m. 3w. Royalty: contact the American Place Theatre.

Set in San Francisco's Chinatown during the Chinese New Year's celebration, 1974. The play deals with two generations of a Chinese-American family and with the emerging consciousness of the new generation. For advanced groups. Ethnic interest: Chinese-American.

Chodorov, Edward. *Kind Lady.* (1934) Based on a story by Hugh Walpole. Melodrama in 3 acts. Interior. Modern costumes. 6m. 8w. Baker $1.75. French $1.75. Royalty $25—$20.

A dignified and aristocratic middle-aged woman in London is surrounded by a family of crooks. They attempt to convince the outside world that she is insane in order to confiscate her property. She finally wins the battle. Tense, exciting drama for all groups.

Christie, Agatha. *Ten Little Indians.* (1946) Mystery-comedy in 3 acts. Interior. Modern costumes. 8m. 3w. Baker $1.75. French $1.75. Royalty $50—$25.

Eight invited weekend guests and two house servants find themselves the subjects of murder plotted on the nursery rhyme of the ten little Indians. Excellent for all groups.

————. *Witness for the Prosecution.* (1954) Melodrama in 3 acts. 2 interiors. Modern costumes. 17m. 5w. 8 nondescript. Baker $1.75. French $1.75. Royalty $50—$25.

A highly suspenseful courtroom mystery of intricate and artfully woven plot in which the murderer almost goes free. Requires mature actors.

Clark, Perry. *Cheaper by the Dozen.* (1950) Based on the book by Frank Gilbreth and Ernestine Gilbreth Carey. Comedy in 3 acts. Interior. Modern costumes. 9m. 7w. Dramatic Publishing Co. $1.75. Eldridge $1.75. Royalty $35.

Dad, a terrific efficiency expert, believes that what will work in his factory will also work in the home. He introduces "organization," equivalent to martial law, into his large family with both hilarious and disastrous results. Recommended for high school groups.

————. *Meet Me in Saint Louis.* (1948) Based on the novel by Sally Benson. Comedy in 3 acts. Interior. Early 20th century costumes. 7m. 9w. Dramatic Publishing Co. $1.75. Eldridge $1.75. Royalty $35.

Four attractive sisters decide to run the family in general, and the romances of their only brother in particular. When father announces that he's been offered a better job in New York, the girls realize that they'll miss the World's Fair, and at this unite for action. Although their strategy almost lands the family in jail, they persist in their battle to stay where they've been so happy. Especially suited for high school groups.

Coffee, Lenore, and Cowen, William Joyce. *Family Portrait.* (1939) Drama in 3 acts. 1 interior, 3 exteriors. Biblical costumes. 12m. 10w. Baker $2.00. French $2.00. Royalty $25—$20.

The last three years of Christ's life, in which we see that the family does not consider him divine. Only Mary senses his role and accepts him as the Messiah. Advanced groups, within range of high school.

Cohan, George M. *Seven Keys to Baldpate.* (1913) Melodramatic farce in 3 acts. Interior. Modern costumes. 9m. 4w. Baker $1.75. French $1.75. Royalty $25—$20.

When a writer goes to a mountain inn to develop a plot for a story, the intrigue and mystery that develop with the others at the inn offer more than he bargained for. Tense; suitable for all groups.

Colton, John, and Randolph, Clemence. *Rain.* (1972) Based on the story "Miss Thompson," by W. S. Maugham. Drama in 3 acts. Interior. Modern costumes. 10m. 5w. French $1.75. Royalty $50—$25.

A missionary on a quarantined Pacific isle seeks to reform a prostitute. The prostitute, Sadie Thompson, discovers that he has information which could send her to prison and agrees to be converted. Sadie appears truly contrite, but when the missionary leaves his family for her, she returns to her old ways, and the missionary is a suicide. For mature groups only.

Conkle, E. P. *Prologue to Glory.* (1938) Historical play in 8 scenes. 5 exteriors, 1 interior. Costumes of 1831. 14m. 7w. extras. French $1.75. Royalty $25—$20.

An account of the life of young Abraham Lincoln, a poor, uneducated rail-splitter, and of his attachment to Ann Rutledge in his early twenties, when he was clerking in a store in New Salem. Advanced groups.

Coppel, Alec. *The Gazebo.* (1959) Comedy-melodrama. Interior. Modern costumes. 9m. 3w. Dramatists Play Service $1.75. Royalty $50—$25.

A writer for TV whodunits with an eye toward inventing the almost-perfect crime gets in a spot where he has to commit a real do-it-yourself murder. To protect his wife from blackmail he places the victim under the concrete of the new gazebo in the backyard. Mature groups only.

Corwin, Norman. *The Rivalry.* (1960) Drama. Series of platforms, no scenery. 1850s costumes. 2m. 1w. 3 bits. Dramatists Play Service $1.75. Royalty $50—$25.

The play discloses the personal issues as well as the political ones during the Lincoln-Douglas debates. Mrs. Douglas ties the proceedings together. Requires actors with unique physical characteristics to be plausible.

Coward, Noel. *Blithe Spirit.* (1941) Farce in 3 acts. Interior. Modern costumes. 2m. 5w. Baker $1.75. French $1.75. Royalty $50—$25.

The ghost of Charles' first wife plots his death so that he may join her. When his second wife is killed by mistake, he is plagued by both women's blithe spirits. Light, humorous; within the range of mature high school groups.

————. *Fallen Angels.* (1925) Comedy. Interior. Modern costumes. 3m. 3w. French $1.75. Royalty $50—$25.

Julia and Jane, best friends, eagerly await the appearance of a past charmer. As their husbands are away, they spend the time discussing the past. They quarrel, make up, and get high on champagne. The day is topped with the husbands coming home early. For advanced groups.

————. *Hay Fever.* (1925) Farcical comedy in 3 acts. Interior. Modern costumes. 4m. 5w. Baker $1.75. French $1.75. Royalty $50—$25.

Weekend guests of the eccentric family of Judith Bliss, retired actress, are confronted by a series of stormy scenes which confuse them but which provide readjustments in the personal lives of Judith and the other members of the family. Suitable for all groups.

————. *Private Lives.* (1931) Comedy in 3 acts. 2 interiors. Modern costumes. 2m. 3w. Baker $1.75. French $1.75. Restricted. Royalty $50—$25.

Two newlywed couples room in adjoining suites. The husband of one and wife of the other were formerly married. After complications, verbal and physical fights, flight and pursuit to Paris, there is a final reshuffling. The couple originally married and divorced are reunited. Mature groups only.

Coxe, Louis O., and Chapman, Robert. *Billy Budd.* (1951) Based on the novel by Herman Melville. Drama. 2 interiors, 1 exterior. British Navy costumes, 1798. 22m. Dramatists Play Service $1.95. Royalty $50—$25.

Billy Budd, a pleasant, guileless sailor, breaks maritime law. While he stoically accepts the death penalty for his act, the officers are troubled over the conflict of humanity versus complete obedience to the law. Requires very sensitive acting and delicate directing.

Crichton, Kyle. *The Happiest Millionaire.* (1957) Suggested by the book *My Philadelphia Father,* by Cordelia Drexel Biddle and Kyle Crichton. Comedy. Interior. Early 20th century costumes. 9m. 6w. Dramatists Play Service $1.75. Royalty $50—$25.

Anthony J. Drexel Biddle is an enthusiastic and unpredictable father. He collects alligators and prizefighters and rules his family by bluster. He meets defeat for the first time when he tries to take over and run the romance of his daughter, Cordelia. Suitable for all groups.

Davenport, Gwen. *Belvedere.* (1949) Comedy in 3 acts. Interior. Modern costumes. 5m. 4w. 2 children. French $1.75. Royalty $25—$20.

An American family is surprised to find that Lynn Belvedere, who answers their ad for a babysitter, is a very precise and impeccable male. The play deals with Belvedere's hilarious adventures with his two charges. Especially recommended for high school.

Davidson, William. *Room for One More.* (1951) Based on the book by Anna Rose Wright. Comedy. Interior. Modern costumes. 4m. 8w. Dramatic Publishing Co. $1.50. Royalty $35.

The Pumpkin Shell, a tiny summer cottage by the ocean, is the home of Poppy and Mother Rose and innumerable homeless waifs. When tragedy strikes the cottage and it is in danger of being sold, Jimmy John, one of the young unfortunates, comes to the rescue. Especially recommended for high school.

Davis, Hallie Flanagan. $E = MC^2$. (1947) Living newspaper. Modern costumes. 6m. 2w. 20 or more extras. French $1.75. Royalty $25—$20.
The atom bomb is discussed in the past, present, and the future through dramatic scenes, music, dance, and movies. The nature of atomic power is explained, and the progress—or doom—that its discovery could bring is dramatized. For advanced groups.

Davis, Owen, and Davis, Donald. *Ethan Frome.* (1936) Based on the novel by Edith Wharton. Drama. Interiors and exteriors. Modern rural costumes. 7m. 4w. extras. Dramatists Play Service $1.75. Royalty $35—$25.
Ethan Frome attempts to escape from his complaining wife Zenobia with Mattie, their house drudge. Their attempts are devastatingly unsuccessful, and the two runaways are reduced to maimed and resentful invalids under the wife's care. Within the range of high school groups.

Dayton, Katherine, and Kaufman, George S. *First Lady.* (1935) Comedy. 2 interiors. Modern costumes. 14m. 11w. Dramatists Play Service, manuscript. Royalty $35—$25.
The conflict centers on the feud between two Washington hostesses who show no quarter in their struggle for the position of First Lady. For advanced groups only.

de Ghelderode, Michel. See Ghelderode, Michel de.

de Hartog, Jan. See Hartog, Jan de.

Denker, Henry. *A Case of Libel.* (1963) Based on Louis Nizer's *My Life in Court.* Melodrama. Interior and inset. Modern costumes. 11m. 3w. 3 extras. French $1.75. Royalty $50—$25.
A story about a celebrated war correspondent's libel suit against a widely syndicated newspaper columnist. The court scenes offer dramatic "fireworks" and also insights into the political philosophies that prompted this case. Advanced groups.

————. *A Far Country.* (1961) Biography. Interior. Late 19th century costumes. 6m. 6w. French $1.75. Royalty $50—$25.
Sigmund Freud's first case in psychoanalysis and the difficulties his theories caused him with the medical academy constitute the body of the play. Advanced groups.

Denker, Henry, and Berkey, Ralph. *Time Limit!* (1956) Melodrama in 3 acts. Interior. Military costumes. 15m. 2w. French $1.75. Royalty $50—$25.

A story of human suffering in a concentration camp in Korea is revealed through flashbacks during the court-martial of one of the prisoners, who is charged with aiding the enemy. Requires mature acting.

Deval, Jacques. *Tovarich.* (1933) Translated by Robert E. Sherwood. Comedy in 3 acts. 4 interiors. Modern costumes. 8m. 7w. French $1.75. Royalty $35—$25.

A tale of impoverished White Russian nobles in Paris following the Bolshevik Revolution. The willingness of the prince and grand duchess to accept work as servants causes confusion and humor but does not destroy their dignity and humanity. Advanced groups.

Duberman, Martin B. *In White America.* (1964) History. Platform stage. 4m. 2w. Baker $1.75. French $1.75. Royalty $35—$25.

An enactment based on actual historical records of the story of black people in America, from slave-trade times to Little Rock. Suitable for all groups.

Dürrenmatt, Friedrich. *The Physicists.* (1961) Translated by James Kirkup. Melodrama. Interior. Modern costumes. 16m. 4w. Baker $1.75. French $1.75. Royalty $50—$25.

The scene is a madhouse, and the focus is on three inmates who are deranged nuclear physicists. At first they appear to be likable lunatics, but they embark on a game which reveals the evil in them and in the world. Requires mature, skilled actors.

————. *The Visit.* (1956) Adapted by Maurice Valency. Morality play. Interior and exterior. Modern middle European costumes. 25m. 5w. 2 children. Baker $1.75. French $1.75. Royalty $50—$25.

An incredibly wealthy woman returns to her hometown, which is in economic trouble. It is hoped that she will come to their aid. She will, but there is a condition: she wants the life of a villager who years before caused her to be expelled from the town in disgrace. Requires mature, skilled actors.

D'Usseau, Arnaud, and Gow, James. *Deep Are the Roots.* (1945) Drama. Interior. Modern costumes. 7m. 4w. Dramatists Play Service $1.75. Royalty $50—$25.

The play explores race prejudice. A black war hero returns to his home in the South and is welcomed by the white family that employed him. However, one of the women of the family falls in love with him, and the hero is overwhelmed by the prejudice which prevents his being treated not only as a hero, but as a man. Advanced groups.

Dyer, Charles. *Rattle of a Simple Man.* (1963) Comedy. Interior. Modern costumes. 2m. 1w. French $1.75. Royalty $50—$25.

A prostitute with an aristocratic background borrowed from novels picks up a lonely man who's come to town for a frolic. One by one their pretentions to worldliness are stripped away, revealing their loneliness, and they offer each other strength and sympathy. Requires mature actors.

Dyne, Michael. *The Right Honourable Gentleman.* (1966) Drama in 2 acts. Divided interior. Victorian costumes. 7m. 7w. Dramatists Play Service $1.75. Royalty $50—$25.

Retells the true-life scandal which destroyed the career of Sir Charles Dilke, who might have been prime minister during Victoria's reign had it not been for rumors and accusations of certain amatory indiscretions. Advanced groups.

Eliot, T. S. *The Cocktail Party.* (1949) Morality play. 2 interiors. Modern costumes. 5m. 4w. Baker $1.75. French $1.75. Royalty $50—$25.

A picture of modern life as it is lived in highly urbane and civilized circles, and an examination of the souls of people seeking identity and truth. We find a man playing host at a cocktail party planned by his wife, with whom he is about to break up. The self-examination begins with the entrance of a mysterious visitor who seems to know so much about each of the guests. Requires skilled acting and exceptional directing.

————. *The Family Reunion.* (1939) Verse play in 2 parts. Interior. Modern costumes. 7m. 4w. French $1.85. Royalty $25—$20.

The son of a contemporary English family is haunted by the impression that he killed his wife. This is an account of what happens to him and the family as they cope with this fear. For advanced groups.

————. *Murder in the Cathedral.* (1935) Poetic drama in 2 acts. 3 interiors. 12th century English costumes. 10m. 9w. Baker $1.75. French $1.45. Royalty $35—$25.

An account of the martyrdom of Archbishop Thomas à Becket, who, though tempted, refused to seize temporal control of England. Suitable for all groups.

Ephron, Phoebe, and Ephron, Henry. *Take Her, She's Mine.* (1962) Comedy. Various sets. Modern costumes. 11m. 6w. Baker $1.75. French $1.75. Royalty $50—$25.

The joys and concerns of the mother and father of two girls going through college. Alarming reports of campus doings, misunderstandings, and character changes make for a hilarious evening. Frothy comedy for mature groups.

Feiffer, Jules. *Little Murders.* (1967) Comedy. Interior. Modern costumes. 6m. 2w. extras. Baker $1.75. French $1.75. Royalty $50—$25.

A satirical study of the modern metropolitan family—matriarchal mother, Milquetoast father, cuddly sister, and brother with sexual hangups—as they try to adjust to the inhumanities of contemporary life. Suitable for advanced high school groups and up.

————. *The White House Murder Case.* (1970) Morality play. Interior, inset. Modern costumes. 9m. 1w. French $1.75. Royalty $50—$25.

Set in the future—the war this time is in Brazil. An attack backfires, and on the eve of the election the president must explain how poison gas for use against the enemy escaped to kill many civilians. The attempt to justify the act involves an examination of the American posture on war, but while the cabinet is concocting a cock-and-bull story for the people, the president's wife is murdered. The duplicity of the president then comes to the fore. For advanced groups.

Feydeau, Georges. *A Flea in Her Ear.* (1968) Translated by Barnett Shaw. Farce. 3 interiors. 19th or 18th century costumes. 9m. 5w. French, manuscript. Royalty $50—$25.

Classic French bedroom farce complete with misdirected letters, confused identities, and zany characters from nowhere. The wife of a lord misinterprets a note and suspects her husband of assignations in a hotel of low repute. She addresses a letter to him in the guise of a smitten lady and goes to the hotel to see how faithful he is. But he gives the letter to a friend, who goes instead. The porter in the hotel looks exactly like the lord, and the complications come fast and furious. Great fun. Needs cast skilled in comedy.

Feydeau, Georges, and Desvallieres, Maurice. *Hotel Paradiso.* (1957) Translated by Peter Glenville. Comedy. 2 interiors. 13m. 8w. extras. French $1.75. Royalty $50—$25.

The story finds an assortment of refined people stealing through the halls and rooms of a cheap hotel comically intent on assignation. There is the hero, a henpecked husband, arrived in disguise with his friend's wife; a tottering octogenarian and a chorus girl; a youth on his first flight with a housemaid; a housing inspector investigating ghosts; and many others, including the police, who raid the hotel at the second act curtain. Requires skill of advanced actors.

Fields, Joseph, and Chodorov, Jerome. *My Sister Eileen.* (1940) Based on stories by Ruth McKenney. Comedy. Interior. Modern costumes. 21m. (several bits) 6w. Dramatists Play Service $1.75. Royalty $35—$25.

Two girls from Ohio, trying to make their way in New York, sign a year's lease on a Greenwich Village basement apartment, and this begins a series of amusing and sometimes catastrophic events, culminating in their eviction. Suitable for all groups; excellent for high school.

————. *The Ponder Heart.* (1956) Based on the story by Eudora Welty. Comedy in 3 acts. 2 interiors, 1 exterior. Modern costumes. 20m. 10w. extras. Baker $1.75. French $1.75. Royalty $50—$25.

The defendant, an amiable Southern gentleman, buys everyone ice cream cones and invites them all, including the prosecutor, to the big murder trial. He is so guileless that he does not realize until the climax of the trial that the state accuses *him* of the murder of his wife. Advanced groups.

Fields, Joseph, and De Vries, Peter. *The Tunnel of Love.* (1957) Based on the novel by Peter De Vries. Comedy in 3 acts. Interior. Modern costumes. 2m. 4w. Baker $1.75. French $1.75. Royalty $50—$25.

A couple plans to adopt a child after five years of a childless marriage. A well-meaning neighbor upsets the plans, and a number of complications ensue before the adoption agency approves. Frothy comedy for mature groups.

Fisher, Bob, and Marx, Arthur. *The Impossible Years.* (1964) Comedy. Interior. Modern costumes. 9m. 5w. Baker $1.75. French $1.75. Royalty $50—$25.

A psychiatrist is writing a book about teenagers, with two teenage daughters of his own plus their host of friends constantly underfoot. The daughters come close to destroying his faith in himself and his theories. Frothy comedy; has appeal to older groups.

Ford, Ruth. *Requiem for a Nun.* (1952) Adapted from the novel/ play by William Faulkner. Tragedy. Unit set. Modern costumes. 5m. 2w. French $6.95. Royalty $50—$25.

Temple Drake, married to the college boy who first led her the wrong way, decides to run away with her latest fancy. When she prepares to take her baby with her, her black maid is horrified and kills the child to stop her. All this we learn in Temple's confession to the governor, to whom she goes in a vain attempt to save the maid's life. Advanced groups only.

Foster, Paul. *Tom Paine.* (1968) Semi-documentary in 2 acts. Open stage. 18th century costumes. 12 actors exchanging roles. French $1.75. Royalty $35—$25.

Using the life of Thomas Paine, whose writings did much to inspire both the American and French revolutions, the play examines the justifiability of using violent means to secure a worthy end. A moving play with great contemporary relevance. For advanced groups only.

Francke, Caroline. *Father of the Bride.* (1951) Based on the novel by

Edward Streeter. Comedy. Interior. Modern costumes. 11m. 7w. 3–4 extras. Dramatists Play Service $1.75. Royalty $35—$25.

A wedding, planned as a simple affair with a few friends, turns out to be an extravaganza, with mass confusion reigning within the family. Recommended for high school groups.

Friel, Brian. *Philadelphia, Here I Come!* (1966) Comedy. Composite interior. Modern costumes. 9m. 4w. Baker $1.75. French $1.75. Royalty $50—$25.

On the night before he is to depart for Philadelphia, an Irishman reflects on the humdrum state of affairs he is leaving and wonders about his future in the new land. Advanced groups.

Frings, Ketti. *Look Homeward, Angel.* (1957) Based on the novel by Thomas Wolfe. Comedy-drama. 2 exteriors and inset. Early 20th century costumes. 10m. 9w. Baker $1.75. French $1.75. Royalty $50—$25.

Concentrating on the last third of Wolfe's novel, the play recreates the family of Eugene Gant: Eliza, his mother, obsessed by her material holdings, raising a barrier against the love of her family; W. O. Gant, father, stonecutter imprisoned by his failures; and Ben, the brother who never broke away. Requires sensitive acting and skilled directing; within the range of advanced high school groups.

Frisch, Max. *Biography: A Game.* Translated by Michael Bullock. Drama. Many scenes. Modern costumes. French $1.75. Royalty $50—$25.

A group of intellectuals debate whether or not their lives had to be the way they were. It is a question of which is more flexible, the human personality or the external world. Offers challenge for those groups playing for "issue"-minded audiences.

Fry, Christopher. *The Lady's Not for Burning.* (1948) Poetic fantasy in 3 acts. Interior. 15th century English costumes. 8m. 3w. Dramatists Play Service $1.75. Royalty $50—$25.

Philosophical humorist Thomas Mendip wants to die, and so confesses to an alleged murder. Jennet Jourdemayne is accused of witchcraft, but does not want to die. Jennet and Thomas fall in love, and live happily on. Delightful romp for advanced groups.

———. *A Sleep of Prisoners.* (1951) Religious play. Simple set. Military uniforms. 4m. Dramatists Play Service $1.75. Royalty $35—$25.

Four prisoners of war locked up in a church struggle to understand themselves and the world. The action comes in a series of dreams in which each prisoner demonstrates his own inner response to events. The immediate surroundings suggest Biblical protagonists to each dreamer, and the attempted murder of one soldier is seen successively as the story of Cain and Abel, David and Absalom, and Abraham and Isaac. Advanced groups only.

————. *Venus Observed.* (1950) Poetic comedy. 1 interior, 1 exterior. Modern costumes. 7m. 4w. Dramatists Play Service $1.75. Royalty $35—$25.

The aging Duke of Altair brings three of his ex-mistresses to his home with the intention of marrying one of them, but he falls in love with the young daughter of his amiably dishonest secretary. For mature groups.

García Lorca, Federico. *The House of Bernarda Alba.* (1936) Translated by James Graham-Luján and Richard O'Connell. Tragedy in 3 acts. 3 interiors. 1890s costumes. 10w. 10–20 extra women. Baker $1.75. French $1.75 (in *Three Tragedies of Lorca*). Royalty $35—$25.

Widowed as the play opens, the stern matriarch Bernarda declares to her five daughters that they will enter a traditional eight-year period of cloistered mourning. One girl revolts, and the family is thrown headlong into a tragic climax of honor and revenge. The greatest of modern Spanish tragedies; within the range of advanced high school groups.

Gardner, Herb. *A Thousand Clowns.* (1962) Comedy. 2 interiors. Modern costumes. 4m. 1w. 1 boy. Baker $1.75. French $1.75. Royalty $50—$25.

When a nonconformist bachelor uncle is left with the responsibility of rearing his precocious nephew, the upbringing that he offers the boy is challenged by the social service team that visits him. He has to go back to work or lose his nephew. Suitable for all groups.

Gazzo, Michael V. *A Hatful of Rain.* (1955) Melodrama. Interior. Modern costumes. 7m. 2w. Baker $1.75. French $1.75. Royalty $50—$25.

In a New York apartment live a husband and wife and the husband's brother. The husband cannot hold a job, having become a dope addict. His card-playing "friends," who come by to collect, and the brother's amorous yearnings finally drive the woman to the edge of hysteria. The husband becomes determined to sweat through a cure. Advanced groups with mature audiences.

Genet, Jean. *The Blacks: A Clown Show.* (1957) Translated by Bernard Frechtman. Drama. Interior. Symbolic costumes, masks. 9m. 5w. French $1.95. Restricted. Royalty $35—$25.

The reenactment of a trial of blacks before a white-masked black jury for the ritualistic murder of a white. When they have played out their crime they turn on their judges and condemn them to death. Then they dance the Mozart minuet with which the play began. Skilled actors and hard directing required.

Gershe, Leonard. *Butterflies Are Free.* (1969) Comedy. Interior. Modern costumes. 2m. 2w. Baker $1.75. French $1.75. Restricted. Royalty $50—$35.

A young bachelor moves into an apartment to escape his domineering mother. Complications arise when a young actress moves in with him. The events are of great interest inasmuch as the young man is blind. Suitable for all.

Ghelderode, Michel de. *Pantagleize.* Translated by George Hauger. Farce. 4 interiors, 1 exterior. Modern costumes. 14m. 2w. extras. French $1.95 (in volume). Royalty $35—$25.

Pantagleize, an innocent pamphleteer caught up in a revolution, must take money from a heavily guarded bank vault and bring it to the conspirators. He returns to the revolutionaries with the money, only to find that his beloved has been killed by the secret policeman who shadows him throughout the play. Advanced groups only.

Gibson, William. *The Miracle Worker.* (1959) Drama. Unit set. 1890s costumes. 7m. 7w. Baker $1.75. French $1.75. Eldridge $1.75. Royalty $50—$25. Restricted to amateur performances before unsegregated audiences.

A dramatization of the real-life struggle of the blind, deaf, and mute Helen Keller when Anne Sullivan comes to care for and teach her. Suitable for all; especially recommended for advanced high school groups.

———. *Two for the Seesaw.* (1958) Comedy. Composite interior. Modern costumes. 1m. 1w. Baker $1.75. French $1.75. Royalty $50—$25. Restricted to amateur performances before unsegregated audiences.

The romance of a Bronx girl and a young lawyer who has run away from his marriage and career brings a few months of happiness into their lives. When it comes time for them to emerge into the world, they both see the hopelessness of the affair. For advanced groups with mature audiences.

Gilroy, Frank D. *The Subject Was Roses.* (1962) Drama. Interior. Modern costumes. 2m. 1w. Baker $1.75. French $1.75. Royalty $50—$25.

When a son who went away to war as a pampered boy comes back as a man, his maturity has a devastating effect on his mother and father, who have been living together in a loveless marriage. This isn't the boy she remembers at all, and the rancour of husband and wife turns sour the love of father and son. For advanced groups; suitable for all age audiences.

———. *Who'll Save the Plowboy?* (1962) Drama. Interior. Modern costumes. 4m. 2w. 1 boy. French $1.75. Royalty $35—$25.

A middle-aged man who has been a failure all his life is visited by a dying friend, who at one time had saved his life. The friend discovers the failure but leaves, allowing the man to think that the truth is unknown. Advanced groups only.

Giraudoux, Jean. *Amphitryon 38*. (1929) Adapted by S. N. Behrman. Comedy. Interior, 3 stylized exteriors. Greek costumes. 6m. 5w. Dramatists Play Service $1.75. Royalty $35—$25.

Follows the outlines of the legend of Amphitryon, Alkmena, and Jupiter, in which Jupiter descends to Earth, impersonates the general Amphitryon—Alkmena's husband—and makes love to her. Sophisticated comedy for advanced groups.

————. *Duel of Angels*. Translated and adapted by Christopher Fry. Comedy. Interiors and exteriors. Mid-19th century costumes. 8m. 5w. extras. Dramatists Play Service $1.75. Royalty $50—$25.

Two ladies of different temperaments are contrasted: the first looks down on those of less exacting standards; the second, to avenge her affairs being made public, drugs the first, who is made to seem that she has slept with a local rake. Advanced groups only.

————. *The Enchanted*. (1950) Adapted by Maurice Valency. Comedy in 3 acts. 1 interior, 1 exterior. Modern costumes. 9m. 11w. Baker $1.75. French $1.75. Royalty $50—$25.

A young lady in a French provincial town is obsessed with spiritualism. The government inspector regards her traffic with the supernatural as a threat to the state and summons all his authority and power to rid her of her obsession. She falls in love, discovers the joys of this world, and accomplishes in one second what the inspector and the law could not do by force. Suitable for all groups.

————. *The Madwoman of Chaillot*. (1943) Adapted by Maurice Valency. Comedy in 3 acts. 1 interior, 1 exterior. Modern costumes. 17m. 8w. Dramatists Play Service $1.75. Royalty $50—$25.

The Madwoman of Chaillot and her eccentric friends foil the plans of a group of greedy prospectors to tear up Paris in search of oil. Suitable for all groups; especially recommended for advanced high school groups.

————. *Ondine*. (1939) Based on the story by La Motte-Fouqué. Translated by Maurice Valency. Tragedy. 3 sets. Stylized costumes. 17m. 11w. Baker $1.75. French $1.75. Royalty $50—$25.

A beautiful nymph falls in love with a handsome knight and they are married at court. All too soon they learn that their love is too ideal to survive the shocks of this world. Advanced groups only. Requires great style.

————. *Tiger at the Gates.* (1935) Adapted by Christopher Fry. Tragedy in 2 acts. Platform stage. Greek costumes. 15m. 7w. Baker $1.75. French $1.75. Royalty $50—$25.

The logic of war is discussed by Hector and Ulysses and it is decided that there is no need for war against the Trojans. In spite of all the logic, other forces cause the war to erupt. Advanced groups only.

Goetz, Augustus, and Goetz, Ruth. *The Heiress.* (1947) Suggested by Henry James's novel *Washington Square.* Drama. Interior. 19th century costumes. 3m. 6w. Dramatists Play Service $1.75. Royalty $50—$25.

Catherine falls prey to a fortune hunter who proposes to her. When her father forbids the marriage, the young man draws away from her proposed elopement. With the death of her father, he again proposes. She leads him on, only to rebuff him in the end. Requires strong leading lady who can portray various ages; suitable for all groups.

Goldman, James. *The Lion in Winter.* (1964) Comedy. Unit set. 12th century English costumes. 5m. 2w. Baker $1.75. French $1.75. Royalty $50—$25.

King Henry II of England has three sons by Eleanor of Aquitaine. He wants to keep the kingdom together after his death, but since all three sons want to rule, it is likely to be torn apart. Henry favors the youngest, John; Eleanor favors the eldest, Richard. We see the aging Henry fight to preserve his country. Requires strong actors with maturity.

Goldman, James, and Goldman, William. *Blood, Sweat and Stanley Poole.* Comedy. Interior. U.S. Army uniforms. 10m. 2w. Dramatists Play Service $1.75. Royalty $50—$25.

Portrays the terrors faced by a battle-hardened combat soldier in the peacetime U.S. Army. The officers must pass a test to prove they have a college education. This requirement causes Stanley Poole to get involved in a number of hilarious situations. Rousing service comedy; best for advanced groups.

Goodrich, Frances, and Hackett, Albert. *The Diary of Anne Frank.* (1956) Drama. Interior. World War II costumes. 5m. 5w. Dramatists Play Service $1.75. Royalty $50—$25.

A dramatization of the famous diary by Anne Frank, who at thirteen was forced into hiding by the Nazi occupation of Amsterdam. Her diary is a document of a fugitive life under terror. A moving, tender story suitable for all groups; especially recommended for high school performance. Ethnic interest: Jewish-American.

————. *The Great Big Doorstep.* (1942) Comedy in 3 acts. Exterior. Modern costumes. 5m. 7w. Dramatic Publishing Co. $1.75. Royalty $35.

When the Crochets, a Cajun family, find a magnificent doorstep floating down the Mississippi River, they set it up in front of their poor shanty and try to live up to its meaning. A heartwarming family story, excellent for high school. Has some involved set problems.

Gordon, Ruth. *Years Ago.* (1946) Comedy. Interior. Early 20th century costumes. 4m. 5w. Dramatists Play Service $1.75. Royalty $35—$25.

The playwright's story of her determination to go on the stage, and how she finally gets her parents' blessings on this venture. A warm story suitable for all groups; well within the range of high school performers.

Gräss, Gunter. *The Plebians Rehearse the Uprising.* (1968) Translated by Ralph Manheim. Documentary. Interior. Modern costumes. 19m. 7w. Harcourt Brace Jovanovich $2.35. Royalty: contact Ninon Karlweis.

Bertolt Brecht's rehearsal of Shakespeare's *Coriolanus* in his East Berlin theater is interrupted by workers seeking his support for their uprising (June 17, 1953) against the tyranny of the Communist regime. Gräss gives his explanation of Brecht's action. Complex story requiring mature actors.

Gray, Simon. *Butley.* Comedy-drama. Interior. Modern costumes. 4m. 3w. Baker $1.75. French $1.75. Royalty $50—$35.

The day in the life of a university professor when he faces up to the ultimate breakdown of his marriage, the estrangement of his best friend, and the realization that the success of his career is questionable. Provides for an excellent virtuoso performance. Requires skilled actors and sophisticated audiences.

Green, Carolyn. *Janus.* (1955) Farce. Interior. Modern costumes. 3m. 2w. Baker $1.75. French $1.75. Royalty $50—$25.

Janus is the joint pen name of a quiet New York schoolteacher and his consort, the respectable wife of a Midwestern tycoon, who turn out an annual bestseller. The husband decides to come by and see his wife in her metropolitan diggings and discovers their romantic goings on. The wife is so charming, however, that the husband can only accept the situation. Light, but emphasis on sex necessitates maturity in cast and audience.

Green, Paul. *The House of Connelly.* (1931) Drama in 4 acts. 1 interior, 2 exteriors. Modern costumes. 4m. 6w. about 20 extras. French, manuscript. Royalty $25.

This play of the old and new South centers on a family to show the contrasts between a decaying society and the new and living forces of the present. Advanced groups.

————. *In Abraham's Bosom.* (1925) Drama in 7 scenes. 2 exteriors, 3 interiors. Modern costumes. 9m. 3w. French $1.95. Royalty $25.

The mulatto son of a white man in a Southern community struggles to achieve status. Although he wants to achieve higher goals for himself and others, he fails because of his own inadequacies and an unfortunate marriage. For advanced groups.

Greene, Graham. *The Potting Shed.* (1957) Melodrama. 3 interiors. Modern costumes. 6m. 5w. Baker $1.75. French $1.75. Royalty $50—$25.

An unwanted son returns home at the time of his father's death. His mother will not permit him to see his father in his last moments. He has been estranged from every member of the family, apparently for an event that occurred when he was 14 years old. The son's mind is blank; his mother is silent. Gradually he pieces together the details of that dark event. Advanced groups.

Greene, Will. *The Riot Act.* (1963) Comedy-drama in 3 acts. Interior. 4m. 5w. 1 boy. Dramatists Play Service $1.75. Royalty $50—$25.

Domineering but hard-working Katie Delaney, Irish Catholic widow, supervises the courtships of her three policemen sons. Amid these and other tangled affairs, she becomes more human and forgiving of filial independence. Set on New York's West Side. For all groups. Ethnic interest: Irish-American.

Guare, John. *The House of Blue Leaves.* (1971) Farce. Interior. Modern costumes. 4m. 6w. Baker $1.75. French $1.75. Royalty $50—$35.

A middle-aged zookeeper has hopes of becoming a songwriter. He invites his famous movie-producer friend to visit the same day the Pope is visiting New York. He has a wacky mistress, a son who is AWOL from the Army, and an insane wife. There is a premature bomb explosion, death, elopements—one zany antic after another. Beneath all the wild antics lies a touch of sadness. Excellent for advanced groups, high school and older.

Hail, Raven. *The Raven and the Redbird.* (1965) Historical drama in 3 acts. Raven Hail $2.50. Royalty to author.

Written by a Cherokee about his people. An account of Sam Houston and his life among the Cherokee Indians, especially his romance with Tiana, the Redbird, his Cherokee wife. Other historical characters include Sequoyah, Davy Crockett, and Blue Jacket the Shawnee. For all groups. Ethnic interest: American Indian.

Hailey, Oliver. *Father's Day.* (1971) Comedy. Exterior. Modern costumes. 3m. 3w. Dramatists Play Service $1.75. Royalty $50—$25.

Left with their alimony and children, three divorcées share their loneliness. When their ex-husbands return to visit the children, the exchange of dialogue reveals the bitterness and hurt of their lives beneath the civilized veneer. A humorous revelation of resignation of these people; for advanced groups only.

Hamilton, Patrick. *Angel Street (Gaslight)*. (1938) Victorian thriller in 3 acts. Interior. 1880s costumes. 2m. 3w. (2 policemen). French $1.75. Royalty $50—$25.
Demoniac story of the Manninghams of Angel Street in the nineteenth century. Handsome, sinister Manningham, under the guise of kindliness, is slowly torturing his wife into insanity. He is under suspicion, and is finally caught for a murder committed fifteen years before in the same house. Suspenseful; suitable for all groups.

————. *Rope (Rope's End)*. (1929) Drama in 3 acts. Interior. Modern costumes. 6m. 2w. French $1.75. Royalty $25—$20.
For the mere sake of adventure, danger, and the "fun of the thing," Wyndham Brandon persuades his weak-minded friend to assist him in the murder of a fellow undergraduate; then invites guests to supper, using as a table the wooden case in which they have hidden the body. Advanced groups only.

Hampton, Christopher. *The Philanthropist*. (1970) Comedy. Interior. Modern costumes. 4m. 3w. Baker $1.75. French $1.75. Royalty $50—$35.
A professor of philology who is incapable of a positive statement is unable to cope with the needs of his fiancée, the supercilious novelist who wins her, or the over-sexed neighbor he obliges. In the end he finds himself quite alone. A witty play for advanced groups with sophisticated audiences.

Hanley, William. *Slow Dance on the Killing Ground*. (1964) Tragedy. Interior. Modern costumes. 2m. 1w. Dramatists Play Service $1.75. Royalty $50—$25. Restricted to amateur performances before unsegregated audiences.
The interaction of a German storekeeper, a black youth, and a young girl seeking an abortionist reveals the strengths and weaknesses of the individuals and the hostile society in which they attempt to survive. Needs strong actors; for advanced groups.

Harris, Elmer. *Johnny Belinda*. (1940) Drama. Unit set. Rural costumes. 16m. 7w. Dramatists Play Service $2.25. Royalty $50—$25.
Hope and cheer are brought into the life of a beautiful deaf-mute, only to be marred by a senseless, brutal murder. She must communicate to save the life of the man who has befriended her. Suspenseful and touching; suitable for all groups.

Hart, Moss, and Kaufman, George S. *You Can't Take It with You.*

(1936) Comedy. Interior. Modern costumes. 9m. 7w. 3 extra men. Dramatists Play Service $1.75. Royalty $35—$25.

The Sycamores live an enchanted, if slightly strange life that is built around the theory that life is a full-time thing to be enjoyed to the utmost—much to the dismay of the conservative world about them. Warm, zany story, suitable for all groups.

Hartog, Jan de. *The Fourposter*. (1951) Comedy in 3 acts. Interior. Costumes, 1890–1925. 1m. 1w. French $1.75. Royalty $50—$25.

A chronicle of the joys, sorrows, quarrels, reunions, and adventures of a husband and wife, from their wedding night in 1890 until they pack and move 35 years later. Within the range of advanced high school actors.

Hayes, Joseph. *The Desperate Hours*. (1955) Drama of suspense in 3 acts. Unit set. Modern costumes. 11m. 3w. French $2.00. Royalty $50—$25.

A home is invaded and its inhabitants held captive by three escaped criminals. In a tense battle of wits, the criminals destroy themselves. Needs advanced actors.

Hecht, Ben, and MacArthur, Charles. *The Front Page*. (1928) Comedy-drama. Interior. Modern costumes. 17m. 5w. French $1.75. Royalty $50—$25.

A reporter is sick of his profession and plans to marry to escape it, only to be pulled back by its irresistible lure. A man about to be hanged escapes, is discovered in the reporter's office, and is saved by the reporter's investigation. The most popular of newspaper stories; suitable for all groups.

Heggen, Thomas, and Logan, Joshua. *Mister Roberts*. (1948) Drama. 3 interiors, 1 exterior. World War II U.S. Navy costumes. 19m. 1w. extras. Dramatists Play Service $1.75. Royalty $50—$25.

The crew of a Navy cargo vessel, faced with the deadly boredom which is part of the routine of war, is given new courage and a sense of worth when a former officer is killed in combat. Funny but touching; "sailor language" may be a bit strong for some high school groups.

Heller, Joseph. *Catch 22*. (1971) Adapted from the author's novel. Comedy. Flexible staging. World War II Air Force costumes. Flexible casting: 9–36m. 2–8w. doubling possible. Baker $1.75. French $1.75. Restricted. Royalty $50—$35.

A satirical look at the Air Force as Captain Yossarian tries to get grounded. Behind this mad zany picture of the service is the serious picture of the insanity of war. Complex to stage; for advanced groups only.

————. *We Bombed in New Haven.* (1967) Morality play. Flexible open stage. Service uniforms. 16m. 1w. Baker $1.75. French $1.75. Royalty $50—$25.

The story of a code-bound captain and the members of the bomber crew he is forced to send to their deaths. In the examination of the morality of war, the action oscillates between reality and unreality, between truth in life and truth in art. Complex story; requires mature actors.

Hellman, Lillian. *Another Part of the Forest.* (1946) Drama. Interior. 19th century costumes. 8m. 5w. Dramatists Play Service $1.75. Royalty $50—$25.

A family drama concerning the parents of the Hubbards of *The Little Foxes.* The story traces the eventual downfall of rich, despotic, and despised Marcus Hubbard. Intense, hard-hitting drama; needs mature actors.

————. *The Children's Hour.* (1934) Drama. 2 interiors. Modern costumes. 2m. 12w. Dramatists Play Service $1.75. Royalty $35—$25.

When a malicious youngster starts an entirely unfounded scandal about two women who run a school for girls, she precipitates tragedy for the two women. Later, it is discovered that the gossip was pure invention, but by that time irreparable damage has been done. A strong story suitable for high schools with mature actors.

————. *The Little Foxes.* (1939) Drama. Interior. 19th century costumes. 6m. 4w. Dramatists Play Service $1.75. Royalty $35—$25.

The prosperous, despotic Hubbard family, who have made a fortune on the Civil War, scheme to steal $80,000 from ailing brother-in-law Horace with the help of his conniving wife, Regina. Popular story; can be handled by high schools with advanced actors.

————. *Toys in the Attic.* (1960) Drama. Interior-exterior. Modern costumes. 4m. 4w. 3 extras. French $1.75. Royalty $50—$25.

An older and younger sister live for the day they will be able to go to Europe. Each time they have the money saved they spend it on their brother. When he gives them the money to go to Europe, they find that their reason for living has been lost. Advanced groups only.

Herlihy, James Leo, and Noble, William. *Blue Denim.* (1958) Drama. Unit set. Modern costumes. 3m. 3w. Baker $1.75. French $1.75. Royalty $50—$25.

A compassionate play dealing with the problem of communications between the younger and older generations. The trouble seems to lie in the fact that they do not speak each other's language. Suitable for all groups; high school actors should be advanced.

Hochhuth, Rolf. *The Deputy*. (1963) Adapted by Jerome Rothenberg. Historical play. Various x-ray sets. Religious and military costumes. 22m. 2w. extras. French $1.75. Royalty $50—$25.

A German officer from a death camp comes to the Papal legate in Berlin with incriminating evidence against the Reich in its annihilation of the Jews, and thus begins the torturous and fruitless effort to interest the Papacy in the cause of the Jews under Hitler. A controversial play requiring advanced actors and skilled direction.

Home, William Douglas. *Lloyd George Knew My Father*. (1972) Drama. Interior. Modern costumes. 5m. 3w. French $1.75. Royalty on application.

Lady Sheila Boothroyd determines to kill herself the moment the bulldozers start cutting through her estate to make a freeway. Her decision to make this sacrifice motivates actions which reveal the feelings and character of her family. Typical British humor; requires skilled, mature performers.

————. *The Reluctant Debutante*. (1955) Comedy. Interior. Modern costumes. 3m. 5w. Baker $1.75. French $1.75. Royalty $50—$25.

A family tries to get the daughter the best match for her marriage. They favor an aristocrat, while she favors the dashing man-about-town. Which finally becomes husband makes for a pleasant romp. Suitable for all groups.

Howard, Sidney. *The Late Christopher Bean*. (1932) Comedy in 3 acts. Interior. Modern costumes. 5m. 4w. Baker $1.75. French $1.75. Royalty $25—$20.

The Haggett family realizes too late the great value of the paintings left by Bean, the deceased artist who had lived with them. The servant, Abby, owns the most precious of the paintings and will not part with it, for Bean had secretly been her husband. Suitable for all groups, especially high school.

————. *The Silver Cord*. (1926) Drama in 3 acts. 2 interiors. Modern costumes. 2m. 4w. French $1.75. Royalty $25—$20.

Left a widow at an early age, Mrs. Phelps works by means that are almost devilish to keep her two sons to herself. One of the sons does escape her domination. Suitable for all groups.

————. *They Knew What They Wanted*. (1924) Comedy-drama in 3 acts. Interior. Modern costumes. 9m. 4w. extras. French $2.00. Royalty $25—$20.

A genial Italian-American grape-grower solicits an attractive young wife by mail. The young woman momentarily falls in love with Joe, Tony's hired hand, and becomes pregnant by him. Nevertheless, Tony accepts her and the baby with philosophical equanimity. For advanced casts.

Appropropriate only if handled sensitively by the teacher and director, since ethnic stereotypes are present. Ethnic interest: Italian-American, Chinese-American.

Ibsen, Henrik. *A Doll's House.* (1879) Translated by Christopher Hampton. Drama in 4 acts. Interior. 19th century costumes. 3m. 4w. 2 children. French $1.75. Royalty $50—$25.
Nora loves her husband Helmer and is willing to commit forgery in order to help him. But he treats her like a plaything, a fixture of his household. Realizing the falseness of her marriage and her need for self-respect, she leaves him. Requires advanced acting.

————. *Hedda Gabler.* (1890) Translated by Christopher Hampton. Tragedy. Interior. 1880s costumes. 3m. 4w. French $1.75. Royalty $50—$25.
Hedda Gabler, frustrated by the boredom of her life, seems capable only of destructiveness. One of her amusements is practicing with a pair of pistols which, when a romantic adventure fails, end the life of a brilliant young scholar as well as her own. Requires advanced acting and directing.

————. *Peer Gynt.* (1867) Adapted by Paul Green. Fantasy. Interiors and exteriors. 19th century costumes. 8m. 12w. French $2.00. Royalty $35—$25.
Peer Gynt, a wild and imaginative mountain lad whose roughness and lying offend people, realizes too late that nobody can exist alone without a commitment to others or to self. Complex story requiring a great number of sets and technical expertise.

————. *The Pillars of Society.* (1877) Translated by Michael Meyer. Drama in 4 acts. Interior. 19th century costumes. 10m. 9w. Dramatists Play Service $2.50 (in volume). Royalty $25.
Johan returns from exile, where he had gone to cover up the wrongdoing of the now successful Bernick. On learning that Bernick has fastened another crime on him which will separate him from his sweetheart Dina, Johan threatens to expose Bernick. Bernick plots his death, only to find out that his own son is endangered. Bernick repents publicly and confesses. One of the simpler plays of Ibsen; still requires advanced acting techniques.

Inge, William. *Bus Stop.* (1955) Comedy. Interior. Modern costumes. 5m. 3w. Dramatists Play Service $1.75. Royalty $50—$25.
A bus out of Kansas City is forced to stop because of a snow storm, and the four or five weary travelers have to wait in a small cafe until morning. We learn of the private loneliness of many of them; Cherie, a dancer, finally accepts the attention of the rough, simple cowboy. Refreshing show requiring mature casts.

————. *Come Back, Little Sheba.* (1950) Drama in 2 acts. **Interior.**
Modern costumes. 8m. 3w. Baker $1.75. French $1.75. Royalty $50—
$25.
The story of a deep-seated frustration brought about by the unfortunate
marriage of Doc and Lola. Doc has become an alcoholic and Lola a
slob—which leads to an inevitable and furious eruption. For advanced
groups only.

————. *The Dark at the Top of the Stairs.* (1957) Comedy-drama.
Interior. Modern costumes. 3m. 2w. 3 boys, 2 girls. Dramatists Play
Service $1.75. Royalty $50—$25.
An account of occurrences in the life of the Flood family of Oklahoma
which lead to a new understanding between mother and father, more
assurance on the part of the teenage daughter, and independence for the
young son. Can be handled by advanced high school groups.

————. *Picnic.* (1953) Comedy. Unit setting. Modern costumes. 4m.
7w. Dramatists Play Service $1.75. Royalty $50—$25.
The action takes place in the joint backyard of two women deserted
by their husbands, the invalid mother of one of them, the two daughters
of the other, and the boarder, a spinster schoolteacher. Into these con-
gested, female surroundings comes a young man whose animal vitality
upsets the entire group. There is a serious story behind the humor.
Requires advanced acting.

Ionesco, Eugene. *Exit the King.* (1963) Translated by Donald Watson.
Drama. Interior. Modern costumes. 3m. 3w. French $1.75. **Royalty**
$50—$25.
The prognosis is that the king will not live out the day. The king does
not want to die and fights desperately against the inevitable. Advanced
groups only.

————. *Rhinoceros.* (1960) Translated by Derek Prouse. Comedy. 1
exterior, 2 interiors. Modern costumes. 11m. 6w. extras. Baker $1.75.
French $1.75. Royalty $50—$25.
The commentary on the absurdity of the human condition made toler-
able by self-delusion. A rhinoceros appears in town and soon the people
are turning into rhinoceroses. The play ends with one character determined not to change. For advanced groups only.

Jeffers, Robinson. *Medea.* (1946) Adapted freely from the play of
Euripides. Tragedy in 2 acts. Exterior. Greek costumes. 5m. 5w. extras.
Baker $1.75. French $1.75. Royalty $50—$25.
The ambitious Jason forsakes Medea, his foreign wife, and takes a new
bride for political advancement. On the day of her banishment, Medea
succeeds in bringing death to the new young bride, and the most wanton

horror to her husband, Jason. Can be handled by advanced high school groups.

Jellicoe, Ann. *The Knack*. (1962) Comedy. Interior. Modern costumes. 3m. 1w. French $1.75. Royalty $50—$25.

Severely tested by three young men, a girl is so distracted that she begins imagining all sorts of involvements with each of them. For mature casts only.

Jerome, Helen. *Jane Eyre*. (1938) Based on the novel by Charlotte Brontë. Drama in 3 acts. 2 interiors. English costumes, 1850. 10m. 12w. French $1.75. Royalty $25—$20.

Offers a more or less complete condensation of the novel. Jane comes to Mr. Rochester's great house to be governess. Rochester, an unhappy man, is beset with a lunatic wife whom he must keep locked up. Jane and Rochester come to an understanding which may lead to marriage, but when Jane finds out about the lunatic wife, she leaves. She is finally able to marry Rochester after his wife succeeds in setting the house on fire and destroying herself in the process. Suitable for all groups.

————. *Pride and Prejudice*. (1935) Based on the novel by Jane Austen. Comedy in 3 acts. 3 interiors. English costumes, 1796. 10m. 16w. Baker $1.75. French $1.75. Royalty $25—$20.

Mrs. Bennet is determined to get her daughters married, especially Elizabeth, who refuses to marry Collins, whom she deplores, and Darcy, whom she secretly adores. The play is the story of the duel between Elizabeth and her pride and Darcy and his prejudice. Before the evening is over, each gives in a little and pride and prejudice meet halfway. For all groups, especially high school.

Job, Thomas. *Uncle Harry*. (1942) Drama in 3 acts. 3 interiors. Costumes, about 1900. 9m. 6w. French $1.75. Royalty $50—$25.

A kindly and benevolent gentleman manages to arrange the murder of one disagreeable sister and the hanging of the other equally unpleasant one. He finds himself tortured to the point of confession, only to be unable to convince anyone that he is guilty. For all groups.

Kanin, Fay, and Kanin, Michael. *Rashomon*. (1959) Suggested by the screenplay by Akira Kurosawa, based on stories by Ryunosuke Akutagawa. Drama. Exterior. 12th century Japanese costumes. 6m. 3w. Baker $1.75. French $1.75. Royalty $50—$25.

Set during the final decay of political power at court, after fire, earthquakes, and famine have wracked the city. Three different, contradictory stories are given of a bandit's assault on a samurai and his wife, the rape of the woman, and the samurai's death. The trial raises the question: What is truth? Intriguing play suitable for all groups.

Kanin, Garson. *Born Yesterday.* (1946) Comedy. Interior. Modern costumes. 12m. 4w. Dramatists Play Service $1.75. Royalty $50—$25.
The highly informal education of ex-chorus girl Billie makes a responsible citizen of her and awakens her to the realization that Harry Brock, the vulgar and egotistical millionaire junkman who had kept her, had used her as a tool for his crooked schemes with Washington higher-ups. For advanced high school groups and older.

————. *A Gift of Time.* (1962) Based on the book by Lael T. Wertenbaker. Drama. 4 sets. Modern costumes. 5m. 5w. extras. French $1.75. Royalty $50—$25.
An American editor resigns his post and moves to France with his wife and two children to spend his time in writing important books. But all too shortly he learns that he is dying of cancer, and forthwith determines to live every day, hour, and minute to the fullest. For advanced groups.

Kaufman, Esther. *A Worm in Horseradish.* (1960) Comedy in 3 acts. Interior. Costumes, 1906. 7m. 3w. French $1.75. Royalty $25—$20.
A comedy of Jewish family life on New York's Lower East Side early in the century. Yonkel, a warm-hearted tailor who sleeps stray friends on the fire-escape, dreams of his son's becoming a doctor. He gains a doctor in the family—a son-in-law. For all groups. Ethnic interest: Jewish-American.

Kaufman, George S., and Connelly, Marc. *Beggar on Horseback.* (1924) Based on the satire by Paul Apel. Fantasy in 3 acts. Several exteriors and interiors. Modern and fantastic costumes. 16m. 5w. Optional pantomime calls for additional 6m. 2w. French $.75. Royalty $50—$25.
The dream of a young composer in which he marries an unattractive girl for her money and becomes a slave of gold and of an impossible family. A rich combination of romance and satire; within the range of advanced high school groups.

Kaufman, George S., and Ferber, Edna. *Dinner at Eight.* (1932) Drama in 3 acts. 6 interiors. Modern costumes. 14m. 11w. French $2.00. Royalty $50—$25.
A small dinner party, honoring a titled Englishman, discloses dramas of love, jealousy, and greed beneath the white ties and pearls. Mature groups only.

————. *The Royal Family.* (1927) Comedy in 3 acts. Interior. Modern costumes. 11m. 6w. French $2.00. Royalty $35—$25.
Three generations of Cavendishes, a great family of the American stage who enjoy great public acclaim, are, in fact, ruled by the courageous, sharp-tongued, sarcastic matriarch, Fanny Cavendish. Can be performed by advanced high school groups.

————. *Stage Door*. (1936) Comedy. Interior. Modern costumes. 11m. 21w. Dramatists Play Service $1.75. Royalty $35—$25.

Sixteen young girls come to New York to study acting and find jobs. The scene is Mrs. Orcutt's boardinghouse, where the hopes, ambitions, and fates of the young women are revealed and contrasted. Suitable for all groups; especially recommended for high school.

Kaufman, George S., and Hart, Moss. *The American Way*. (1939) Patriotic drama in 2 acts. 4 interiors, 13 exteriors (pageant effect possible with curtains). 27m. 17w. 7 boys, 3 girls. Band, soldiers, citizens, as desired. Dramatists Play Service, manuscript. Royalty $35—$25.

The saga of a German immigrant to America, Martin Gunther, who welcomes his wife in 1896. By his honesty and skill, he attains peace and happiness in their family group. He later loses a son in the World War and lives through the depression of 1933, when he sacrifices all for his family. In 1939, when his grandson is about to join a fascist group, Martin interferes and is killed by the mob, fighting still for freedom. For all groups. Ethnic interest: German-American.

————. *The Man Who Came to Dinner*. (1940) Comedy. Interior. Modern costumes. 15m. 9w. extras. Dramatists Play Service $1.75. Royalty $35—$25.

The egotist Sheridan Whiteside, popular columnist and traveler, having dined at the home of the Stanleys, slips on their doorstep and breaks his hip. The six weeks of confinement at their home involve a series of tumultuous and bizarre happenings. Wild and frenetic; suitable for all groups.

Kaufman, George S., and Marquand, John P. *The Late George Apley*. (1945) Based on Marquand's novel. Comedy. 2 interiors. Modern costumes. 8m. 8w. Dramatists Play Service, manuscript. Royalty $50—$25.

George Apley is the personification of old Boston tradition. The story centers on his two children, who heroically strive to break away from the shackles of family and tradition. One succeeds; the other is defeated. Suited for all groups; requires a mature lead.

Kelly, George. *Craig's Wife*. (1924) Drama in 3 acts. Interior. Modern costumes. 5m. 6w. French $1.75. Royalty $50—$25.

Mrs. Craig, unassailably selfish, succeeds during one evening in alienating the affections not only of her husband, who is driven from his home, but also of her friends and relatives. Biting satire requiring skilled acting; for advanced groups only.

————. *The Show-Off*. (1924) Comedy in 3 acts. Interior. Modern costumes. 6m. 3w. French $1.75. Royalty $50—$25.

Aubrey Piper struggles to satisfy his enormous egotism and at the same time preserve his self-respect in the presence of cynical relatives and discouraging obstacles. Suitable for all groups.

————. *The Torchbearers.* (1922) Satire in 3 acts. 2 interiors. Modern costumes. 6m. 6w. Baker $2.00. French $2.00. Royalty $50—$25.

Fred Ritter, a sane and capable gentleman, has to resort to heroic methods to save Paula, his wife, from the idea that she is a great actress, which idea has been inculcated by Mrs. Pampinelli, the overpowering director of the local little theater. Brilliant and classic satire on the little theater movement. Fun to do; suitable for all groups.

Kerr, Jean. *Mary, Mary.* (1961) Satire. Interior. Modern costumes. 3m. 2w. Dramatists Play Service $1.75. Royalty $50—$25.

Mary is a contrary person because of her basic insecurity. She appears at the apartment of her former husband to work on his income tax returns with a lawyer. Before the end of the play, she and her husband have gotten together again. For advanced actors and mature audiences.

————. *Our Hearts Were Young and Gay.* (1946) Based on the book by Cornelia Otis Skinner and Emily Kimbrough. Comedy in 3 acts. Unit set. Modern costumes. 8m. 9w. Dramatic Publishing Co. $1.75. Royalty $35.

The sparkling and exuberant escapades of two girls determined to prove how mature and cosmopolitan they can be on an uproarious and enchanting trip to Europe. Recommended for high school.

Kerr, Jean, and Brooke, Eleanore. *King of Hearts.* (1954) Comedy. Interior. Modern costumes. 6m. 2w. 2 small boys, 1 dog. Dramatists Play Service $1.75. Royalty $50—$25.

Larry Larkin, who draws a comic strip, is also the world's no. 1 egotist. Larry's fiancée is rescued from a fate worse than death by Dignan, who originally was to take Larry's place during the latter's honeymoon—at the drawing board, that is. Witty; for advanced actors and mature audiences.

Kerr, Jean, and Kerr, Walter. *The Song of Bernadette.* (1946) Based on the novel by Franz Werfel. Play in 3 acts. Interiors, exteriors; curtain set may be used. Modern costumes. 7m. 11w. extras. Dramatic Publishing Co. $1.50. Royalty $35.

Day-dreaming Bernadette has a vision and is disbelieved by the entire village. The civil authorities are bent on shutting her up in an asylum. After she enters a convent, the divine origin of her vision is accepted. Suitable for all groups.

Kesselring, Joseph. *Arsenic and Old Lace.* (1941) Comedy. Interior.

Modern costumes. 11m. 3w. Dramatists Play Service $1.75. Royalty $35—$25.

Two charming and innocent ladies who populate their cellar with the remains of socially and religiously "acceptable" roomers, and the antics of their brother, who thinks he is Teddy Roosevelt, are the subject of this ready-made hit. Possibly the best American farce; suitable for all groups.

Kingsley, Sidney. *Darkness at Noon.* (1951) Based on the novel by Arthur Koestler. Tragedy in 3 acts. Interior. Modern and Russian military costumes. 18m. 3w. French $1.75. Royalty $50—$25.

A Soviet commissar with considerable power in the party is jailed for treason. The play deals with his torment and frustration in his cell, with flashbacks explaining his sentence and the unjust hearings leading up to his execution. Powerful, suspenseful play. For advanced groups only.

————. *Dead End.* (1935) Drama. Exterior. Modern costumes. 22m. 6w. extras. Dramatists Play Service, manuscript. Royalty $35—$25.

A group of hardboiled street urchins turn to the devious methods of their elders in making their hard way of life. A story of young love is combined with the last efforts of a gangster to see his mother. Serious social comment; for advanced groups.

————. *Detective Story.* (1949) Drama. Police station interior. Modern costumes. 24m. 8w. doubling possible, extras. Dramatists Play Service $1.75. Royalty $50—$25.

McLeod, a detective, has a mania for punishing lawbreakers to the point where he often loses sight of human values and compassion. When he learns about his wife's premarital abortion, McLeod's world collapses about him. He is murdered with his own gun, trying to disarm a hardened criminal. For advanced groups with mature actors.

————. *The Patriots.* (1942) Historical play in prologue and 3 acts. 7 interiors. Revolutionary War costumes. 19m. 5w. Dramatists Play Service $7.95 (in volume). Royalty $35—$25.

This beautiful tribute to the American spirit is a chronicle of the important years in the life of Thomas Jefferson. For all groups.

Kipphardt, Heinar. *In the Matter of J. Robert Oppenheimer.* (1968) Translated by Ruth Speirs. Documentary drama. Interior. Modern costumes. 14m. 9w. extras. French $1.75. Royalty $50—$35.

A dramatization of the trial of J. Robert Oppenheimer as he seeks government security clearance. Using the actual transcripts, the play examines the dangers that lurk in governmental invasions of privacy and the stagnation of creative thought resulting from governmental conformity. Requires mature actors.

Knott, Frederick. *Dial "M" for Murder.* (1952) Melodrama. Interior. Modern costumes. 5m. 1w. Dramatists Play Service $1.75. Royalty $50—$25.

A man plans to murder his wife for her money. When the murderer he hired is unwittingly killed, the husband takes the opportunity to have his wife convicted of the murder, almost succeeding in his plan. Suitable for all groups.

Kober, Arthur. *"Having Wonderful Time."* (1937) Comedy. Modern costumes. 2 sets. 17m. 14w. Dramatists Play Service $1.75. Royalty $35—$25.

A comedy about those city men and women who seek relaxation in two short summer weeks at a camp. For advanced groups.

Kopit, Arthur. *Indians.* (1969) Drama in 13 scenes. 1 basic set. Period costumes. 20m. 3w. extras. Baker $1.65. French $1.65. Royalty $50—$35.

A series of scenes about the opening of the West in which Buffalo Bill Cody dramatizes his misgivings about the excesses committed by white men against the Indians. The characters of Buffalo Bill's past pass in review as he seeks to justify his life and defend his position as an American hero. Wild Bill Hickok, Jesse James, and Billy the Kid contrast sharply with Buffalo Bill's victims—Geronimo, Chief Joseph, and Sitting Bull. Advanced high school groups and older. Ethnic interest: American Indian.

———. *Oh Dad, Poor Dad, Mamma's Hung You in the Closet and I'm Feeling So Sad.* (1961) Farce. 2 interiors. Modern costumes. 4m. 2w. extras. Baker $1.75. French $1.75. Royalty $50—$25.

A widow and her son arrive at a hotel, tipping the bellboys with rare coins for carrying their luggage—tall plants, coffin, aquarium with piranha, and so on. A babysitter enters from across the way; she sits for the children of a man and woman who never come home. A yachtsman with a mile-long yacht throws himself at the widow's feet. Affairs continue in this fashion until the sitter attempts to seduce the son. At this point dear dead old dad falls out of the closet. A biting play, verging on the absurd. For advanced groups only.

Kramm, Joseph. *The Shrike* (1952) Drama. Unit set. Modern costumes. 17m. 5w. doubling possible. Dramatists Play Service $2.00. Royalty $50—$25.

The bitter story of Jim Downs, who must make a compromise and choose the lesser of two evils. He chooses life with his evil wife over life in the asylum she has sent him to. For advanced actors and mature audiences.

Krasna, Norman. *Sunday in New York.* (1962) Comedy. Interior.

Modern costumes. 4m. 3w. Dramatists Play Service $1.75. Royalty $50—$25.
The plight of a young lady from Albany who comes to visit her brother in New York, having discovered that she has exhausted the supply of eligible young men at home. A small fib grows and she is hard-pressed to convey the truth. Mature groups and audiences.

Laurents, Arthur. *A Clearing in the Woods.* (1957) Drama. Unit set. Modern costumes. 5m. 4w. 1 small girl. Dramatists Play Service $1.75. Royalty $50—$25.
The entire life of a young woman is shown during the course of the play. Virginia is an afflicted woman who cannot make peace with life and is tormented with memories of the past. Advanced groups only.

————. *Home of the Brave.* (1945) Drama. 2 interiors, 2 exteriors. World War II costumes. 6m. Dramatists Play Service $1.75. Royalty $35—$25.
A play of several short scenes taking place on a Pacific island during World War II. Coney, a Jew, feels that he has failed in his duty toward a dying buddy. His guilt complex so grips him that he literally becomes paralyzed until a sympathetic doctor makes him realize that he is no different from anyone else, that being a Jew and the victim of prejudice has not made him a coward. Requires advanced acting skills. Ethnic interest: Jewish-American.

————. *Invitation to a March.* (1961) Comedy. 2 exteriors, one very simple. Modern costumes. 3m. 4w. 1 boy. Dramatists Play Service $1.75. Royalty $50—$25.
This story deals with the conflict between summer visitors to Long Island's South Shore and two of the permanent residents who become entangled in their lives. Advanced groups only.

Lavery, Emmet. *The Magnificent Yankee.* (1946) Drama in 3 acts. Interior. Costumes, 1902–1933. 15m. 2w. Baker $2.00. French $2.00. Royalty $50—$25.
The marriage that lasted 57 years—that of Justice Oliver Wendell Holmes and his wife—and the critical years between the administrations of Theodore Roosevelt and Franklin Delano Roosevelt. A great piece of Americana; requires strong character actors.

Lawrence, Jerome, and Lee, Robert E. *Auntie Mame.* (1956) Based on the novel by Patrick Dennis. Comedy. Interiors and exteriors. Late 1920s to present-day costumes. 25m. 12w. 3 boys; doubling possible. Dramatists Play Service $1.75. Royalty $50—$25.
Episodes from the life of an uninhibited female who brightens American society with her whimsical gaiety, her slightly madcap adventures, and

her devotion to her young nephew. For mature high school groups and older.

———. *The Gang's All Here.* (1959) Drama. 4 interiors. 1920s costumes. 15m. 4w. French $1.75. Royalty $50—$25.
The story of the compromise candidate for the presidency, Griffith P. Hastings, and his political intrigues and chicanery. The easy-going president does not realize the extent of political corruption in his cabinet, but when the shady dealings are revealed, this fictional president has the courage to fire his friends. Spotlights the crime of not electing responsible officials. Requires a great number of character actors.

———. *Inherit the Wind.* (1955) Semi-historical drama. Unit set. 1920s costumes. 21m. 6w. 1 girl, 2 boys, extras. Dramatists Play Service $1.75. Royalty $50—$25.
An account of the famous Scopes trial centering on Henry Drummond, a public-spirited lawyer dedicated to the search for truth, and his conflicts in a community aroused by religious fundamentalism against the teaching of evolution. An excellent vehicle for advanced high school groups and older.

———. *The Night Thoreau Spent in Jail.* (1970) Biographical drama. Open stage. 19th century costumes. 11m. 5w. extras. Baker $1.75. French $1.75. Royalty $50—$35.
Opens with Thoreau in jail for refusing to pay taxes for support of the Mexican War. In a series of flashbacks, Thoreau's life is revealed. There is also a dream of the future. Excellent for all groups.

———. *Only in America.* (1959) Adapted from the book by Harry Golden. Comedy. Interior-exterior, inset. 17m. 5w. 3 extras. French $1.75. Royalty $50—$25.
This comedy is an account of an eastside New York Jew who sets up a humorous journal in North Carolina, "The Carolina Israelite." His publication, filled with witty aphorisms and homespun humor, soon becomes a success, and Harry becomes an accepted member of the community. For all groups. Ethnic interest: Jewish-American.

Leontovich, Eugenie. *Anna K.* Based on Tolstoi's novel *Anna Karenina.* Drama. Multiple sets, bare stage. 19th century costumes. 6m. 5w. extras. French $1.75. Royalty $50—$35.
A play-within-a-play approach to the telling of the Tolstoi novel. Suitable for all groups; offers possibilities for exciting ensemble effects.

Levin, Ira. *No Time for Sergeants.* (1955) Based on the novel by Mac Hyman. Comedy. Unit set. Military uniforms. 34m. 3w. doubling possible. Dramatists Play Service $1.75. Royalty $50—$25.

The story of a good-natured hillbilly who finally gets into the Air Force despite his father's propensity for tearing up his draft papers. He creates devastation among the generals, sergeants, his fellow servicemen, and a military psychiatrist. Requires advanced comic techniques, even though many of the scenes seem "naturals."

Levitt, Saul. *The Andersonville Trial*. (1960) Drama. Military courtroom interior. Civil War military uniforms and costumes. 28m. doubling possible. Dramatists Play Service $1.75. Royalty $50—$25.

A courtroom drama based on the famous military trial of Henry Wirz, commander of the Confederate prison for Northern soldiers in Andersonville during the Civil War. Raises the question of when the responsibility of the individual to his conscience supersedes military duty to follow orders of superiors. Requires mature, skilled actors.

Lindsay, Howard, and Crouse, Russel. *The Great Sebastians*. (1957) Melodramatic comedy. Interiors. Late 1940s costumes. 15m. 6w. Dramatists Play Service $1.75. Royalty $50—$25.

The story of a husband and wife vaudeville team who are performing their mind-reading act in Czechoslovakia at the time of the Communist coup (1948). How they get out of the country alive makes for great fun. Sparkling show for all groups.

———. *Life with Father*. (1939) Based on the book by Clarence Day. Comedy. Interior. Late 1880s costumes. 8m. 8w. Dramatists Play Service $1.75. Royalty $50—$25.

Father and his wife Vinnie, their young sons, relatives and friends, are all involved in the tremendous struggle between father and mother to have father properly baptized. Delightful study of family life, especially recommended for high school.

———. *Life with Mother*. (1948) Based on the book by Clarence Day. Comedy. 2 interiors. Late 1880s costumes. 8m. 8w. Dramatists Play Service $1.75. Royalty $50—$25.

Further adventures of the Day family in which mother attempts to provide an engagement ring for one of her sons, who wants it for his fiancée. Delightful family show, especially good for high school.

———. *State of the Union*. (1945) Satire. 4 interiors (3 are essential). Modern costumes. 11m. 6w. 3 nonspeaking men. Dramatists Play Service $1.75. Royalty $50—$25.

A successful businessman is urged to consider running for the presidency while taking a cross-country tour to inspect his plants and to make speeches en route. He expresses some opinions that are too radical for the politicians who had urged him to run. At a final meeting with the politicians at his home, he gives up the idea because of his differences with them. Requires a mature cast.

Livings, Henry. *Eh?* (1965) Farce. Interior. Modern costumes. 4m. 2w. Dramatists Play Service $1.75. Royalty $50—$25.

Set in a factory boiler room, with the main prop the boiler itself. The play details the plight of a hardy individualist caught in the over-protective web of a mechanized, computerized, and dehumanized modern industry. For advanced groups only.

Logan, Joshua. *The Wisteria Trees.* (1950) Based on Chekhov's *The Cherry Orchard.* Drama. Interior. Southern costumes. 8m. 6w. Dramatists Play Service, manuscript. Royalty $50—$25.

The story of "progress" necessitating the alteration of traditions and modification of the extravagances of life. Requires mature actors and delicate direction.

Long, Sumner Arthur. *Never Too Late.* (1957) Comedy. Interior. Modern costumes. 6m. 3w. Baker $1.75. French $1.75. Royalty $50—$25.

A married man in his fifties suddenly learns that he is to become a father again. This news has a great effect on his 24-year-old daughter. Frothy, escapist comedy for mature groups and older audiences.

Loos, Anita. *Gigi.* (1951) Based on the novel by Colette. Comedy. 2 interiors. Early 20th century costumes. 2m. 5w. Baker $1.75. French $1.75. Royalty $50—$25.

Gigi is a young French girl brought up by her mother, grandmother, and aunt to be a stylish cocotte. Gigi maintains her innocence and maneuvers the most important catch of Parisian society into asking her to marry him. Delightful show; suitable for all groups.

Lorca, Federico García. See García Lorca, Federico.

MacLeish, Archibald. *J. B.* (1958) Based on the Book of Job. Verse drama. Interior. Modern costumes. 12m. 9w. Baker $1.75. French $1.75. Royalty $50—$25.

The Biblical story of Job, set in a circus tent with God and the Devil arguing over Job's soul. J. B., a modern businessman rich with blessings, is brought down by the terrible afflictions of our century. J. B. does not curse God for his misfortunes, but remains unswerving in his devotion. Thought provoking; requires mature actors.

Mandel, Loring. *Advise and Consent.* (1961) Based on the novel by Allen Drury. Drama. Flexible staging. Modern costumes. 18m. 4w. 12 extras. French $1.75. Royalty $50—$25.

A melodrama about backstage politics in Washington during a sub-committee investigation of a man proposed for secretary of state. Presents a vivid picture of people and issues in government. For advanced groups only.

Manhoff, Bill. *The Owl and the Pussycat.* (1965) Comedy. Interior. Modern costumes. 1m. 1w. Baker $1.75. French $1.75. Royalty $50—$25.

In a loft in San Francisco lives a prim, stuffy author. Observing the neighborhood through his binoculars, he spots a prostitute plying her trade. He reports her, and she is thrown out of her apartment. She moves in with him, and both their lives are altered. For advanced casts and mature audiences.

Marchant, William. *The Desk Set.* (1956) Comedy. Interior. Modern costumes. 8m. 8w. Baker $1.75. French $1.75. Royalty $50—$25.

Bunny Watson, one of the "desk set"—a group of girls in the reference department of a television network—finds herself competing with the new electronic brains that have been placed around the office. Bunny, with her encyclopedic knowledge, is able to best them at every turn. Pleasant comedy suitable for all groups.

Marqués, René. *The Oxcart.* Translated by Charles Pilditch. Drama in 3 acts. 3 interiors. Modern costumes. 6m. 6w. In *Eight American Ethnic Plays*, ed. by Francis Griffith and Joseph Mersand. Royalty to author.

Set in the mountains outside San Juan, in La Perla, a San Juan slum district, and in the Spanish district of the Bronx. The play recounts the hopes and aspirations of Puerto Ricans who come to the mainland and their despair on arrival. The story covers a wide spectrum of Puerto Rican experience: those who are attached to the land; those who seek a better life in a large city; those who believe that only a trip to the mainland will improve their lot; those who ultimately return to the island in search of what has eluded them—economic security and inner contentment. For mature groups. Ethnic interest: Puerto-Rican-American.

Martínez Sierra, Gregorio. *The Cradle Song.* (1911) English version by John Garrett Underhill. Romantic drama in 2 acts. 2 interiors. Modern and religious costumes. 4m. 10w. extras. Baker $1.75. French $1.75. Royalty $50—$25.

Teresa, a foundling, is brought up in a convent, where the nuns lavish upon her all the tenderness generally absent from their lives. She finally falls in love and leaves them on her wedding day. A charming, amusing, and pathetic story told with Spanish grace and a delicate touch. Suitable for all groups.

Maugham, W. Somerset. *The Circle.* (1921) Social comedy. Interior. 1920s costumes. 4m. 3w. servants. Baker $1.75. Royalty $25.

Lady Kitty returns to her family with Lord Porteous, for whom she deserted her husband and son Arnold thirty years before. The spectacle of their degeneration delays, but fails to deter, Elizabeth, Arnold's unhappy wife, from deserting him and eloping with Teddie. Requires excellent character actors.

McCullers, Carson. *The Member of the Wedding*. (1950) Based on the author's novel. Drama. Unit set. Modern costumes. 6m. 7w. Dramatists Play Service $1.50. Royalty $50—$25.
Perceptive portraits of a lonely harum-scarum adolescent girl passing into maturity, a sympathetic black servant, and the little boy next door. Heartwarming show; must have sympathetic older actress for the black lead. Suitable for all groups.

McEnroe, Robert E. *The Silver Whistle*. (1948) Comedy. Exterior. Modern costumes. 10m. 5w. Dramatists Play Service $1.75. Royalty $50—$25.
A romantically minded tramp finds a birth certificate made out in the name of Oliver Erwenter, age 77. He then impersonates Erwenter, gets admitted to an old-age home, and proceeds to bring new life and happiness to the other inmates. Suitable for all groups.

McGreevey, John. *The Robe*. (1952) Based on the novel by Lloyd C. Douglas. Drama in 3 acts. Early Christian and Roman costumes. 13m. 9w. extras. Dramatic Publishing Co. $1.50. Royalty $35.
Christ's robe, won in a throw of dice by Marcellus, the young Roman officer who crucified him, is instrumental in the latter's repentance and conversion. Suitable for all groups.

Michaels, Sidney. *Dylan*. (1964) Based on memoirs by Caitlin Thomas and John M. Brinnin. Biography. Various sets. Modern costumes. 15m. 13w. French $1.75. Royalty $50—$25.
Explores the hectic, humorous, often bawdy life of Dylan Thomas at the time he began to travel and lecture. For advanced actors and mature audiences.

Miller, Arthur. *All My Sons*. (1947) Drama. Exterior. Modern costumes. 6m. 4w. Dramatists Play Service $1.75. Royalty $35—$25.
The story is concerned with the fortunes of the Keller and Deever families during World War II. There has been war profiteering, sabotage, and death. The play ends with the guilty father realizing that all young men are his sons. Within the range of advanced high school groups.

————. *The Crucible*. (1953) Drama. Unit set. 17th century Puritan costumes. 10m. 10w. Dramatists Play Service $1.75. Royalty $50—$25.
Witchcraft hysteria hits old Salem and many are threatened by the trials. The Proctor family is marked by a jealous serving girl, who maliciously causes the wife's arrest. Proctor takes the girl to court to

admit the lie but finds himself accused instead. He refuses to make a false confession to save his life. Suitable for all groups.

————. *Death of a Salesman.* (1948) Tragedy. Interior-exterior unit set. Modern costumes. 8m. 5w. Dramatists Play Service $1.75. Royalty $50—$25.
The tragic story of Willie Loman who, in his last days as a failing salesman, seeks to find out just where and how he has failed to win success and happiness with his wife, his sons, and his business associates. An American classic; has been done at high schools where there is an actor capable of portraying age.

————. *Incident at Vichy.* (1964) Tragedy. Interior. Modern costumes. 21m. Dramatists Play Service $1.75. Royalty $50—$25.
During the German occupation of France, eight men are brought in to the detention room of a Vichy police station for examination. None can comprehend that they will be sent to concentration camps. Requires mature actors.

————. *A View from the Bridge.* (1955) Revised, full-length version. Tragedy. Interior. Modern costumes. 12m. 3w. Dramatists Play Service $1.75. Royalty $50—$25.
Set near the New York waterfront. The story of Eddie Carbone, long-shoreman, whose misplaced love for his niece blurs his judgment about the one she loves and brings on tragedy for all. Exciting; for advanced groups. Ethnic interest: Italian-American.

Moll, Elick. *Seidman and Son.* (1963) Based on the author's novel. Comedy. 5 interiors. Modern costumes. 9m. 10w. French $1.75. Royalty $50—$25.
Morris Seidman has come through life the hard way and discovers that the problems don't stop. His son comes to work for him, and employees and clients are ready to leave. Morris uses his natural resources and sets the world right. Can be done by high school groups with actors capable of portraying age.

Molnár, Ferenc. *Liliom.* (1908) Translated by Benjamin F. Glazer. Fantasy in 7 scenes and prologue. 1 interior, 4 exteriors. Modern costumes. 17m. 5w. extras. Baker $1.75. French $1.75. Royalty $25.
Liliom was a ne'er-do-well who stabbed himself to death rather than be caught for a robbery he committed to provide for his unborn child. In heaven he is sentenced to years of purification fires, after which he may return to earth to perform one good deed. Excellent for all groups.

————. *The Play's the Thing.* (1925) Adapted by P. G. Wodehouse. Comedy in 3 acts. Interior. Modern costumes. 8m. 1w. French $1.75. Royalty $50—$25.

Turai, a playwright, brings Albert, his composer, on a surprise visit to an Italian castle. Albert overhears his fiancée making love to someone in her boudoir. Turai consoles him, making it appear that the conversation was actually a rehearsal for a play. To support this fabrication, he must stay up all night writing the play which includes the same conversation which the youth overheard. For advanced casts playing to mature audiences.

————. *The Swan.* (1914) Translated by Melville Baker. Romantic comedy in 3 acts. Interior. Court costumes. 9m. 8w. extras. David McKay $1.75. Royalty $25.

Duty and love conflict when a young princess loses her heart to her brother's tutor, but realizes that she must make a marriage benefitting her station. Imaginative and effective play combining sentiment and comedy. Offers a challenge for high school performers.

Morley, Robert, and Langley, Noel. *Edward, My Son.* (1947) Drama. 6 interiors. Modern costumes. 10m. 4w. Dramatists Play Service $1.75. Royalty $35—$25.

An ambitious and unscrupulous man is shown at various periods during his spectacular career. His life is motivated largely by devotion to his only son, who turns out to be a failure. Requires actors capable of playing mature roles.

Mortimer, John. *A Voyage round My Father.* (1970) Comedy. Open stage. Modern costumes. 12m. 7w. French $1.75. Restricted. Royalty $50—$35.

Through the eyes of the son we see the effect of the father upon the boy's life and that of the family. A touching, perceptive account of father and son. A sensitive story for advanced groups.

Mosel, Tad. *All the Way Home.* (1960) Based on James Agee's novel *A Death in the Family.* Drama. Composite interior-exterior. Early 20th century costumes. 6m. 7w. 1 child, extras. Baker $1.75. French $1.75. Royalty $50—$25.

The play tells what happens to the family when the father who goes to visit his dying father is killed along the way. A sensitive play requiring actors who can portray older characters.

Nichols, Anne. *Abie's Irish Rose.* (1922) Comedy in 3 acts. 2 interiors. Modern costumes. 6m. 2w. French $1.75. Royalty $25—$20.

Abraham Levy brings home, as his bride, Rosemary Murphy, to the resentment of both families. To appease them, the couple are married three times: by the Methodist minister, by the Jewish rabbi, and by the Catholic priest. For all groups. Ethnic interest: Jewish-American, Irish-American.

Nichols, Peter. *Joe Egg*. (1967) Comedy. Interior. Modern costumes. 2m. 3w. 1 child. Baker $1.75. French $1.75. Royalty $50—$25.

The love and marriage of a couple with a ten-year-old spastic child. The tortures, heartaches, and fears that hang over the parents of such a child are examined in a most humorous but tender manner. Sensitive play for advanced high school groups.

Obey, André. *Noah*. (1931) Adapted from the French by Arthur Wilmurt. Fantasy in 3 acts. 3 exteriors. Biblical costumes. 5m. 4w. extras. Baker $1.75. French $1.75. Royalty $25—$20.

The story of Noah, a kindly, simple old man who grows lonely in his faith, who pilots his craft safely to shore in the midst of doubts, and who is rudely deserted by the young folks the moment they touch foot to land. Excellent for high schools.

O'Casey, Sean. *Juno and the Paycock*. (1924) Tragedy in 3 acts. Interior. Modern costumes. 14m. 5w. French $1.75. Royalty $25.

A compelling story dealing with urban family life after the Irish Revolution. Exceptional example of keen character analysis. Quite difficult.

————. *The Plough and the Stars*. (1926) Drama in 4 acts. 3 interiors, 1 exterior. Modern costumes. 10m. 5w. French $1.75. Royalty $25—$20.

The futile efforts of the leader of one of the Irish revolutions. He is finally killed and his wife goes mad after losing her unborn child. Gripping and difficult; for advanced groups.

————. *Red Roses for Me*. (1942) Drama. Interior, exteriors. Early 20th century costumes. 21m. 9w. Dramatists Play Service, manuscript. Royalty $35—$25.

The theme is the lives of people—their valor, joy, love, religious devotion, loyalty, and belief in the future. The action takes place during the strike in Dublin in 1913–14 that led to the bloody Easter Week Rising of 1916. Special groups only.

————. *The Shadow of a Gunman*. (1923) Tragedy. Interior. Modern costumes. 8m. 3w. French $1.75. Royalty $25—$20.

One of two roommates, in reality a dreaming poet, is thought to be a gunman in the service of the Irish Republican Party. A Republican calls and leaves a bag containing bombs. When the house is raided by the authorities, Minnie, a friend, takes the bag to her room, thinking they will not search her. The deed is discovered and Minnie is shot, and the others find themselves deeply involved. Advanced groups only.

Odets, Clifford. *The Big Knife*. (1949) Drama. 8m. 4w. Dramatists Play Service $1.75. Royalty $50—$25.

Tells of the last few days of a movie star and former idealist whose years of compromise with his beliefs for the sake of a Hollywood career have resulted in the slow destruction of his personality. We see his struggles to escape from the net of insincerity and falsehood in which he has trapped himself, and his ultimate defeat. Mature groups only.

————. *The Country Girl.* (1950) Drama. 5 simple interiors. Modern costumes. 6m. 2w. Dramatists Play Service $1.75. Royalty $50—$25.

Georgie Elgin, the country girl, is a lovable, faithful, forgiving woman whose long years of devotion to her actor husband Frank have almost obliterated her own personality. She strives to save him from downfall and despair between jobs, but only in the tragic end of the play is her work recognized. Requires skillful character portrayal.

————. *Golden Boy.* (1937) Drama in 3 acts. 4 interiors, 2 exteriors. Modern costumes. 17m. 2w. Dramatists Play Service $1.75. Royalty $35—$25.

The account of a young Italian-American, Joe Bonaparte, who had some hope of becoming a great violinist before inordinate ambition led him to the prize ring, where his talent as a fighter—and ultimate tragedy— cut him off from music forever. Sharp dialogue and vivid characterization. For advanced groups. Ethnic interest: Italian-American.

O'Neill, Eugene. *Ah, Wilderness!* (1933) Comedy in 3 acts. 3 interiors, 1 exterior. Costumes, about 1900. 9m. 6w. Baker $2.00. French $2.00. Royalty $50—$25.

Richard, a high school senior and a confirmed rebel, disturbs his family and the average Connecticut small town they live in with his anarchic views and his violent behavior. He falls passionately in love with a neighbor's girl, and, despite several discouraging events, the play ends on a tenderly understanding, warm note. Excellent for groups with actors who can portray older characters.

————. *Anna Christie.* (1921) Drama. 2 interiors, 1 exterior. Waterfront costumes. 8m. 2w. extras. Dramatists Play Service $1.95 (in volume). Royalty $35—$25.

A character study of Anna Christie, a prostitute, who turns toward a clean life and unsullied love, only to be beaten down by the two men closest to her. Play recounts the struggle she undergoes to deserve the love she inspires. For advanced groups and mature audiences. Ethnic interest: Irish-American.

————. *Beyond the Horizon.* (1920) Tragedy in 3 acts. 1 interior, 2 exteriors. Modern rural costumes. 6m. 4w. Dramatists Play Service $1.75. Royalty $35—$25.

Robert Mayo discovers too late that his marriage with Ruth is a mistake. He struggles against maladjustment until misery and poverty ruin his home, crush Ruth's spirit, and break his own health. Then he welcomes death as an escape into the wide world of his dreams. Poetic and interesting; for very advanced groups only.

————. *Desire under the Elms.* (1924) Tragedy in 3 acts. Interior. Modern rural costumes. 4m. 1w. many extras. Dramatists Play Service $1.95 (in volume). Royalty $35—$25.
Eben, though fighting his young stepmother Abbie for the inheritance of the farm, is seduced by her. His unsuspecting old father wills the farm to the illegitimate baby. To prove to Eben that she really loves him and did not intend to trick him in this way, Abbie kills the infant. For advanced groups only.

————. *The Emperor Jones.* (1920) Drama in 8 scenes. 1 interior, 6 exteriors. West Indies costumes. 3m. 1w. many extras. Dramatists Play Service $1.95 (in volume). Royalty $35—$25.
Emperor Jones, once a pullman porter and convict, finds himself fleeing from his tribal subjects. The memories of his misdeeds, in the form of hallucinations and sounds, pursue him through the forest to his death from an avenging silver bullet. A tense, poetic study of primitive fear. Limited to groups with skillful character actors.

————. *The Great God Brown.* (1926) Fantastic drama in 4 acts. 1 exterior, 5 interiors. 9m. 5w. Dramatists Play Service $4.95 (in volume). Royalty $35—$25.
Dion Anthony, the artistic, and Billy Brown, the practical, are rivals for Margaret's hand. Dion wins her, but his genius fails to materialize and he is forced to take a job under Billy's management. Dion drinks himself to death, and Billy assumes his personality and attempts to live a double life. Eventually Billy is shot by the police when, as Dion, he supposedly murders Billy. A complicated production necessitating the clever use of masks to show variations in personality and requiring very expert acting and direction.

————. *The Hairy Ape.* (1922) Drama. 5 interiors, 2 exteriors. Modern costumes. 6m. 2w. extras. Dramatists Play Service $1.95 (in volume). Royalty $35—$25.
When a stoker is described as a "filthy beast," he begins to realize that he does not belong to the human family. He wanders around New York and finally ends up at the zoo, where he hails the gorilla as brother, only to be crushed to death by it. One of O'Neill's most striking dramas; for advanced groups and mature audiences only.

————. *Long Day's Journey into Night.* (1940) Autobiographical drama. Interior. Costumes of 1912. 3m. 2w. Dramatists Play Service $2.95. Royalty $50.
In the space of one day the tortured family background which created

the elusive yet magnificent talent of the author is given. Requires outstanding talent and sensitive direction.

————. *A Moon for the Misbegotten.* (1943) Drama. Exterior with scrim. Modern costumes. 3m. 1w. French $1.75. Royalty $50—$25.
Deals with just one of the "four haunted Tyrones" and follows in sequence *Long Day's Journey into Night.* James Jr., believed to be the counterpart of O'Neill's older brother, is a hard-drinking, self-destructive Broadway playboy who attempts unsuccessfully to blot out a haunting memory. Advanced groups only. Ethnic interest: Irish-American.

————. *A Touch of the Poet.* (1947) Drama. Interior. Costumes of 1828. 7m. 3w. Dramatists Play Service $1.75. Royalty $50—$25.
Con Melody, a proud and profane Irishman, owns a tavern near Boston. He is forever boasting of his wealthy background and military commission, which only antagonizes the Yankees and alienates him from his own daughter. Finally he realizes his situation and shoots his mare, symbol of his past pretensions. Possible for advanced groups. Ethnic interest: Irish-American.

Osborn, Paul. *A Bell for Adano.* (1944) Based on the novel by John Hersey. Drama in 3 acts. Interior. World War II costumes. 22m. 5w. Dramatists Play Service, manuscript. Royalty $35—$25.
Major Joppolo, an Italian from New York, comes to a small Sicilian town just after its liberation in World War II, restores order, and inspires its residents with a feeling of confidence and affection. They want a bell, symbol of the town's former well-being; Major Joppolo secures one from the Navy, although this act brings about his doom in the Army. Excellent for demonstrating democracy in action; interesting but dated. Suitable for all groups. Ethnic interest: Italian-American.

————. *On Borrowed Time.* (1938) Based on the novel by L. E. Watkins. Fantasy. 1 set. Modern costumes. 11m. 3w. Dramatists Play Service $1.75. Royalty $35—$25.
Death is chased up an apple tree by a boy and his grandfather. The exchange is interesting and touching. Possible for advanced groups.

Osborne, John. *The Entertainer.* (1956) Drama. Modern costumes. 5m. 2w. Dramatic Publishing Co. $1.75. Royalty $50.
Archie Rice is a glib, cheap, unscrupulous actor and promoter who is going down for the last time and dragging everyone else with him. Out of range and interest of high school groups.

————. *Epitaph for George Dillon.* (1958) Drama. 1 set. Modern costumes. 5m. 4w. Dramatic Publishing Co. $1.75. Royalty $50.
George Dillon cries out against himself after selling out his purpose-

fulness to secure commercial success. Out of range and interest of high school.

————. *Inadmissible Evidence.* (1965) Drama. Interior and fragment. Modern costumes. 3m. 5w. Dramatic Publishing Co. $1.75. Royalty $50. The self-destruction of a man begins in the courtroom and then goes to his office, where he alienates himself from all his close friends, including himself. Advanced groups and mature audiences only.

————. *Look Back in Anger.* (1956) Drama. 1 set. Modern costumes. 3m. 2w. Dramatic Publishing Co. $1.75. Royalty $50. In Jimmy Porter's boiling resentment at not being able to find himself in his own generation, he makes life impossible for those he most cherishes. Possible for mature high school groups.

————. *Luther.* (1961) Drama. Numerous simple sets. Clerical costumes. 12m. 1w. extras. Dramatic Publishing Co. $1.75. Royalty $50. A look at the man beneath the cowl, the mind behind the dramatic split in Christianity that launched the Reformation. Mature acting required; out of range of high school groups.

Owens, Robert. *Nineteen Eighty-Four.* (1963) Based on the novel by George Orwell. Drama. 1 basic set. Costumes of the future. 14 persons (2m. 2w. others flexible). Dramatic Publishing Co. $1.75. Royalty $35. The scene is London in 1984, a world where science has abandoned man for the state, a world where every citizen knows that war is peace, freedom is slavery, ignorance is strength. Possible for most groups.

Panetta, George. *Comic Strip.* (1958) Comedy in 3 acts. Unit set. Modern costumes. 12m. 3w. French $1.75. Royalty $35—$25. Humorous account of what happens to Jimmy Potts when he gets a haircut and *doesn't* get hit by a truck. Set against the background of the LaGuardia administration. Firello, the man of the comic strip, is the inspiration for the play. For all groups. Ethnic interest: Italian-American.

————. *Kiss Mama.* (1964) Comedy in 2 acts. Interior. Modern costumes. 4m. 4w. French $1.75. Royalty $35—$25. Play about Mama Caparuta, the power behind the throne, who settles on some compromises to make peace with her Jewish daughter-in-law. For all groups. Ethnic interest: Italian-American, Jewish-American.

Patrick, John. *The Curious Savage.* (1950) Comedy. Interior. Modern costumes. 5m. 6w. Dramatists Play Service $1.75. Royalty $35—$25. Mrs. Savage, a widow, wants to dispose of $10 million in the best possible way, in spite of the efforts of her grown-up stepchildren to get their hands on it. She leads these children on a merry chase, which takes her even into a sanatorium. There she is relieved to find people interested in her, not her money. With the help of the friends in the sanatorium, she arrives at a solution. Excellent for high school.

————. *The Hasty Heart.* (1945) Comedy-drama. Interior. World War II costumes. 8m. 1w. Dramatists Play Service $1.75. Royalty $50—$25.

A wounded Scottish soldier's last few weeks of life in a hospital in the Orient are changed by the sympathetic treatment his fellow patients try to give him. The man's stubborn rejection nearly wrecks the good intentions of those who want to make him happy, but at last he learns the true meaning of love for his neighbor. Requires mature acting and sensitive directing.

————. *The Teahouse of the August Moon.* (1953) Based on the novel by Vern J. Sneider. Comedy in 3 acts. U.S. Army and Japanese costumes. 18m. 8w. 3 children, 1 goat. Dramatists Play Service $1.75. Royalty $50—$25.

The comic confrontation between American occupation forces on Okinawa, determined to Americanize the entire culture, and the local residents, who have no intention of changing their customs. Funds allocated for the construction of a school are diverted and used to build a teahouse, which opens, of course, precisely when the colonel comes to make his inspection. Within the range of high school.

Percy, Edward, and Denham, Reginald. *Ladies in Retirement.* (1939) Mystery-drama. Interior. Modern costumes. 1m. 6w. Dramatists Play Service $1.75. Royalty $35—$25.

Lucy Fiske, ex-actress, is murdered by her companion Ellen so that Ellen's two eccentric sisters may share the cottage with her. For all groups; good for high school.

Piñero, Miguel. *Short Eyes.* Drama in 3 acts. Interior. Modern costumes. 16m. Royalty to French.

Set in the Dayroom, Men's House of Detention. A searing trip into the realities of prison life as told from the inmates' point of view. Blacks, Puerto Ricans, and whites clash in the ultimate struggle for survival. A true story by those who were there. Not for the squeamish. Ethnic interest: Puerto-Rican-American, Afro-American.

Pinter, Harold. *The Caretaker.* (1961) Comedy-drama. Interior. Modern costumes. 3m. Dramatists Play Service $1.75. Royalty $50—$25.

An old bum receives shelter in a cluttered room of an abandoned house. At first a comical character, the tramp soon becomes pitiful, finally alienating the two brothers who have separately offered him a job as caretaker of the premises. For advanced groups; out of range of high school.

————. *The Homecoming.* (1965) Drama. Interior. Modern costumes. 5m. 1w. Baker $1.95. French $1.95. Royalty $50—$25.

In a London home live four men: a widower with his two grown sons, and his brother, their uncle. Back into their life comes the third son, who six years earlier married a woman whom he has brought back with him. She fits into this tension-ridden household quite cannily. For advanced groups; out of range of high school.

Pratt, Theodore. *Seminole: A Drama of the Florida Indian.* (1953) Historical drama in 15 scenes. 50 characters; extras, fiddler, choir. University of Florida Press $2.00. Royalty to estate of Theodore Pratt.

The story of the Seminole leader Osceola and his treacherous capture by the United States Army after he had been brought in under a flag of truce. The plot follows historical documents of 1821–37 closely. A play written for outdoor amphitheater presentation but adaptable for school or community theater presentation. For advanced groups. Ethnic interest: American Indian.

Priestley, J. B. *Dangerous Corner.* (1932) Drama in 3 acts. Interior. Modern costumes. 3m. 4w. French $1.75. Royalty $25—$20.

The gradual revelation of the truth about a murdered man disrupts his family and friends and shows them up for the rotters they are. A combination mystery play and psychological study. For mature casts only.

————. *An Inspector Calls.* (1947) Drama. Interior. Modern costumes. 4m. 3w. Dramatists Play Service $1.75. Royalty $50—$25.

An eminently respectable British family is subjected to a routine inquiry in connection with a young girl's suicide. The family, close-knit and friendly at the beginning of the evening, is shown up as self-centered and cowardly as the inspector implicates all members of the group in the girl's undoing. Suitable for all groups; good for high school.

Rama Rau, Santha. *A Passage to India.* (1960) Based on the novel by E. M. Forster. Drama. 3 interiors, 1 exterior. Western and Indian costumes. 13m. 6w. French $1.75. Royalty $50—$25.

The irreconcilable ideas of Eastern and Western cultures and their pitiless dramatic conclusions are the basis of this play about an Indian doctor, an English professor, and an English girl who claims that the Indian doctor molested her. For advanced groups only.

Rattigan, Terence. *Ross.* (1961) Biography. 7 insets and sets. Modern and Arabian costumes. 21m. French $1.75. Royalty $50—$25.

The story of Lawrence of Arabia, now a middle-aged, undistinguished soldier, a man crippled in body and spirit. In a malarial dream he goes back over the courageous events of his life—how he lead the Arabs in an impossible march that led to victory over the Turks—and finally to that fatal event that broke his will and made him wince at the touch of any man. Suitable for mature groups only.

————. *Separate Tables.* (1954) Two dramas: "Tables by the Window" and "Table Number Seven." 2 interiors. Modern costumes. 3m. 8w. Baker $1.75. French $1.75. Royalty $50—$25.
Set in the dining room and lounge of a small hotel. In "Tables by the Window," a journalist is confronted by his former wife, who had provoked him to violence and led him to prison and ruin. In "Table Number Seven," a bogus army officer and a neurotic girl are attracted to each other, but a scandal threatens to keep them apart irrevocably. In both cases it is Miss Cooper, the hotel manager, who comes to the rescue and finds a way to repair their broken lives. Suitable for mature groups only.

————. *The Winslow Boy.* (1946) Drama. Interior. Modern costumes. 7m. 4w. Dramatists Play Service $1.75. Royalty $50—$25.
A youngster in an English governmental school is expelled for an alleged theft, of which he is innocent. The boy's father proceeds to contest the decision, and the issue, which began as a private matter, grows into a cause célèbre involving individuals challenging the forces of bureaucracy. Must have actors capable of portraying age.

Redgrave, Michael. *The Aspern Papers.* (1959) Based on the story by Henry James. Melodrama. Interior. Modern costumes. 2m. 4w. French $1.75. Royalty $50—$25.
An American publisher arrives at an old palazzo in Venice which is inhabited by a woman of 90 and her niece. He is in search of the writings of a dead author who had loved the aunt. It is his belief that the writings will prove the author's greatness. For advanced groups; possible for mature high school.

Resnick, Muriel. *Any Wednesday.* (1964) Comedy. Interior. Modern costumes. 2m. 2w. Dramatists Play Service $1.75. Royalty $50—$25.
The story deals with four engaging and believable people: a millionaire businessman, his disarmingly innocent mistress, his hoodwinked wife, and an irate victim of his sharp practice. Their paths cross under the most unexpected and hilarious circumstances. For mature groups only.

Rice, Elmer. *The Adding Machine.* (1923) Drama in 7 scenes. 5 interiors, 2 exteriors. Modern costumes. 14m. 9w. French $2.00. Royalty $50—$25.
The play shows, in stark outline, the life history and, in its later scenes, the death history of Mr. Zero, a cog in the vast machine of modern business. Powerful and expressionistic play, suitable only for very advanced amateurs and sophisticated audiences.

————. *Dream Girl.* (1945) Comedy-fantasy. Simple sets suggesting dream scenes. Modern costumes. 25m. 7w. Dramatists Play Service $1.75. Royalty $50—$25.

A charming but dreamy and overimaginative young woman who runs a bookstore finds escape into a romantic world of unreality by day-dreaming. The play is a dramatization of some of these dreams. Possible for advanced high school casts.

————. *Street Scene.* (1929) Drama in 3 acts. Exterior. Modern costumes. 16m. 11w. French $2.00. Royalty $50—$25.

A mood picture of the comedy and tragedy of daily life in a poor urban neighborhood. Anna, hungry for the love which her husband denies her, carries on an affair with the milkman. When her husband discovers them together, he shoots them. This incident crystalizes the viewpoints and very human reactions of the family and entire neighborhood. For advanced groups only.

Richardson, Howard, and Berney, William. *Dark of the Moon.* (1945) Folk play. Various sets. Rural costumes. 28 roles. Baker $2.25. French $1.75. Royalty $50—$35.

Based on the haunting ballad of Barbara Allen, the play recounts the story of a witch boy who one day beholds the beautiful Barbara Allen and immediately falls in love with her. A compact is made by which he is given human form to woo and marry her. In a frenzy of religious revival, Barbara betrays her husband. Excellent for advanced groups.

Riggs, Lynn. *Green Grow the Lilacs.* (1930) Romantic drama in 6 scenes. Modern costumes. 10m. 4w. extras. French $2.00. Royalty $50—$25.

Laurey's love for Curly, the cowhand, inflames the jealous Jud Fry, whose threatening presence hangs over their romance even after they are married, and whom Curly is forced to kill. Suitable for high school production.

Rinehart, Mary Roberts, and Hopwood, Avery. *The Bat.* (1920) Based on Rinehart's novel *The Circular Staircase.* Mystery-comedy in 3 acts. 2 interiors. Modern costumes. 7m. 3w. French $1.75. Restricted. Royalty $25—$20.

The thrilling solution to a bank robbery is made in the dead banker's summer house, where four people, believing him to be secretly alive, are trying to secure the treasure they think he has hidden there. The real culprit is unsuspected until the very end. One of the best of the thrillers; good characters. Exciting for high school groups.

Roman, Lawrence. *Under the Yum Yum Tree.* (1961) Comedy. Interior. Modern costumes. 3m. 2w. Dramatists Play Service $1.75. Royalty $50—$25.

Hogan is the landlord who lives next door. He is a man on the prowl and he lies, eavesdrops, and intrudes on his gorgeous tenant, Robin Austin. Robin is in love with a young lawyer named Dave Manning. She thinks before their marrying they ought to test their compatibility. Gay fluff, but not suitable for high school.

Rostand, Edmond. *Cyrano de Bergerac.* (1897) Adapted and arranged by Edna Kruckemeyer. Heroic comedy in 5 acts. 2 interiors, 3 exteriors. 17th century French costumes. 30m. 16w. Baker $1.75. French $1.75. Royalty on application (budget play).

Cyrano, a clever but homely cavalier, loves Roxane, who in turn loves a handsome but stupid soldier, Christian. Cyrano woos Roxane for Christian and does many noble, unselfish deeds; years later, as he is dying, Cyrano learns that Roxane loves him. In this version, the more difficult scenes have been simplified. Offers excellent parts to a large number of actors; suitable for all groups.

Rotter, Fritz, and Vincent, Allen. *Letters to Lucerne.* (1941) Drama in 3 acts. 2 interiors. Modern costumes. 4m. 9w. French $1.75. Royalty $35—$25.

The animosity a Polish girl feels toward her German friend Erna, whose brother she had loved at the outbreak of the war, is dispelled when she learns that Erna's brother preferred suicide to bombing Warsaw. Suitable for high school.

Saroyan, William. *The Beautiful People.* (1941) Comedy in 3 acts. Interior. Modern costumes. 7m. 2w. French $1.75. Royalty $25—$20.

An assortment of charming, weird characters and their idiosyncrasies represent Saroyan's belief that love is the only thing that matters in the world. Offers challenge to advanced groups, including high school.

————. *The Cave Dwellers.* (1957) Comedy. Bare stage. Modern costumes. 9m. 5w. Baker $1.75. French $1.75. Royalty $50—$25.

The adventures of some penniless people who have camped out on the stage of an abandoned theater that is about to be destroyed for a housing project. Unsuitable for high school.

————. *My Heart's in the Highlands.* (1939) Fantasy. Simple sets. Modern costumes. 13m. 2w. extras. French $1.75. Royalty $25—$20.

Through his warm characters, the author dwells on themes of war and of love, of the place of money and of art in the world, of life and its wonders. The characters are the innocents of this world who long dimly for a beauty they but vaguely understand. Sensitive characterizations required; a challenge for high school groups.

————. *The Time of Your Life.* (1939) Comedy in 3 acts. 2 interiors. Modern costumes. 18m. 7w. French $2.00. Royalty $35—$25.

Joe's search for happiness and for the answers to the far-reaching enigmas of life takes him to a waterfront saloon, where the vivid characters wandering in and out are as unsure as Joe about how to get more living done. For advanced groups only.

Sartre, Jean-Paul. *The Flies.* (1943) Adapted from the French by Paul Bowles. Tragedy in 3 acts. 2 interiors, 2 exteriors. Greek costumes. 8m. 6w. extras. French $1.75 (in volume with "No Exit"). Royalty $25—$20.
The ancient Greek legend of Orestes, wherein Orestes returns to his homeland after a long exile to find his father, the king, dead, and his mother married to the murderer. The flies are the furies, who feed upon the political corruption and are the source of excruciating conscience and remorse. For mature, advanced groups only.

———. *No Exit.* (1946) Adapted from the French by Paul Bowles. Fantasy in 2 acts. 75 minutes. Interior. Modern costumes. 2m. 2w. French $1.75 (in volume with "The Flies"). Royalty $25—$20.
Two women and one man are locked up together for eternity in one hideous room in Hell. Ironically, the torture is not of rack and fire, but of the burning humiliation of each soul as it is stripped of its pretenses by the curious souls of the damned. For advanced groups.

Schary, Dore. *The Devil's Advocate.* (1961) Based on the novel by Morris L. West. Drama. 5 interiors. Modern costumes. 9m. 2w. extras. Baker $1.75. French $1.75. Royalty $50—$25.
A dying priest is sent by his superiors in the role of devil's advocate to investigate and, if possible, discredit a dead man's claims to sanctity. The man, an Italian patriot, had been beaten by Communists and finally killed by Nazis. Miracles are attributed to him. Was he a holy man or sinner? He was, it turns out, a bit of both. For advanced groups.

———. *Sunrise at Campobello.* (1958) Drama. Interiors. 1920s costumes. 19m. 5w. Dramatists Play Service $1.75. Royalty $50—$25.
The play covers the life of F. D. Roosevelt from his attack of infantile paralysis to the day at Madison Square Garden when he was able to stand and nominate Al Smith for president of the United States. Requires unique physical characteristics; limited possibilities.

Schulberg, Budd, and Breit, Harvey. *The Disenchanted.* (1958) Based on the novel by Budd Schulberg. Drama. 3 interiors. Modern costumes. 10m. 4w. extras. French $1.75. Royalty $50—$25.
The love affair of Manley Halliday and his wife is over. While she is under psychiatric care, he is trying to recover his place in the world by writing a new novel. To relieve the financial crisis, he accepts an offer to write a filmscript, though he has nothing but contempt for this very commercial venture. For mature, advanced groups only.

Segall, Harry. *Heaven Can Wait.* (1938) Comedy-fantasy. Interior. Modern costumes. 12m. 6w. Dramatists Play Service $1.75. Royalty $35—$25.

Joe Pendleton, a prizefighter who refuses to admit that he's dead, returns to earth in the bodies of various recently deceased people and creates much comic confusion. Suitable for high school.

———. *Mister Angel.* Comedy-fantasy. Interior. Modern costumes. 5m. 8w. Dramatists Play Service $1.75. Royalty $35—$25.

Item, a small girl angel, encounters many problems waiting to be born to a certain couple who are too busy with the theater at the moment to consider such an event. Suitable for high school.

Semple, Lorenzo Jr. *Golden Fleecing.* (1959) Comedy. Interior. Modern costumes and uniforms. 11m. 2w. French $1.75. Royalty $50—$25.

When the Navy pays a courtesy call in Venice, a lieutenant, an ensign, and a civilian scientist take up residence in a plush hotel in order to execute a fantastic scheme: with the aid of a spotter in a local roulette palace they plan to relay numbers from one particular wheel to the secret computer aboard the cruiser and thereby break the bank. Limited appeal and value for high school.

Shaffer, Peter. *Five Finger Exercise.* (1958) Tragedy. Composite interior. Modern costumes. 3m. 2w. Baker $1.75. French $1.75. Royalty $50—$25.

A German orphan goes to England to tutor the daughter of a nouveau riche family. Although he hopes to be absorbed by the country and the love of the family, he encounters selfish passions instead. Advanced groups only.

———. *The Royal Hunt of the Sun.* (1966) History. Cyclorama, drops and insets. Conquistador and Incan costumes. 22m. 2w. extras. Baker $1.75. French $1.75. Royalty $50—$25.

A history of the expedition of the Spanish under Pizzaro to Peru. Although the Inca pays the 9000 pounds of gold ransom for his release, he is tried in a kangaroo court and executed. For advanced groups.

Shaw, George Bernard. *Androcles and the Lion.* (1912) Comedy in prologue and 2 acts. 2 exteriors, 1 interior. Early Christian and Roman costumes. 14m. 2w. 2 nondescript, extras. Baker $1.95. French $.95. Royalty $25.

A Christian tailor, Androcles, pulls a thorn from the foot of a lion, and later, in the arena in Rome, is thrown to the same lion, who recognizes and saves him. A satire on persecutions; mad and hilarious. Excellent for high school.

———. *Arms and the Man.* (1894) Comedy in 3 acts. 2 interiors, 1 exterior. Balkan costumes of 1885. 5m. 3w. Baker $1.75. French $1.75. No royalty in U.S.; $25 in Canada.

Captain Bluntschi, a Serbian soldier fleeing from the Bulgarians, is sheltered by Raina Petchoff, a Bulgarian lady engaged to Sergius. After the war Bluntschi returns on military business with Major Petchoff and wins Raina from Sergius, who marries Raina's maid. Brilliant and worthwhile comedy requiring good acting.

―――. *Candida.* (1895) Comedy in 3 acts. Interior. Costumes, 1905 or modern. 4m. 2w. Baker $.95. French $.95. No royalty in U.S.; $25 in Canada.

Candida, the charming wife of a clergyman, has to choose between her husband and a young poet, Marchbanks. Finally she chooses her apparently self-sufficient husband as "the weaker." Fast and witty. Needs experienced actors.

―――. *The Devil's Disciple.* (1897) Drama in 3 acts. 2 interiors, 1 composite interior, 1 exterior. Costumes of the American Revolution. 10m. 5w. extras. Baker $.80. French $.75. No royalty in U.S.; $25 in Canada.

Dick Dudgeon, the "devil's disciple," is unable to live up to his misanthropic ideals. He finds himself saving the life of a clergyman, but gets sentenced to death by the British. Reprieve comes just as he is about to die heroically. Suitable for advanced groups.

―――. *Fanny's First Play.* (1911) Comedy in prologue, 3 acts, and epilogue. 3 interiors. Modern costumes. 12m. 5w. French $7.50. Royalty on application.

Fanny O'Dowda has written a play to which well-known critics are invited. The play: Mr. and Mrs. Lilley are disgraced because their son, who was to marry Margaret Knox, is thrown in jail after a brawl. However, Margaret is also in jail for hitting a policeman, so the young people are thrown together. The critics declare the play a success. Witty and interesting play, sometimes played by colleges.

―――. *Major Barbara.* (1905) Satiric comedy in 3 acts. 1 interior, 2 exteriors. Modern costumes. 9m. 7w. Baker $1.35. French $.75. Royalty $25.

Barbara, who has renounced her social position to become a Salvation Army major, refuses as "tainted money" the generous donations of Bodge, whiskey distiller, and Undershaft, her father, only to discover the Army's view that money from whatever source is desirable. Completely converted, she marries a man who takes a position in her father's munitions factory. Brilliant and playable. Requires experienced actors.

―――. *Man and Superman.* (1905) Satiric comedy in 4 acts. 1 interior, 3 exteriors. Modern costumes. 18m. 7w. Baker $1.25. French $1.25. No royalty.

Jack Tanner, who has been appointed Anne's guardian, discovers that she is interested in him romantically. He flies from her in his motor, but she follows and captures him. Witty exposition of the "life force." Difficult staging; needs cutting. For advanced amateurs only.

————. *Pygmalion.* (1913) Comedy in 5 acts. 3 interiors, 2 exteriors. Early 20th century costumes. 6m. 6w. extras. Baker $.65. French $.65. Royalty $25.

Higgins, a crank on phonetics, enters into a bet with a friend that he can transform Eliza, a flower girl, into a duchess and pass her off at a court function. He succeeds, but complications arise when the affair is over and Eliza is no longer needed as a subject for experimentation. Difficult, but good for advanced groups.

————. *Saint Joan.* (1923) Drama. 6 interiors, 1 exterior. Modern and 15th century costumes. 21m. 2w. extras. Baker $.95. French $.85. Royalty $25.

Traces the life of Joan of Arc from the time she appeared to her regional governor to her death at the stake. Requires mature, experienced actors.

————. *You Never Can Tell.* (1896) Comedy in 4 acts. 2 interiors, 1 exterior. Early 20th century costumes. 6m. 4w. French $1.75. No royalty in U.S.; $25 in Canada.

The children of a "new woman" who has left her husband, the husband himself, and a struggling young dentist become involved in complicated interrelations. Brilliant comedy of witty talk; for advanced amateurs.

Shaw, Irwin. *The Gentle People.* (1939) Comedy. 3 interiors, 2 exteriors. Modern costumes. 10m. 3w. Dramatists Play Service $1.75. Royalty $35—$25.

Two middle-aged cronies who love to fish seek in each other's company a refuge from domestic difficulties. Their peace is threatened by a gangster, who is quickly taken for a boat ride from which he fails to return. Advanced groups only.

Shaw, Robert. *The Man in the Glass Booth.* (1967) Drama. 3 interiors. Modern costumes. 18m. 3w. French $1.75. Restricted. Royalty $50—$35.

A man claiming to be a Jew is captured by Israeli agents and tried as a Nazi officer. He confesses; however, he is later identified by other Jews as being, in fact, a Jew. A study of a man's struggle with identity and expiation. Requires experienced actors.

Sherriff, Robert C. *Journey's End.* (1929) Drama in 3 acts. Interior.

British military uniforms. 10m. Baker $1.75. French $1.75. Royalty $50—$25.
Shows the effect of war on a small group of English officers. A tragic and moving piece; for advanced casts only.

Sherwood, Robert E. *Idiot's Delight.* (1936) Satire. Interior. Modern costumes. 17m. 10w. Dramatists Play Service, manuscript. Royalty $35—$25.
A group of international vacationers are marooned in an inn high in the Alps just before the outbreak of what threatens to be a world war. An American vaudeville couple are the only ones left, as the others make good their escape. These two succumb to the first onslaught of war with bravery and a useless sort of idealism. Satire on warmongering. For advanced groups.

————. *The Petrified Forest.* (1935) Drama. Interior. Modern costumes. 18m. 3w. Dramatists Play Service $1.75. Royalty $35—$25.
A group of gangsters take over a lunchroom in the Arizona desert where Alan Squier, a disillusioned sophisticate on his way to the Petrified Forest—i.e., self-destruction—has given his insurance policy to Gaby, a waitress, so that she might go to Europe. The gangsters accommodate Alan by killing him. For advanced groups only.

————. *The Queen's Husband.* (1928) Comedy in 3 acts. Interior. Royal court costumes. 11m. 4w. extras. David McKay $1.50. Royalty $30.
King Eric, who has always been ruled by his wife and the scheming statesmen, finally asserts himself and averts the marriage of his daughter Anne to a prince whom she does not love. He helps her elope with his secretary. Excellent plot; difficult to direct.

————. *There Shall Be No Night.* (1940) Drama. 3 interiors. Modern costumes. 13m. 4w. Dramatists Play Service, manuscript. Royalty $35—$25.
The effect on people's lives of the Russian invasion of Finland, and the necessity for individual courage. Advanced casts only.

Shyre, Paul. *The Child Buyer.* (1962) Based on the novel by John Hersey. Drama. Interior. Modern costumes. 10m. 4w. 1 child. French $1.75. Royalty $35—$25.
A corporation comes up with the idea of "buying" child prodigies, wiping out their memories, and then reeducating them for use in a project for the government. For advanced groups.

Sills, Paul. *Story Theatre.* Fables. Open stage, projections. Costumes. 5m. 3w. Baker $1.75. French $1.75. Restricted. Royalty $50—$35.

The improvised telling of favorite fables—Henny Penny, The Golden Goose, Venus and the Cat, The Fisherman and His Wife, The Robber Baron, and others. Requires skilled ensemble work with people skilled in body movement, pantomime, and improvisation. Suitable for all groups.

Simon, Neil. *Barefoot in the Park.* (1963) Comedy. Interior. Modern costumes. 4m. 2w. Baker $1.75. French $1.75. Royalty $50—$35.
A serious young lawyer and his new, free-spirited wife try married life in a fifth-floor walk-up apartment in New York. Complications are created by the appearance of his mother-in-law and the aging, outlandish gourmet who lives in the loft above them. Within the range of high school groups.

————. *Come Blow Your Horn.* (1961) Comedy. Interior. Modern costumes. 3m. 4w. Baker $1.75. French $1.75. Royalty $50—$25.
Harry Baker, the father of two sons, is the owner of the largest artificial fruit business in the East. Buddie, hitherto an obedient son, moves into the apartment of his older, playboy brother, leaving behind a rebellious letter by way of explanation. A rich variety of complications ensue. Suitable for high school.

————. *The Odd Couple.* (1965) Comedy. Interior. Modern costumes. 6m. 2w. Baker $1.75. French $1.75. Royalty $50—$35.
A slob, who is divorced, and his meticulous friend, who has just been separated from his wife, decide to room together. The patterns of their own disastrous marriages begin to reappear, with hilarious results. Suitable for high school.

————. *The Star-Spangled Girl.* (1966) Comedy. Interior. Modern costumes. 2m. 1w. Dramatists Play Service $1.75. Royalty $50—$35.
Two dedicated young men, who are enduring near starvation in order to publish a protest magazine, find themselves the neighbors of an all-American girl. The three find that interaction is somewhat complicated by misunderstandings. Suitable for high school.

————. *The Sunshine Boys.* Comedy. 1 set. Modern costumes. 5m. 2w. French $1.75. Restricted. Royalty $50—$35.
Two vaudeville performers have split at the height of their successful career. After eleven years they are asked to do a comedy special. The old wounds have not healed, and the attempt at reconciliation is a fiasco. Crisp, funny dialogue; for advanced groups only.

Sommer, Edith. *Roomful of Roses.* (1956) Comedy-drama. Interior. Modern costumes. 3m. 5w. 1 boy. Dramatists Play Service $1.75. Royalty $50—$25.
Bridget, a young girl, does not feel it wise to love anyone after being

passed from her father to her rewed mother. Suitable for advanced groups.

Spewack, Bella, and Spewack, Samuel. *Boy Meets Girl.* (1935) Comedy. 2 interiors. Modern costumes. 14m. 5w. Dramatists Play Service $1.75 (in volume with "Spring Song"). Royalty $35—$25.
A studio waitress and her unborn child get involved with two Hollywood writers, who get the idea of starring the infant in a western. When their plan falls through, they attempt to get their revenge. Suitable for mature high school groups.

———. *My Three Angels.* (1953) Based on *La Cuisine des Anges*, by Albert Husson. Comedy. Interior. Modern costumes. 7m. 3w. Dramatists Play Service $1.75. Royalty $50—$25.
Three convicts of French Guiana are employed as roofers by a harassed household. The three—two murderers and one swindler—are passionate believers in the "robinhood" of man. Possessing every criminal art, they proceed to set things straight. Suitable for high school groups.

Spigelgass, Leonard. *Dear Me, The Sky Is Falling.* (1963) Based on a story by Gertrude Berg and James Yaffe. Comedy. Interior and inset. Modern costumes. 5m. 7w. Baker $1.75. French $1.75. Royalty $50—$25.
A matriarch fearlessly takes on all the problems of the neighborhood, in addition to those of her husband and her last unmarried daughter. The husband and daughter decide to have things their own way for once. Suitable for high school groups.

———. *A Majority of One.* (1959) Comedy in 3 acts. 4 interiors. Modern and Japanese costumes. 6m. 8w. Baker $1.75. French $1.75. Royalty $50—$25.
A Jewish widow from Brooklyn accompanies her daughter and son-in-law on a delicate diplomatic mission to Japan. The son-in-law becomes concerned with the growing friendship that develops between his mother-in-law and an influential Japanese gentleman. Japanese and Jewish-American culture are contrasted, never in serious conflict. Within the range of high school groups. Ethnic interest: Jewish-American.

Stein, Joseph. *Enter Laughing.* (1963) Based on the novel by Carl Reiner. Comedy. Stage, wagons and insets. Modern costumes. 7m. 4w. Baker $1.75. French $1.75. Restricted. Royalty $50—$25.
The account of a stage-struck youth who works as the delivery boy for a sewing machine factory. Although his parents want him to be a druggist, as soon as he has saved enough money he enlists in a semi-professional company that will put anybody in any play for the right amount. Within the range of high school.

Steinbeck, John. *Of Mice and Men.* (1937) Based on the author's novel. Drama. 2 interiors, 1 exterior. Modern costumes. 9m. 1w. Dramatists Play Service $1.75. Royalty $35—$25.

A character study of two roving farmhands, one of whom, "with the strength of a gorilla and the mind of an untutored child," unwittingly murders a woman and is killed by his friend to prevent him from falling into the hands of the law. Requires advanced groups.

Stoppard, Tom. *Rosencrantz and Guildenstern Are Dead.* (1967) Comedy. Unit set. Elizabethan costumes. 14m. 2w. 12 extras, 6 musicians. Baker $1.75. French $1.75. Restricted. Royalty $50—$35.

Rosencrantz and Guildenstern, fellow students of Hamlet, reveal what happened behind the scenes in Shakespeare's play. Suitable for advanced high school groups.

Storey, David. *The Contractor.* (1970) Drama. Exterior. Modern costumes. 9m. 3w. French $1.75. Restricted. Royalty $50—$25.

A group of laborers are putting up a tent on the employer's estate for the wedding of his daughter. As the men put up the tent, decorate it, and then dismantle it, we learn of the sorrows and joys, strengths and weaknesses of those involved. Play revolves around the erection of the tent. For advanced casts with skilled technical assistance.

Synge, John Millington. *The Playboy of the Western World.* (1907) Comedy in 3 acts. Interior. Modern costumes. 7m. 5w. French $1.95. Royalty $25—$20.

A rollicking poetic comedy about a young man who thought he had murdered his father. He becomes the hero of the countryside, only to lose all when it is learned that his father is still alive. For all groups.

Tarkington, Booth. *Seventeen.* (1918) Based on the author's novel. Comedy in 4 acts. Exterior, 2 interiors. Can be arranged for 1 interior throughout. Modern costumes. 8m. 6w. French $1.75. Royalty $25—$20.

Silly Bill falls in love with Lola, the Baby-Talk Lady, a vapid if amiable little flirt. Recommended for high school production.

Taylor, Samuel. *The Happy Time.* (1950) Based on stories by Robert Fontaine. Comedy. 2 interiors. Modern costumes. 8m. 4w. Dramatists Play Service $1.75. Royalty $50—$25.

Bibi Bonnard, the youngest member of a gay, uninhibited French-Canadian family in Ottawa, grows up and learns what it truly is to be a man. A happy and carefree theatrical treat. Suitable for high school and older groups.

————. *Sabrina Fair.* (1953) Romantic comedy. Exterior. Modern costumes. 7m. 7w. Dramatists Play Service $1.75. Royalty $50—$25.

In this modern Cinderella fable the chauffeur's daughter marries the son of her father's wealthy employer. Wonderful character parts (the chauffeur is a millionaire too, but keeps his job because he wants to read on someone else's time). Suitable for high school and older groups.

Taylor, Samuel, and Skinner, Cornelia Otis. *The Pleasure of His Company.* (1958) Comedy. Interior. Modern costumes. 5m. 2w. Dramatists Play Service $1.75. Royalty $50—$25.
A somewhat tarnished international playboy returns to the home of his former wife to give away their daughter in marriage. When he turns on his charm, his daughter is transported. The mother and fiancé are helpless. Fun for high school groups and older.

Teichmann, Howard. *The Girls in 509.* (1958) Comedy. Interior. Modern costumes. 9m. 3w. Baker $1.75. French $1.75. Royalty $50—$25.
When a no longer fashionable hotel in New York is being demolished, a pair of hermit ladies are discovered in one of the back suites. They went into hiding when Herbert Hoover was defeated by Roosevelt and resolved never to emerge until FDR was out of office. The action that ensues involves both major political parties. Suitable for high school and older.

Teichmann, Howard, and Kaufman, George S. *The Solid Gold Cadillac.* (1953) Comedy. Simple, stylized sets. Modern costumes. 11m. 6w. Dramatists Play Service $1.75. Royalty $50—$25.
The wicked board of directors of General Products is foiled with the help of a little old lady who owns $10 worth of stock and who cares. Fun show for high school and older.

Terry, Megan. *Viet Rock.* (1966) Drama. Bare stage. Modern costumes. 8 to 20 characters. French $2.95 (in *Viet Rock and Others*). Royalty $35—$25.
Through the use of dialogue, music, chant, dance, pantomine, and image, the play satirizes attitudes toward the Vietnam War. The action of the play follows several soldiers from birth to induction, to indoctrination, to battle overseas, to fraternization, and to death. Requires mature, advanced actors.

Thomas, Brandon. *Charley's Aunt.* (1892) Farcical comedy in 3 acts. 1 exterior, 2 interiors. Costumes of 1892. 6m. 4w. Baker $2.00. Eldridge $2.00. French $2.00. Royalty $25. No royalty in Canada.
When an Oxford undergraduate impersonates a wealthy aunt for his two friends, all three become involved in a mad, comic tangle with their sweethearts, especially when the real aunt turns up under an assumed name. Suitable for all groups.

Thomas, Dylan. *Under Milk Wood.* (1953) Drama. Area setting and staging. Modern costumes. 17m. 17w. Baker $1.50. French $1.50. Royalty $50—$25.
A look into a smug and ingrown Welsh fishing village and the lives of its inhabitants: a sea captain dreaming of the dead, a draper making love promises to his wife, a schoolteacher waiting for someone—anyone, a lunatic with 66 clocks eating from a dog's dish, children playing a kissing game. These vignettes are threaded together and unified by the "Onlooker." Suitable for high school and older.

Thurber, James. *A Thurber Carnival.* (1960) Revue. 5m. 4w. (more if desired). Baker $1.75. French $1.75. Royalty $50—$25.
This is a revue for those with little or no musical talent; therefore there is little or no music between the humorous scenes of American life. Includes "The Night the Bed Fell," "The Unicorn in the Garden," "Gentlemen Shoppers," "The Secret Life of Walter Mitty," "File and Forget." Suitable for high school and older.

Thurber, James, and Nugent, Elliott. *The Male Animal.* (1940) Comedy in 3 acts. Interior. Modern costumes. 8m. 5w. Baker $2.00. French $2.00. Royalty $50—$25.
Tommy Turner insists on standing up for his rights and the four freedoms at the risk of losing his wife and a comfortable teaching job at the university. Suitable for all groups.

Tiller, Ted. *Count Dracula.* Based on the novel by Bram Stoker. Mystery-comedy. Interior with inset. 19th century costumes. 7m. 2w. Baker $2.00. French $2.00. Royalty $50—$25.
The account of the successful attempts to conquer the vampire Count Dracula, this popular "horror" provides for innumerable scenic gimmicks and funny lines. Should prove a scary, zany evening for high school and other groups.

Turner, Philip. *Christ in the Concrete City.* Drama. 1 hour. Bare stage with rostrum. Modern costumes. 4m. 2w. Baker $1.25. Royalty $15.
Sets before the audience the Passion of Christ. The actors play both the historical characters of the Bible story and their own lives, passing freely from one to the other. Suitable for all groups.

Ustinov, Peter. *The Love of Four Colonels.* (1953) Comedy. Stylized sets, interiors and exteriors. Modern costumes. 6m. 2w. Dramatists Play Service $1.75. Royalty $50—$25.
The colonels, representing four major world powers, are given the opportunity to waken and claim the Sleeping Beauty. Each of the colonels sees her as embodying his own particular ideal. Each fails, surrendering the illusion he had long cherished. For advanced groups.

————. *Romanoff and Juliet.* (1956) Comedy. Unit set. Modern costumes. 9m. 4w. Dramatists Play Service $1.75. Royalty $50—$25.
The smallest of mythical countries lies between the East and the West, so each of these world divisions seeks to make an ally. The Russian has a son and the American has a daughter and the two fall in love. For advanced groups.

————. *The Unknown Soldier and His Wife.* (1967) Comedy. X-ray or platform set. Military costumes. 15m. 2w. Baker $1.75. French $1.75. Royalty $50—$25.
Two acts of war separated by a truce for refreshment. The common soldier who is about to be buried with honors turns out, on investigation, to be the same fall-guy throughout the world's history, dragging his wife along with him. In fact, the general and priest are the same, too; over and over the same war recurs and the same common soldier is buried with honors. For advanced groups only.

van Druten, John. *Bell, Book and Candle.* (1950) Comedy. Interior. Modern costumes. 3m. 2w. Dramatists Play Service $1.75. Royalty $50—$25.
Gillian Holroyd, a modern day witch, casts a spell over an unattached publisher. He falls in love with her, but she cannot fall in love. This imperfection leads to a number of difficulties. Suitable for all groups.

————. *I Am a Camera.* (1951) Based on *The Berlin Stories,* by Christopher Isherwood. Drama. Interior. 1930s costumes. 3m. 4w. Dramatists Play Service $1.75. Royalty $50—$25.
A look at life in a tawdry Berlin roominghouse of 1930 concerned for the most part with the mercurial and irresponsible moods of a girl named Sally Bowles. For mature groups only.

————. *I Remember Mama.* (1944) Based on the novel *Mama's Bank Account,* by Kathryn Forbes. Comedy-drama in 2 acts. Unit set. Early 20th century costumes. 9m. 13w. Dramatists Play Service $1.75. Royalty $50—$25; high school version $35—$25.
The story of a Norwegian-American immigrant family in San Francisco guided by a loving, understanding mother. With the help of her husband and Uncle Chris, Mama protects her family from harm, even from the reality that there exists no bank account at all. Excellent for high school. Ethnic interest: Norwegian-American.

————. *The Voice of the Turtle.* (1943) Comedy. Interior. Modern costumes. 1m. 2w. Dramatists Play Service $1.75. Royalty $50—$25.
It is wartime and a charming young man and an equally attractive young woman gradually fall in love. For advanced groups.

van Druten, John, and Morris, Lloyd. *The Damask Cheek.* (1942)

Comedy in 3 acts. Interior. Costumes of 1909. 3m. 6w. French $1.75. Royalty $35—$25.

A literate and charming comedy of manners concerning a middle-aged and repressed English spinster who is sent to America to live with her aunt in the hope of finding a husband. For advanced groups.

Vane, Sutton. *Outward Bound.* (1923) Comedy-drama in 3 acts. Interior. Modern costumes. 6m. 3w. Baker $1.75. French $1.75. Royalty $25—$20.

A group of oddly assorted characters are passengers on an ocean liner whose destination is unknown. Suddenly the bewildered and puzzled passengers realize that they are all dead and headed for Judgment Day. Suitable for all groups.

Vidal, Gore. *The Best Man.* (1960) Drama. Interiors. Modern costumes. 14m. 6w. Dramatists Play Service $1.75. Royalty $50—$25.

The politics involved at the presidential nominating convention, as the ex-president and the party choose between the ex-secretary of state, a scholar beloved by the liberal intellectuals, and a ruthless and hard-driving young man. For advanced groups.

Vonnegut, Kurt Jr. *Happy Birthday, Wanda June.* (1970) Based on the author's novel. Comedy. Interior with scrim. Modern costumes. 5m. 2w. 2 children. Baker $1.75. French $1.95. Restricted. Royalty $50—$35.

A famous big game hunter who has been missing for years returns just as his wife is to be declared a widow. There are two men waiting to ask her hand in marriage. The exchange between the suitors and the hunter, who is not as heroic and noble as believed, makes for a delightful evening. For advanced groups only.

Wallach, Ira. *The Absence of a Cello.* (1965) Comedy. Interior. Modern costumes. 3m. 4w. Dramatists Play Service $1.75. Royalty $50—$25.

A brilliant but indigent scientist tries to land a much-needed job with a large corporation. The family and friends "play the game" as the personnel man comes to interview him. A bit of fluff suitable for all groups.

Weiss, Peter. *The Persecution and Assassination of Jean-Paul Marat as Performed by the Inmates of the Asylum of Charenton under the Direction of the Marquis de Sade (Marat/Sade).* (1965) English version by Geoffrey Skelton. Verse adaptation by Adrian Mitchell. Drama. Bare stage. 9m. 3w. many extras. Dramatic Publishing Co. $1.75. Special license required. Royalty $75—$50.

As an inmate of the Asylum of Charenton, the Marquis de Sade wrote and staged plays that were performed by fellow inmates. Here is a suggestion of what might have been presented. Requires advanced actors; has been done at the high school level.

Wesker, Arnold. *Chips with Everything*. (1962) Drama. Various settings. Military uniforms. 23m. French $4.50. Royalty $50—$25.

The central character in an Air Force training camp is a patrician youth who has all the qualifications for Officers Candidate School. The circumstances leading to the graduation of the recruits comment on contemporary society. Advanced groups only.

Wheeler, Hugh. *Big Fish, Little Fish*. (1961) Comedy. Interior. Modern costumes. 5m. 2w. Dramatists Play Service $3.95. Royalty $50—$25.

The big fish is a former professor whose career ended when a trustee's daughter committed suicide, leaving a note that compromised him. Since then he has lived in oblivion, maintaining an apartment which has become the nesting place of an incredible assortment of friends. For advanced groups only.

Wibberley, Leonard. *The Mouse That Roared*. (1963) Comedy. Simple set. Modern costumes. 13m. 16w. extras if desired. Dramatic Publishing Co. $1.75. Eldridge $1.75. Royalty $50.

To solve the near bankruptcy of her microscopic country, the Duchess Gloriana decides to declare war on the United States, knowing from history that aid, relief, and rehabilitation will follow her defeat. When the war is carried through, the impossible occurs—she wins. Suitable for all groups.

Wilde, Oscar. *The Importance of Being Earnest*. (1895) Farcical English social comedy in 3 acts. 1 exterior, 2 interiors. Late 19th century costumes. 5m. 4w. Baker $1.50. French $1.75. No royalty.

Jack, in order to escape from his usual surroundings, has invented a wild younger brother, Earnest, who takes the fancy of Cecily Cardew, his ward. Complications ensue when Jack's friend Algernon introduces himself to Cecily as Earnest. Witty; very popular with all groups.

———. *Lady Windermere's Fan*. (1892) Comedy in 4 acts. 3 interiors. 19th century English costumes. 7m. 6w. Baker $1.50. French $1.50. No royalty.

Lady Windermere is about to leave her husband, but is saved from this and other fatal steps by Mrs. Erlynne, a notorious lady to whom she objects, but who is really her own mother. Mrs. Erlynne has made the mistakes in the past from which she saves her daughter. Brilliant, but difficult and sophisticated. Considered Wilde's best play.

Wilder, Thornton. *The Matchmaker.* (1955) A revision of Wilder's *The Merchant of Yonkers* (1938). Based on Johann Nestroy's play *Life Is a Joke to Him,* based on John Oxenford's *A Well Spent Day.* Farce in 4 acts. 4 interiors. 9m. 7w. Costumes of the 1880s. Baker $1.75. French $1.75. Royalty $50—$25.

Horace Vandergelder, a 60-year-old, successful and miserly merchant, decides to marry and enlists the help of a matchmaker, a volatile lady of uncertain means. Subsequently they become involved with two of his clerks, assorted young ladies, and the headwaiter at an expensive restaurant. When matters are straightened out and all have their heart's desire, Vandergelder finds himself affianced to the astute matchmaker herself. Hilarious show, suitable for all groups.

————. *Our Town.* (1938) Drama in 3 acts. Bare stage. Costumes of 1901. 17m. 7w. extras. Baker $1.75. Eldridge $1.75. French $1.75. Royalty $25—$20.

This is a tender and romantic recollection of the life of a New Hampshire village, with its humor, picturesqueness, and pathos. Deeply moving. Suitable for all groups.

————. *The Skin of Our Teeth.* (1942) Fantasy in 3 acts. 1 exterior, 1 interior. Various costumes. 4–5m. 4–5w. many bit parts, extras; doubling possible. Baker $2.00. French $2.00. Royalty $50—$25.

The extraordinary adventures of the Antrobus family down through the ages. They have survived flood, fire, pestilence, locusts, the ice age, the black plague, a dozen wars and as many depressions. They are the stuff of which heroes and buffoons are made. A testament of faith in humanity. All groups.

Williams, Emlyn. *The Corn Is Green.* (1938) Comedy. Interior. Modern costumes. 10m. 5w. extras. Dramatists Play Service $1.75. Royalty $50—$25.

Miss Moffat, an English spinster, settles in a Welsh mining village. There, against the prejudices of local folk and the wealthy squire, she starts a school for the boys of the neighborhood. Her star pupil wins a university scholarship. Suitable for all groups.

————. *Night Must Fall.* (1935) Melodrama in 3 acts. Interior. Modern costumes. 4m. 5w. Baker $1.75. French $1.75. Royalty $25—$20.

Dan, a completely selfish, self-centered psychopath with no feelings and a vast imagination, is a bellhop who has already murdered one woman and will soon murder another. This dashing young assassin is only unhappy because he cannot share his secret with the world. Requires skillful acting, but well within the range of high school.

Williams, Tennessee. *Cat on a Hot Tin Roof.* (1955) Drama. Interior.

Modern costumes. 8m. 5w. 4 children. Dramatists Play Service $1.75.
Royalty $50—$25.

A family has gathered at the huge plantation of the patriarch, Big
Daddy, to celebrate his birthday. The mood is one of tension, as the
insecurity of the lives of the family prevents trust and love. For very
advanced and mature groups only.

————. *The Glass Menagerie.* (1945) Drama. Interior. Modern costumes. 2m. 2w. Dramatists Play Service $1.75. Royalty $50—$25.

Amanda Wingfield, a faded, tragic remnant of Southern gentility, lives
in poverty in a dingy St. Louis apartment with her son Tom and
daughter Laura. Tom is a dreamer and poet, and Laura lives in a world
of illusions bordered by a zoo of delicate glass animals. Suitable for all
groups.

————. *The Night of the Iguana.* (1959) Adapted from a story by
the author. Drama. Exterior. Modern costumes. 8m. 6w. Dramatists
Play Service $1.75. Royalty $50—$25.

The pervading mood at this cheap Mexican resort hotel is one of loneliness and despair. The desolation, the emptiness, are in the people:
the tough, sex-starved widow who runs the hotel, the neurotic, defrocked
minister, and the gentle maiden lady from New England. For advanced
groups only.

————. *Period of Adjustment.* (1960) Serious comedy. Interior. Modern costumes. 4m. 5w. Dramatists Play Service $1.75. Royalty $50—$25.

The play presents the stories of two marriages at points of acute crisis.
One couple has broken up after five years together, the other couple
after one day of wedlock. The play explores the sources of the crises.
Difficult to do; for advanced groups.

————. *The Rose Tattoo.* (1951) Drama. Unit set showing interior
and exterior. 9m. 14w. Dramatists Play Service $1.75. Royalty $50—$25.

Set in a village of Sicilian-American fishermen somewhere between New
Orleans and Mobile. The account of Seraphina, a restless widow, and
her glorified dream of "lost love," symbolized by her departed husband's
rose tattoo, which remains fixed in her memory. She is able to love another only after admitting her husband's infidelity to her during his
lifetime. For advanced groups. Ethnic interest: Italian-American.

————. *A Streetcar Named Desire.* (1947) Drama. Interior. Modern
costumes. 6m. 6w. Dramatists Play Service $1.75. Royalty $50—$25.

The life of Blanche du Bois, undermined by romantic frustrations, has
led her to reject reality. The pressures brought to bear upon her by
her sister, intensified by her sister's earthy husband, lead to a revelation
of her self-delusion and eventually to madness. For advanced groups.

————. *Summer and Smoke.* (1948) Drama. Simple unit set. Modern costumes. 8m. 6w. Dramatists Play Service $1.75. Royalty $50—$25.

The love story of a somewhat puritanical young Southern girl and a free-and-easy young doctor. The latter realizes, years later, that the girl had been right, but time and circumstances won't let the two come together. For advanced groups; within the range of mature high school groups.

————. *Sweet Bird of Youth.* (1958) Drama. Interiors. Modern costumes. 15m. 7w. Dramatists Play Service $1.75. Royalty $50—$25.

Chance Wayne, a young hustler, and the Princess, an aging motion-picture actress, return to his hometown so that he can see the young woman with whom he had had an affair and whom he still loves. The girl's father is waiting to avenge the wrong that Chance caused before he left. For mature groups only.

Willingham, Calder. *End as a Man.* (1953) Melodrama in 3 acts. 2 interiors. Military uniforms. 14m. French, manuscript. Royalty $35—$25.

Life in a military academy is the process by which boys are turned into men. Jocko, a rich, spoiled, brutal and vicious upperclassman, abuses the lowerclassmen until he is finally court-martialed and expelled. Excess of violence; for advanced groups only.

Wishengrad, Morton. *The Rope Dancers.* (1957) Drama. Interior. Early 20th century costumes. 5m. 4w. French $1.75. Royalty $50—$25.

The story of an Irish-American couple whose daughter was born with six fingers on her left hand. Later she becomes the victim of an ailment that appears to be St. Vitus's dance. Who is to blame for these circumstances? The mother believes it to be God's punishment and has become bitter, resentful, and ingrown. Difficult; for advanced groups only.

Wouk, Herman. *The Caine Mutiny Court-Martial.* (1954) . Based on the author's novel. Tragedy in 2 acts. Interior. World War II U.S. Navy uniforms. 19m. (6 nonspeaking) . Baker $1.75. French $1.75. Royalty $50—$25.

The court-martial proceedings against a young lieutenant who relieved his captain of command in the midst of a harrowing typhoon on the grounds that the captain was psychopathic and was directing the ship and its crew to destruction. Powerful psychological drama requiring skilled acting.

Yaffe, James. *The Deadly Game.* (1960) Adapted from the novel *Trapps,* by Friedrich Dürrenmatt. Melodrama. Interior. Modern costumes. 6m. 2w. Dramatists Play Service $1.75. Royalty $50—$25.

Three retired men of law on a remote mountain in Switzerland amuse themselves by going through the legal action of prosecuting anyone who drops in. When they have an American salesman as their guest, they make his case real out of phantoms. Complicated; for advanced groups and special audiences only.

Musical Plays

Musical plays stand as the principal contribution of the United States to world theater, having their roots in popular entertainment forms—the minstrel show, vaudeville, light operetta, and revue. In 1929 Jerome Kern and Oscar Hammerstein created *Show Boat,* a musical play based on Edna Ferber's novel, that was an artistic entity, having a logical story line and incorporating music, dance, and comedy as integral parts of the stage action. This approach or form offered great creative possibilities. In 1943 Richard Rodgers and Oscar Hammerstein collaborated on *Oklahoma,* based on Lynn Riggs' play *Green Grow the Lilacs,* which was a landmark development of a distinctly American art form. The popularity of the musical has grown and the form gained world-wide acceptance. The success of the musical play has resulted in a broadening of its subject matter beyond an emphasis solely on comedy. Today many musicals treat the most serious and significant of social subjects, and in the United States they represent the most popular and financially successful of all theater forms.

The producer of the musical play may choose from a wide variety of musical plays. Each play is unique, not only in its subject matter, but also in the way it emphasizes and blends the various elements. One play will require certain vocal qualities, another will emphasize dance, while a third will depend on specific scenic devices. One musical play will require but a minimum number of people—perhaps only six or seven—while another would be meaningless without a cast of ten and a chorus of thirty to fifty. Depending on the play, the producer may have the opportunity to utilize any of a variety of musical arrangements—from piano and percussion, rock group, or small pit orchestra, to an orchestra of symphony size. Because of the variety of production possibilities, the producer must contact the agency or firm in control of performance rights and determine the limitations of the production before royalty and rental fees can be established.

Bibliography

Engel, Lehman. *The American Musical Theatre: A Consideration.* New York: Macmillan Co., 1967.

Ewen, David. *New Complete Book of the American Theater.* Illustrated. New York: Holt, Rinehart and Winston, 1970.

————. *The Story of America's Musical Theatre.* Rev. ed. Philadelphia: Chilton Book Co., 1968.

Green, Stanley. *The World of Musical Comedy.* Rev. 2nd ed. New York: A. S. Barnes and Co., 1973.

Laufe, Abe. *Broadway's Greatest Musical Hits.* 3rd ed. New York: Funk and Wagnalls, 1973.

————. *Broadway's Greatest Musicals: The New Illustrated Edition.* New York: Funk and Wagnalls, 1970.

Smith, Cecil. *Musical Comedy in America.* New York: Theatre Art Books, 1950.

Summaries of Plays

Abbott, George. *The Boys from Syracuse.* (1938) Based on Shakespeare's *The Comedy of Errors.* Lyrics by Lorenz Hart. Music by Richard Rodgers. 1 basic set. Mixed cast. Rodgers and Hammerstein $2.00. Terms quoted on application.

Antipholus of Syracuse and his servant Dromio come to Ephesus, where they are confused with the local Antipholus and Dromio. The mistaken identity involves both Antipholuses in a series of amusing romantic mishaps, reaching a hilarious climax of complications. Within the range of all groups.

————. *Where's Charley?* (1948) Based on Brandon Thomas's play *Charley's Aunt.* Lyrics and music by Frank Loesser. 3 exteriors, 6 interiors. Late 19th century costumes. 8m. 5w. Music Theatre International. Terms quoted on application.

Charley and his roommate Jack invite their sweethearts to their room for lunch, and since Charley's rich aunt from Brazil will be there to chaperone, the girls agree. But the aunt fails to arrive on schedule, and Charley, dressed as an elderly woman for the school play, must play her part. When the real aunt turns up under an assumed name, the tangle becomes even more complicated. An excellent vehicle for a strong male dancer.

Abbott, George, and Bissell, Richard. *The Pajama Game.* (1954) Based on Bissell's novel *7½ Cents.* Lyrics and music by Richard Adler and Jerry Ross. 3 exteriors, 7 interiors. 12m. 6w. extras. Music Theatre International. Terms quoted on application.

A fast-moving story of attempts to unionize a pajama factory. Sid, just hired as foreman, falls for redhead Babe, head of the workers' grievance committee. The inevitable conflicts between them are not helped by Hines, the efficiency expert, and Gladys, the boss's secretary, for in order to resolve the dispute, Hines must make a play for her in order to get the key to the company books. Excellent character roles; needs mature performers and audience.

Abbott, George, and Wallop, Douglass. *Damn Yankees.* (1955) Based on Wallop's novel *The Year the Yankees Lost the Pennant.* Lyrics and music by Richard Adler and Jerry Ross. 1 exterior, 8 interiors. 14m. 6w. extras. Music Theatre International. Terms quoted on application.

A fast-moving fantasy in which Joe, a fanatic, middle-aged baseball fan, sells his soul to the Devil and becomes an outstanding ball player so that the Washington Senators, his favorite team, can beat the New York Yankees. Despite the fact that the Devil introduces Joe to Lola, his prize worker, Joe outwits him when it comes time to live up to his part of the bargain. An excellent vehicle for a strong female dancer.

Barrie, James M. *Peter Pan.* (1954) Lyrics by Carolyn Leigh, Betty Comden, and Adolph Green. Music by Mark Charlap and Jule Styne. 4 exteriors, 2 interiors. 28 characters, extras. French, manuscript. Restricted. Terms quoted on application.
Musical version of Barrie's popular play for children; appeals to adults as well. The classic story of a boy and a girl who follow Peter Pan and Tinker Bell, the invisible fairy, into Never Land, where they outwit Captain Hook and his pirates. Requires technical skill to fly Peter Pan and the children, but can be done without flying.

Bart, Lionel. *Oliver!* Based on the works of Charles Dickens. Lyrics and music by Lionel Bart. 6 interiors, 2 exteriors. Mid-19th century costumes. 10m. 7w. extras. Tams-Witmark. Terms quoted on application.
Oliver is sold by the owners of the workhouse to an undertaker, but he escapes and falls in with Fagin and Sikes, two thieves. They welcome him to their group of boys and send him out with the others to pick pockets. When Oliver comes under the protection of a rich benefactor, Fagin and Sikes dispatch Nancy to abduct him, fearful that he will give away their set-up. Her efforts to return him result in tragedy. Suitable for all groups. Provides many roles for adolescents and children.

Behrman, S. N., and Logan, Joshua. *Fanny.* (1954) Based on a trilogy of plays by Marcel Pagnol. Lyrics and music by Harold Rome. 9 interiors, 6 exteriors. 23m. 6w. few extras. Tams-Witmark. Terms quoted on application.
Marius, victim of his love for the sea, sails away despite his love for Fanny. Without his knowledge, she is pregnant by him, and when he is gone she marries an older man who accepts the child. When Marius returns, he and Fanny discover that their love for one another is not dead. More serious than most musicals; tender, heartwarming, and full of compassion. Requires delicate performances and directing.

Besoyan, Rick. *Little Mary Sunshine.* (1959) Lyrics and music by Rick Besoyan. 4 exteriors, 2 interiors. 6m. 3w. French, manuscript. Score $12.50. Terms quoted on application.
A lampoon of old-time American melodramas and operettas, with deliberately corny songs and naive situations. Includes government rangers, a stalwart captain, good and bad Indians, a lovely maiden, a chorus of schoolgirls, and dastardly villains. For all groups.

Brecht, Bertolt. *The Threepenny Opera.* (1928) Based on John Gay's *The Beggar's Opera.* Music by Kurt Weill. English adaptation by

Marc Blitzstein. 6 interiors. 15m. 10w. extras. Tams-Witmark. Terms quoted on application.

When the Peachums' beautiful daughter Polly marries the master criminal Macheath (Mack the Knife), Peachum arranges with the police commissioner to have him put out of the way. Jenny, one of Mack's old girls, reports him to the police, but he soft-talks Lucy Brown, the commissioner's daughter, into freeing him from jail. Betrayed again by the girls, he is freed at the last minute by the newly crowned Queen Victoria. A bitter indictment of life and manners in the twentieth century. Requires sophisticated performers and mature audience.

Bricusse, Leslie, and Newley, Anthony. *The Roar of the Greasepaint— The Smell of the Crowd.* Lyrics and music by Leslie Bricusse and Anthony Newley. 1 basic set. 4m. 2w. extras. Tams-Witmark. Terms quoted on application.

Sir, one of the "haves," and Cocky, one of the "have nots," meet to play the game. Sir insists that the haves must retain their position even if the rules of the game must be constantly changed. Cocky tries again and again to play, but with each defeat the rules become more restrictive. Cocky revolts and is crowned "king." When someone even more downtrodden than Cocky enters the game, Cocky becomes as overbearing as Sir. Relies heavily on pantomime and commedia dell'arte training.

————. *Stop the World—I Want to Get Off.* (1963) Lyrics and music by Leslie Bricusse and Anthony Newley. 1 basic set. 1m. 3w. extras. Tams-Witmark. Terms quoted on application.

The life of Littlechap, from childhood to senility. Remarkably, Littlechap manages to achieve all that he had dreamed of—wealth, power, travel, romance, political acclaim—but he never finds the power and strength to make himself, his wife and daughters, or anyone else truly happy. Only when senility crowds out the mental calculations necessary to life in the scuffling business world does he see the ultimate failure of his glorious, but so superficial, successes. Needs performers capable of pantomime and commedia dell'arte technique.

Burrows, Abe, Weinstock, Jack, and Gilbert, Willie. *How to Succeed in Business without Really Trying.* (1961) Based on the novel by Shepherd Mead. Lyrics and music by Frank Loesser. 2 exteriors, 8 interiors. 5m. 2w. extras. Music Theatre International. Terms quoted on application.

The fast-moving story of a "promoter" who starts as a window washer and ends up as the chairman of the board of a great corporation through his clever manipulation. Office life is turned inside out as he makes his climb. An excellent satire, complete with office party, board meeting, office wolf, dangerous secretary, and boss's nephew. All groups.

Comden, Betty, and Green, Adolph. *Applause.* (1970) Based on the screenplay *All about Eve,* and the story by Mary Orr. Lyrics by Lee Adams. Music by Charles Strouse. 16m. 5w. Tams-Witmark. Terms quoted on application.

"What is it that we're living for?" "Applause, Applause!" These lyrics epitomize the motives of all the characters in this story about the plots and intrigues of life backstage. An aspiring young actress successfully dethrones the established star, but in the process relinquishes any redeeming qualities and becomes the producer's plaything. The star, in turn, realizes that there is another life besides the one on stage and that the applause is, after all, hollow. Provides two strong character parts for women.

————. *Bells Are Ringing.* (1956) Lyrics by Betty Comden and Adolph Green. Music by Jule Styne. 10 interiors, 8 exteriors. 14m. 9w. extras. Tams-Witmark. Terms quoted on application.

Sue and her cousin Ella, who run a telephone answering service, get involved in the lives of two of their accounts. Sue falls in love with Sandor, head of Titanic Records—a front for a book-making concern— and Ella falls for Jeff Moss, a writer in need of inspiration. After a series of hilarious complications, Ella gets her man. Relatively simple sets; within the range of all groups.

Coopersmith, Jerome. *The Apple Tree.* (1966) Based on stories by Mark Twain, Frank R. Stockton, and Jules Feiffer. Lyrics by Sheldon Harnick. Music by Jerry Bock. Three 1-act musicals. 3 sets. 2m. 1w. extras. Individual acts available separately. Music Theatre International. Terms quoted on application.

Act one, "The Diary of Adam and Eve," recreates Twain's witty account of the first two people. Act two, "The Lady or the Tiger," is the classic story of the dilemma of choice, set in a mythical rock 'n' roll barbarian kingdom. The last act, "Passionella," tells the story of a chimney sweep who becomes a movie star. A light evening with some fine satirical touches. Good vehicle for three outstanding performers; can also feature nine people in strong roles. Within reach of all.

Driver, Donald. *Your Own Thing.* (1968) Based on Shakespeare's *Twelfth Night.* Lyrics and music by Hal Hester and Danny Apolinar. 1 basic set. 6m. 3w. Tams-Witmark. Terms quoted on application.

When a member of the rock group Apocalypse is drafted into the Army, Viola assumes a disguise to be his replacement. Viola's brother, believed dead, arrives and the resulting mistaken identity is compounded romantically. Set in the 1960s; slightly dated. Can be costumed in fashions of the 70s or of the future. Very gay, light evening.

Fields, Herbert, and Fields, Dorothy. *Annie Get Your Gun.* (1946)
Lyrics and music by Irving Berlin. 1 basic exterior set. 10m. 9w. extras.
Rodgers and Hammerstein $2.00. Terms quoted on application.

The story of the female sharpshooter Annie Oakley as she gains recognition and love in the Wild West Shows of the late nineteenth century.
Includes famous Western characters, such as Buffalo Bill, Sitting Bull,
and others. Popular with all groups.

Fields, Joseph, and Chodorov, Jerome. *Wonderful Town.* (1953)
Fields and Chodorov's play *My Sister Eileen,* based on stories by Ruth
McKenney. Lyrics by Betty Comden and Adolph Green. Music by
Leonard Bernstein. 2 exteriors, 6 interiors. 16m. 15w. extras. Tams-
Witmark. Terms quoted on application.

The saga of two sisters from Ohio trying to make their way in New
York. Ruth, the elder, has motherly instincts and wants to become a
writer. Eileen is a coquette who can't help making men her slaves.
Beginning in their Greenwich Village apartment, the narrative shifts
to the subway, the editorial offices of a magazine, the Brooklyn Navy
Yard, ending with great enthusiasm in one of the Village's torrid night
spots. Provides numerous opportunities for character roles.

Furth, George. *Company.* (1970) Lyrics and music by Stephen Sondheim. 1 basic set. 6m. 12w. Music Theatre International. Terms
quoted on application.

Bobby, a bachelor afraid of not being married, is nevertheless dis-
trustful after sizing up the imperfections in the marriages of his friends.
This provocative picture of the manners and morals of New York City
in the 60s and 70s takes our antihero through a series of encounters with
April, the stewardess, Kathy, who's going to marry someone else, Marta,
the "peculiar" one, and his good but somewhat crazy married friends.
For sophisticated performers and audience.

Gesner, Clark. *You're a Good Man Charlie Brown.* (1967) Based on
the comic strip *Peanuts,* by Charles M. Schulz. Lyrics and music by
Clark Gesner. 1 set. 3m. 3w. 1 dog. Tams-Witmark. Terms quoted
on application.

Incidents in a day in the life of Charlie Brown, hero or antihero of the
popular comic strip, including lunch on the school playground, Lucy's
true love for Schroeder, Linus and his blanket, Lucy's five-cent psy-
chiatry booth, Snoopy and the Red Baron, a baseball game, homework
assignments. Easily staged, this is a warm, funny evening of theater.
Well within the range of all groups.

Goldman, James. *Follies.* Lyrics and music by Stephen Sondheim. One
set. Elaborate costumes for showgirls. Large cast. Music Theatre International. Terms quoted on application.

A group of former showgirls return to the theater in which they once starred, and which will soon be torn down, for a farewell party. As the aging performers mingle with the ghosts of their former selves, two unhappily married couples make a last frantic attempt to relive their pasts. The empty stage bursts into a true *Follies* production, exposing the follies of youth and love, and the couples realize they must leave the ghosts of their youth behind at the doomed theater. For mature groups. Heavy on nostalgia.

Green, Paul. *Johnny Johnson.* (1936) Revised by the author. Lyrics by Paul Green. Music by Kurt Weill. Legend in 3 acts. 13 simple sets. Modern costumes. 49m. 6w. French $2.00. Terms quoted on application.

Assured by President Wilson that World War I will end all wars, pacifist Johnny enlists. He becomes disillusioned and ends up selling toys on the street. Strong antiwar statement; needs mature actors. Good opportunity for experimental interpretation and creative choreography.

Haimsohn, George, and Miller, Robin. *Dames at Sea.* (1968) Music by Jim Wise. 2 sets. 4m. 3w. 2 extras, chorus. French $2.00. Terms quoted on application.

A sweet little girl from faraway hometown arrives in New York, planning to make it big. But who should she meet but the hometown boy, now a sailor, who has ambitions to become a songwriter. A triangle develops, but the songwriter saves the show with a smash tune, and the hometown girl achieves stardom. A spoof on all the Busby Berkeley movie musicals of the 1930s.

Hammerstein, Oscar II. *Carousel.* (1945) Based on Ferenc Molnár's *Liliom.* Lyrics by Oscar Hammerstein II. Music by Richard Rodgers. 8 exteriors. Large cast. Rodgers and Hammerstein $2.00. Terms quoted on application.

The romance and marriage of Billy, a handsome, tough, irresponsible young man, and Julie, the girl he meets at the amusement park. Though she worries whether he can be dependable enough to be a good father, she knows that she loves him, and this is all that counts. Knowing that they will need money to support their child, Billy gets involved in a holdup, but kills himself to avoid capture. The tragedy is dispelled by love and forgiveness. Popular with all groups.

————. *The King and I.* (1951) Based on Margaret Landon's novel *Anna and the King of Siam.* Lyrics by Oscar Hammerstein II. Music by Richard Rodgers. 6 interiors, 3 exteriors. Elaborate Oriental costumes. 9m. 4w. extras. Rodgers and Hammerstein $2.00. Terms quoted on application.

Anna comes to Siam from England to teach the royal princes and princesses. The King is bewildered by Western ways, and Anna is equally dogmatic, finding him unreasonable and overbearing. Gradually they learn to understand and admire one another. An innovative musical providing opportunities for young children in a colorful ballet. Within range of all groups.

————. *Oklahoma!* (1943) Based on Lynn Riggs' play *Green Grow the Lilacs*. Lyrics by Oscar Hammerstein II. Music by Richard Rodgers. 5 exteriors, 1 interior. 14m. 9w. extras. Rodgers and Hammerstein $2.00. Terms quoted on application.
The love triangle between Curly, Laurey, and Jud Fry, and a story of the struggles between farmers and ranchers in early Oklahoma. This authentic American folk play was the first musical to combine music, dialogue, and the ballet in an indivisible entity. Still a popular production.

————. *Show Boat*. (1927) Based on the novel by Edna Ferber. Lyrics by Oscar Hammerstein II. Music by Jerome Kern. 4 exteriors, 6 interiors. 3m. 3w. extras. Rodgers and Hammerstein $2.00. Terms quoted on application.
Life aboard a Mississippi riverboat in the 1880s. Magnolia, the captain's daughter, falls in love with a riverboat gambler and runs off with him to Chicago. His gambling life poisons their marriage, however, and they part. After the birth of their daughter, Magnolia earns her living as a performer. Her father takes her back to the riverboat, where she and her husband are reconciled. Considered the first modern musical play. Requires skilled design and technical support.

Hammerstein, Oscar II, and Fields, Joseph. *Flower Drum Song*. (1958) Based on a novel by C. Y. Lee. Lyrics by Oscar Hammerstein II. Music by Richard Rodgers. 10 interiors, 3 exteriors. 11m. 7w. Rodgers and Hammerstein $2.00. Terms quoted on application.
A story of conflict between the older generation of San Francisco's Chinatown, who wish to preserve traditions, and the younger generation, who wish to become Americanized. Presents ethnic stereotypes; appropriate only if handled sensitively by the director. Provides a variety of roles for adolescents and children. A colorful play for all groups. Ethnic interest: Chinese-American.

Hammerstein, Oscar II, and Logan, Joshua. *South Pacific*. (1949) Based on stories from James Michener's *Tales of the South Pacific*. Lyrics by Oscar Hammerstein II. Music by Richard Rodgers. 6 exteriors, 5 interiors. 20m. 5w. extras. Rodgers and Hammerstein $2.00. Terms quoted on application.
A story of love and Navy life in the South Pacific during World War II. In the love of Emile de Becque, a wealthy middle-aged French planter with two Eurasian children, and Nellie Forbush, a Navy ensign,

and in the romance of Lieutenant Cable and the Tonkinese girl Liat, the play makes a strong plea for racial tolerance. Popular with all groups.

Harbach, Otto, and Mandel, Frank. *No, No, Nanette.* (1925) Lyrics by Irving Caesar and Otto Harbach. Music by Vincent Youmans. 2 interiors, 1 exterior. 3m. 7w. extras and chorus. Tams-Witmark. Terms quoted on application.

The recent revamped production of this 1925 musical has been credited with starting the nostalgia craze on Broadway. A melange of innocent affairs, marriages on the brink, love affairs ended, threats of scandal and blackmail, all deriving from the fact that everyone has decided to go to Atlantic City for the weekend, and end up at the same cottage. Set to a lighthearted score; a pleasant evening.

Harburg, E. Y., and Saidy, Fred. *Finian's Rainbow.* (1947) Lyrics by E. Y. Harburg. Music by Burton Lane. 6 exteriors. 11m. 2w. extras. Tams-Witmark. Terms quoted on application.

Believing that he has discovered the secret of wealth, Finian, an Irishman, steals a leprechaun's pot of gold and brings it to America to bury in the ground near Fort Knox. The leprechaun pursues, uttering dire warnings of misery as he attempts to retrieve his gold. Both Finian's theories of wealth and the leprechaun's predictions prove true, but in the process, the Southern community is rid of its racial intolerance. A serious statement in a fast-moving, fun-filled show.

Hart, Moss. *Lady in the Dark.* (1941) Lyrics by Ira Gershwin. Music by Kurt Weill. 5 interiors, 2 exteriors. 9m. 11w. Dramatists Play Service, book $1.75, score $12.50. Royalty $50—$25.

Liza, successful editor of a magazine, is lost in the maze of her own unhappiness and seeks help in psychoanalysis. Through the analysis of a series of dreams—in which she is surrounded by men who admire her, or is a circus queen, or is a young girl in school rejected by a callow youth—the doctor gives her back her belief in herself, and she finds her true love. Requires complicated technical effects.

Hirson, Roger O., and Frings, Ketti. *Walking Happy.* Based on Harold Brighouse's play *Hobson's Choice.* Lyrics by Sammy Cahn. Music by James Van Heusen. 3 exteriors, 4 interiors. 14m. 7w. French $2.00. Terms quoted on application.

A miserly bootmaker has three eligible daughters and thinks he runs a shop of giddy girls. In reality, the eldest daughter is the only level-headed person in the establishment, and she rebels, setting up her own shop and marrying her father's best bootmaker. For all groups.

Jacobs, Jim, and Casey, Warren. *Grease.* Lyrics and music by Jim

Jacobs and Warren Casey. Multi set. Late 1950s costumes. 9m. 8w. French $2.00. Restricted. Terms quoted on application.
A salute to the rock 'n' roll era of the 1950s. While hip Danny and wholesome Sandy—members of the class of '59 at Rydell High—resolve the problems of their mutual attraction, the gang sings and dances its way through such fifties institutions as the pajama party, the prom, the burger hangout, and the drive-in. Simple, fast moving story with opportunity for dancing. Best suited for young casts.

Jones, Tom. *Celebration.* (1969) Music by Harvey Schmidt. 1 basic set. Fantastic costumes, masks, torches. 9m. 7w. Music Theatre International. Terms quoted on application.
The ritual conflict between an old man and a young man, set on New Year's Eve. Looking for his lost garden of beautiful peace, a young man becomes entangled with a host of bizarre characters, including the richest man in the Western world, who becomes his rival in love. Described as a fable "about the time and life cycle passing through the cold winter season to the inevitable spring of rebirth, renewal, and love." Considered one of the most artistic works of the musical theater. For advanced groups and sophisticated audiences.

————. *The Fantasticks.* (1960) Based on Edmond Rostand's play *The Romancers.* Music by Harvey Schmidt. 1 basic set, minimum of props. 8 characters. Music Theatre International. Terms quoted on application.
The story of two sentimental youngsters who refuse to cooperate with their parents' wishes that they marry. After their fathers pretend a mortal enmity, building a huge wall between their homes, the young people are brought together, but only after they have left home and returned disillusioned. Can be staged very simply. Within the range of all groups.

————. *I Do! I Do!* (1966) Based on Jan de Hartog's play *The Four-poster.* Music by Harvey Schmidt. 1 basic set. 1m. 1w. Music Theatre International. Terms quoted on application.
The moving chronicle of a marriage, from wedding night through old age. The birth of children, quarrels, money problems, love—all are told in a warm and sentimental style. Delightful, intimate production for two strong performers.

Kaufman, George S., and Ryskind, Morrie. *Of Thee I Sing.* (1931) Lyrics by Ira Gershwin. Music by George Gershwin. Various simple interiors and exteriors. 14m. 5w. extras. French, libretto $2.00, vocal score $15.00. Terms quoted on application.
A political satire which follows the presidential campaign and election of John B. Wintergreen, who promises to marry the winner of a beauty

contest after proposing to her in every state. Includes the misadventures of Throttlebottom, the new vice-president, and a supreme court that sings and dances its way through important decisions. A prize-winning play that still retains its topicality. Within the range of all groups.

Laurents, Arthur. *Gypsy*. (1959) Lyrics by Stephen Sondheim. Music by Jule Styne. 13 interiors, 4 exteriors. 15m. 12w. extras. Tams-Witmark. Terms quoted on application.

Suggested by the memoirs of Gypsy Rose Lee, this is the story of a bullying, ruthless stage mother who attempts to drive her two daughters into show business. Together they travel the entire country, playing in seamy small-town theaters. One daughter elopes; the other, realizing that vaudeville is dying except for burlesque, breaks away from her mother and becomes a star. Serious comment, but fun-filled evening. The mother must be a strong performer.

————. *West Side Story*. (1957) Based on Shakespeare's *Romeo and Juliet*. Lyrics by Stephen Sondheim. Music by Leonard Bernstein. 6 interiors, 6 exteriors. 28m. 11w. Music Theatre International. Terms quoted on application.

Tony, member of a street gang called the Jets, falls in love with Maria, sister of the leader of the rival gang, the Sharks. The young lovers are tortured by insurmountable barriers of hate and fear, but manage to find a few tender moments together until the gangs meet for a rumble in which Tony kills Maria's brother. Maria and Tony are reunited for a fleeting moment before they are discovered by the Sharks and Tony is killed. Good opportunity for dancing. For all groups. Ethnic interest: Puerto Rican-American, Italian-American.

Lawrence, Jerome, and Lee, Robert E. *Mame*. (1966) Lawrence and Lee's play *Auntie Mame,* based on the novel by Patrick Dennis. Lyrics and music by Jerry Herman. 4 exteriors, 7 interiors. 18m. 12w. extras. Tams-Witmark. Terms quoted on application.

Auntie Mame raises her orphaned nephew by inviting him to the banquet of life and urging him to help himself. Just as his need for her rescued her from the shallow diversions of the twenties, she helps to save him from the toils of conformity and a life of "Darien drabness and snobbery." Fast moving; popular with all groups.

Lederer, Charles, and Davis, Luther. *Kismet: A Musical Arabian Night*. (1953) Based on the play by Edward Knoblock. Lyrics and music by Robert Wright and George Forrest, from melodies by Aleksandr Borodin. 7 exteriors, 6 interiors. Arabian Nights costumes. Large mixed cast. Music Theatre International. Terms quoted on application.

The adventures of a handsome and poetic beggar in ancient Baghdad, and a tale of the ironic twists of fate. Hajj comes to town with his beautiful daughter Marsineh, for whom he has plans that she marry the caliph. This he accomplishes; he also elopes to an oasis with Lalume, the beautiful widow of the police wazir, and competes successfully with Omar the tentmaker in the writing of verses.

Lennart, Isobel. *Funny Girl.* (1964) Based on a story by Isobel Lennart. Lyrics by Bob Merrill. Music by Jule Styne. 15 interiors, 2 exteriors. Large mixed cast. Tams-Witmark. Terms quoted on application.

Based on the life of Fanny Brice, from her rise to fame in the Ziegfield Follies through her broken marriage with the gambler Nick Arnstein. Conflicts arise when he discovers that Fanny has put up the money for his gambling ventures. Incensed that he is so dependent on his wife, Nick gets involved in a shady bond deal and goes to prison for embezzlement. When he returns, the couple realize they cannot be happy and reluctantly part. Provides a star vehicle for a strong female performer.

Lerner, Alan Jay. *Brigadoon.* (1947) Lyrics by Alan Jay Lerner. Music by Frederick Loewe. 2 interiors, 4 exteriors. 10m. 4w. Tams-Witmark. Terms quoted on application.

Tommy and Jeff, two American travelers in Scotland, come upon a mysterious village that appears and comes to life once every hundred years. Enraptured by the beautiful Fiona, Tommy cannot decide whether to remain with her or to return to his familiar, unsatisfying life, but at the end of the day he leaves with Jeff for America. Restless and unhappy, Tommy finally yields to his memories and finds his way back to Brigadoon. Good opportunity for colorful Scottish dancing.

————. *Camelot.* (1960) Based on T. H. White's *The Once and Future King.* Lyrics by Alan Jay Lerner. Music by Frederick Loewe. 5 interiors, 13 exteriors. Medieval costumes. 23m. 4w. extras. Tams-Witmark. Terms quoted on application.

Hearing word of King Arthur's Round Table, Lancelot journeys to Camelot, where he falls in love with Queen Guenevere. Guenevere is arrested and sentenced to burn at the stake for her love of Lancelot, but she escapes with Lancelot to France. Arthur ultimately forgives them both, but his dreams of love and the new principles of the Round Table have been shattered, and he is left sad and disillusioned. Lends itself to beautiful visual production.

————. *Gigi.* (1958) Based on the novel by Colette. Lyrics by Alan Jay Lerner. Music by Frederick Loewe. Multi set. 4m. 4w. extras and chorus. Tams-Witmark. Terms quoted on application.

Set in Paris around the turn of the century, this is the story of the charming young girl who has been raised by her grandmother and grandaunt to become a mistress, but who maintains her purity and marries the richest, handsomest, most desired bachelor in Paris.

————. *My Fair Lady.* (1956) Based on George Bernard Shaw's *Pygmalion.* Lyrics by Alan Jay Lerner. Music by Frederick Loewe. 7 exteriors, 3 interiors. 18m. 9w. extras. Tams-Witmark. Terms quoted on application.

Professor Henry Higgins, a phonetics expert and confirmed bachelor, wagers that he can transform a common flower girl with a cockney accent into a lady of lovely voice and pass her off in high society. He succeeds but fails to recognize her own personal achievement in the matter. Only when she angrily storms out does he realize that he will have a difficult time living without her. Within range of most groups.

————. *On a Clear Day You Can See Forever.* (1965) Lyrics by Alan Jay Lerner. Music by Burton Lane. 1 exterior, 3 interiors. 14m. 7w. Tams-Witmark. Terms quoted on application.

Under hypnosis to stop smoking, an American college student with extrasensory perception relapses into the life of an eighteenth century Englishwoman. The psychiatrist falls in love with this character, but discovers that it is the student he really wants. Limited appeal.

————. *Paint Your Wagon.* (1951) Lyrics by Alan Jay Lerner. Music by Frederick Loewe. 8 exteriors, 3 interiors. 24m. 11w. Tams-Witmark. Terms quoted on application.

Set in the old West, this is the story of a wandering gold miner, Ben Rumson, who discovers gold and has the town named after him. He soon becomes restless, begins to dream, and prepares to roam once again after his wand'rin star. Music based on folk music of the early West.

Lindsay, Howard, and Crouse, Russel. *The Sound of Music.* (1959) Suggested by Maria Augusta Trapp's *The Trapp Family Singers.* Lyrics by Oscar Hammerstein II. Music by Richard Rodgers. 3 exteriors, 4 interiors. 3m. 3w. children, extras. Rodgers and Hammerstein $2.00. Terms quoted on application.

The story of the escape of the Trapp family from Austria after the Nazi takeover prior to World War II. Maria, hired as governess for the captain's seven children, teaches them to sing, filling the house with warmth, gentleness, and enthusiasm. Very sentimental. Provides good roles for adolescents and children. Within range of all.

Longstreet, Stephen. *High Button Shoes.* (1947) Based on the author's novel. Lyrics by Sammy Cahn. Music by Jule Styne. 11 exteriors, 1 interior. Costumes of 1913. 9m. 3w. extras. Tams-Witmark. Terms quoted on application.

Two swindlers arrive in New Brunswick, New Jersey, where they sell underwater real estate, try to fix the Rutgers-Princeton game, and otherwise attempt to obtain an easy buck. A charming piece of Americana and a blend of burlesque, vaudeville, gags from silent film, and musical comedy. Requires strong character performers.

Loesser, Frank. *The Most Happy Fella.* (1956) Based on Sidney Howard's play *They Knew What They Wanted.* Lyrics and music by Frank Loesser. 2 interiors, 4 exteriors. 21m. 16w. extras. Music Theatre International. Terms quoted on application.

Tony writes to a waitress he had met while traveling. During their courtship by mail, they exchange photographs, but Tony substitutes one of his young, handsome foreman. The young woman, who accepts his offer of marriage, arrives disillusioned, for she has fallen in love with the hired hand. She becomes pregnant by him, but Tony accepts her and the child, and an understanding love develops between them. Requires sensitive handling of ethnic stereotyping. For all groups. Ethnic interest: Italian-American.

Marx, Arthur, and Fisher, Robert. *Minnie's Boys.* (1970) Lyrics by Hal Hackady. Music by Larry Grossman. Multi set. Large cast. French, manuscript. Terms quoted on application.

The story of Minnie Marx and her sons Groucho, Harpo, Chico, Zeppo, and Gummo. The heartwarming story of a tender, gutsy, energetic woman and her outrageous family, and a celebration of show business.

Masteroff, Joe. *Cabaret.* (1966) Based on John van Druten's play *I Am a Camera,* and stories by Christopher Isherwood. Lyrics by Fred Ebb. Music by John Kander. Multi set. 5m. 4w. extras and chorus. Tams-Witmark. Terms quoted on application.

The life of Cliff Bradshaw, a young American writer, and Sally Bowles, an English cabaret performer, in Berlin in 1929. A strong picture of middle-class decadence and the beginnings of the Nazi rise to power. Though Cliff wants to take Sally home to America to raise a family, Sally refuses to leave. Her life is in Berlin, and Cliff sadly leaves her in the doomed city. For mature casts only.

Miles, Bernard. *Lock Up Your Daughters.* Based on Henry Fielding's comedy *Rape upon Rape.* Lyrics by Lionel Bart. Music by Laurie Johnson. Multi set. 18th century English costumes. 15m. 4w. French $2.00. Terms quoted on application.

A delightful romp of confusion as two virtuous lovers, attempting to elope, get embroiled in a street fracas and are brought before a corrupt judge. While the judge makes a play for the heroine, his wife makes one for the dashing new man-about-town. Letters intercepted in the nick of time and an honorable hero save all.

Montgomery, James. *Irene.* (1919) Lyrics by Joseph McCarthy. Music by Harry Tierney. 3 interiors. Large cast. Tams-Witmark. Terms quoted on application.

The cinderella story of a beautiful shopgirl who catches the eye of a rich young man. He gets her a job in a fashionable dress shop and then falls in love with her. Another of the early musicals that has been revived and is popular in the seventies.

Morris, Richard. *The Unsinkable Molly Brown.* (1960) Lyrics by Meredith Willson. 7 exteriors, 6 interiors. 2m. 1w. extras. Music Theatre International. Terms quoted on application.
The story of the trials and tribulations, battles and victories, of Molly Brown, legendary heroine of Denver, gold-mining boom town. A vivid portrayal of frontier society, taking this indomitable Irish lass from the Missouri backwoods to the royal palaces of Europe. Not even the *Titanic* can defeat Molly Brown. Within the range of all groups.

Nash, N. Richard. *The Happy Time.* Based on the play by Samuel Taylor and book by Robert Fontaine. Lyrics by Fred Ebb. Music by John Kander. 2 interiors. 8m. 11w. Dramatic Publishing Co. $1.50. Royalty on application.
The story of Bibi, a French-Canadian boy. When his romantic, adventuresome uncle returns to the village to recover the good times of his childhood, Bibi is fascinated and proposes to drop out of school to become his uncle's assistant. The ensuing conflicts between adventure and life at home reach a climax when Bibi's gay-blade grandfather intervenes.

O'Hara, John. *Pal Joey.* (1940) Based on stories by the author. Lyrics by Lorenz Hart. Music by Richard Rodgers. 2 exteriors, 3 interiors. 1m. 2w. extras. Rodgers and Hammerstein. Terms quoted on application.
Joey Evans is a cheap opportunist who gives up his girl for a wealthy, hard-boiled matron who sets him up in his own swanky night club. Joey soon wearies of her and begins to look elsewhere. Eventually both women decide they've had enough of him, and Joey, a victim of blackmail, is left broke and alone. A bitter story and one of the few serious musicals to command audience support. For mature performers and sophisticated audiences only.

Panama, Norman, and Frank, Melvin. *Li'l Abner.* (1956) Lyrics and music by Johnny Mercer and Gene de Paul. 6 exteriors, 5 interiors. 29m. 2w. extras. Tams-Witmark. Terms quoted on application.
Al Capp's comic strip characters placed in a colorful musical extravaganza, full of hillbilly nonsense and sharp critical humor. Dogpatch is picked as the site for nuclear tests, but the decision is delayed when the miraculous effects of Yokumberry Tonic are discovered. Plotting government agents allow Abner to be caught in the Sadie Hawkins Day race, but in the end Dogpatch is saved by the dead Confederate General Cornpone.

Patrick, John. *Lovely Ladies, Kind Gentlemen.* Patrick's play, *Teahouse of the August Moon,* based on the novel by Vern J. Sneider. Lyrics and music by Stan Freeman and Franklin Underwood. Several sets. U.S. military and Japanese costumes. 17m. 4w. extras and chorus. French $2.00. Terms quoted on application.

The comic confrontation between American occupation forces on Okinawa, determined to Americanize the entire culture, and the local residents, who have no intention of changing their customs. Funds allocated for the construction of a school are diverted and used to build a teahouse, which opens, of course, precisely when the colonel comes to make his inspection. Good opportunity for large chorus.

Ragni, Gerome, and Rado, James. *Hair.* (1968) Lyrics by Gerome Ragni and James Rado. Music by Galt MacDermot. 1 basic set. 10m. 11w. extras, chorus, dancers. Tams-Witmark. Terms quoted on application.

The first and most successful of the rock musicals, epitomizing the utopian philosophy of the flower children of the sixties. Comprised almost entirely of musical numbers and unified by Claude's ambivalent feelings about escaping the draft, the play provides a vehicle for considerations of love, freedom, identity, the dreary existence of the establishment, the spirit of communal living, reality and illusion, politics and war. Advisable for special groups only.

Rice, Elmer. *Street Scene.* (1947) Lyrics by Langston Hughes. Music by Kurt Weill. Exterior. 16m. 11w. Royalty to French.

Anna, hungry for love which her husband denies her, carries on an affair with the milkman. When her husband returns home unexpectedly and finds the two together, he shoots them and is arrested. This tragedy convinces daughter Rosa that she must not ask boyfriend Sam to give up his studies to marry her, and she flees with her younger brother to find a new life. Mature groups only.

Shevelove, Burt, and Gelbart, Larry. *A Funny Thing Happened on the Way to the Forum.* (1962) Based on situations from the comedies of Plautus. Lyrics and music by Stephen Sondheim. One basic set. Roman costumes. Large cast. Music Theatre International. Terms quoted on application.

A mad blend of zany nonsense, confusion, and gags from Roman comedy and burlesque, centering on the connivings of the slave Pseudolus to achieve his freedom. His young master, Hero, promises Pseudolus his freedom if he can obtain for Hero the beautiful girl Philia. A frivolous, fast-moving laugh production. Requires mastery of comic timing.

Simon, Neil. *Little Me.* Based on a novel by Patrick Dennis. Lyrics by Carolyn Leigh. Music by Cy Coleman. 11 exteriors, 13 interiors. 28m. 7w. extras. Tams-Witmark. Terms quoted on application.

The story of Belle Poitrine's ascent from the wrong side of the tracks in Venezuela, Illinois, to the exquisite luxury of Southhampton, Long Island, and success. A sophisticated show.

————. *Promises, Promises.* (1968) Based on the screenplay *The Apartment,* by Billy Wilder and I.A.L. Diamond. Lyrics by Hal David. Music by Burt Bacharach. 2 exteriors, 11 interiors. 14m. 11w. extras. Tams-Witmark. Terms quoted on application.

The story of Chuck Baxter, a young man eager to get ahead in business and romance. The only way he can get a promotion, however, is to lend out the key to his apartment, and soon he must give exclusive rights to the apartment to Sheldrake in personnel. Chuck discovers that Fran, whom he likes, is the girl Sheldrake sees in his apartment. Only after Fran's attempted suicide does Chuck throw Sheldrake out and find a promise of romance. A serious comment on business ethics.

————. *Sweet Charity.* Based on the screenplay *The Nights of Cabiria,* by Federico Fellini. Lyrics by Dorothy Fields. Music by Cy Coleman. 5 exteriors, 11 interiors. Large cast. Tams-Witmark. Terms quoted on application.

The story of a dance hall hostess of easy virtue whose great desire for love and a naive trusting nature cause her to always give her heart to the wrong man. Filled with deceptively charming character types—her cynical, hard-core trio of girlfriends, the phoney evangelist, the Coney Island "fun people," the Central Park "strollers," and, of course, her heroes—the animal-magnetism type, the continental type, the better-than-nothing type. Romantic; provides strong roles for females.

Spewack, Samuel, and Spewack, Bella. *Kiss Me Kate.* (1948) Based on Shakespeare's *The Taming of the Shrew.* Lyrics and music by Cole Porter. 4 exteriors, 5 interiors. 12m. 3w. Tams-Witmark. Terms quoted on application.

The backstage life of an actor and actress, formerly married, which closely parallels their roles as Katharina and Petruchio in a production of Shakespeare's *The Taming of the Shrew.* Colorful vehicle requiring strong performers in leads.

Starkie, Martin, and Coghill, Nevill. *Canterbury Tales.* Based on translations from Geoffrey Chaucer's work by Nevill Coghill. Lyrics by Nevill Coghill. Music by Richard Hill and John Hawkins. 1 basic set. 12m. 6w. Music Theatre International. Terms quoted on application.

A witty medley of four tales told by the pilgrims on their way to Canterbury: The Miller's Tale, The Steward's Tale, The Merchant's Tale, and The Wife of Bath's Tale. Offers opportunity for imaginative, stylized staging.

Stein, Joseph. *Fiddler on the Roof.* (1964) Based on stories by Sholem

Aleichem. Lyrics by Sheldon Harnick. Music by Jerry Bock. 3 interiors, 3 exteriors. 14m. 10w. villagers. Music Theatre International. Terms quoted on application.

The story of a hard-working and devout Jewish family living in a small peasant town in tsarist Russia early in the 1900s. Trying to survive the persecutions of the times and the changes which would destroy the family and revered traditions, the family realizes that the old ways do not always work, and they set out to find new lives in new lands.

————. *Zorba.* (1968) Based on Nikos Kazantzakis's novel *Zorba the Greek.* Lyrics by Fred Ebb. Music by John Kander. 1 basic set. 22m. 13w. French, manuscript. Terms quoted on application.

The story of Zorba, the carefree vagabond, and the bookish, inhibited Nikos he chooses as his friend and master. Zorba loves the aging but lusty Hortense, but Nikos' romance with the beautiful widow begins a feud which results in her death. Advanced groups only.

Stein, Joseph, and Glickman, William. *Plain and Fancy.* (1955) Lyrics by Arnold B. Horwitt. Music by Albert Hague. 3 interiors, 12 exteriors. 19m. 11w. extras. French, libretto $2.00, vocal score $15.00. Terms quoted on application.

A sophisticated New Yorker and his girlfriend learn about life among the Amish in the Pennsylvania Dutch country—customs of love and betrothal, a barn raising, religious and household life, and a brilliant carnival. For all groups. Ethnic interest: Amish.

Stein, Joseph, and Russell, Robert. *Take Me Along.* Based on Eugene O'Neill's *Ah, Wilderness!* Lyrics and music by Bob Merrill. 9 exteriors, 6 interiors. 11m. 6w. extras. Tams-Witmark. Terms quoted on application.

The sentimental story of a boy becoming a man in the early 1900s in New England. Richard, a confirmed rebel, disturbs his family and the average Connecticut small town they live in with his anarchistic views and violent, erratic behavior. He falls passionately in love with the neighbor's girl and, despite discouraging events, the play ends on a tenderly understanding note. Fine for all groups.

Stewart, Michael. *Bye Bye Birdie.* (1960) Lyrics by Lee Adams. Music by Charles Strouse. 7 interiors, 9 exteriors. 11m. 11w. extras. Tams-Witmark. Terms quoted on application.

An account of what happens when the national rock 'n' roll teen hero is inducted into the Army. As a final publicity stunt, Birdie will bid a typical American teenage girl goodbye with an all-American kiss, a plan which completely upsets the girl's household and sends their small Ohio town into a real spin. Many excellent roles for young performers. Popular with all groups.

————. *Carnival!* (1961) Lyrics and music by Bob Merrill. 9 interiors, 1 exterior. 9m. 7w. plus performers of the carnival. Tams-Witmark. Terms quoted on application.

The sentimental story of a young country girl who joins a third-rate carnival and becomes the pawn in a fierce rivalry for her affection between Marco, the troupe's magician, and Paul, a shy puppeteer with a game leg. Opportunity for a great many carnival acts—jugglers, clowns, aerialists, harem girls, strong man, gypsies—and a delicate, intimate story for sensitive performers and director.

————. *Hello, Dolly!* (1964) Based on Thornton Wilder's play *The Matchmaker.* Lyrics and music by Jerry Herman. 5 exteriors, 4 interiors. 8m. 6w. extras. Tams-Witmark. Terms quoted on application.

Set in New York in the nineties, this comedy centers on the busy schemes of a shrewd, volatile matchmaker who, on the pretext of arranging the marriage of the miserly merchant Vandergelder, succeeds in getting him herself. A hilarious climax of complications. Requires a "star" performer. Popular with all groups.

Stewart, Michael, Pascal, John, and Pascal, Fran. *George M!* (1968) Lyrics and music by George M. Cohan, revised by Mary Cohan. 6m. 5w. extras. Tams-Witmark. Terms quoted on application.

A musical biography of George M. Cohan, towering giant of the American musical theater, from the 1890s to his last stage appearance in 1937. Leading character must be strong stylist, need not try to imitate Cohan.

Stone, Peter. *1776.* (1969) Lyrics and music by Sherman Edwards. 1 basic set. 24m. 2w. Music Theatre International. Terms quoted on application.

The play commences in May, as we find the representatives to the Continental Congress braving the humidity and flies of the stuffy chamber. It continues through June, with countless votes and arguments, climaxing on July 4, 1776, as the Declaration of Independence, somewhat modified from Jefferson's original, is passed and signed. Excellent for a predominantly male group.

————. *Sugar.* Based on the screenplay *Some Like It Hot,* by Billy Wilder and I.A.L. Diamond, and the story by Robert Thoeren. Lyrics by Bob Merrill. Music by Jule Styne. Multi set. 5m. 2w. extras and chorus. Tams-Witmark. Terms quoted on application.

Set in the depression. Two out-of-work musicians witness a gangland killing and are forced to join an all-female band and flee in women's attire to save their lives. Complications arise when they fall in love with one of the girls who has befriended them and an aging playboy starts to make advances. When the killers arrive in town by chance and recognize the two "girls," the chase is on. Fast and funny nonsense.

———. *Two by Two*. Based on Clifford Odets' play *The Flowering Peach*. Lyrics by Martin Charnin. Music by Richard Rodgers. 4m. 4w. Rodgers and Hammerstein. Terms quoted on application.
The story of Noah and his family as they survive the Great Flood. Noah persuades his skeptical family that God has given them a mission, and though they bicker, they do the job obediently. The voyage concludes triumphantly with the grounding of the ark and the departure of the family to replenish the earth.

Swerling, Jo, and Burrows, Abe. *Guys and Dolls: A Musical Fable of Broadway*. (1950) Based on stories by Damon Runyon. Lyrics and music by Frank Loesser. 5 interiors, 3 exteriors. 6m. 2w. extras. Music Theatre International. Terms quoted on application.
Nathan Detroit, an inveterate gambler, has been engaged to Miss Adelaide for fourteen years. She wants him to go legit, but Nathan is more interested in raising $1000 to obtain a place to hold his floating crap game. Nathan tricks Sky Masterson into betting that Sky can get Sarah Brown, who runs a street-corner mission, to go with him to Havana. Great opportunity for a variety of character types.

Tebelak, John-Michael. *Godspell*. Based on the Gospel According to Matthew. Lyrics and music by Stephen Schwarts. One set. 5m. 5w. Theatre Maximus. Terms quoted on application.
The Gospel story is retold through group improvisation and 60s rock music. Simple but effective. A colorful and touching production within the grasp of all groups. Especially popular with young adults.

Thompson, Jay, Barer, Marshall, and Fuller, Dean. *Once upon a Mattress*. Based on "The Princess and the Pea," by Hans Christian Andersen. Lyrics by Marshall Barer. Music by Mary Rodgers. Unit set. 16m. 10w. extras. Music Theatre International. Terms quoted on application.
The King has been cursed by a witch and will not speak until "the mouse devours the hawk." The Queen has decreed that no one shall wed until the Prince is married to a true Princess. Eleven have failed the Queen's royalty test, but when Princess Winnifred fails to fall asleep on twenty mattresses when one pea is placed beneath, the Queen is livid. The Prince shouts her down—the mouse devours the hawk— and the kingdom is restored to order. Relatively simple to stage and popular with all groups.

Wasserman, Dale. *Man of La Mancha*. (1965) Based on Cervantes' novel *Don Quixote*. Lyrics by Joe Darion. Music by Mitch Leigh. 1 basic set. 17m. 5w. Tams-Witmark. Terms quoted on application.
Miguel de Cervantes Saavedra, aging and an utter failure, awaits in prison his trial by the Inquisition. In order to prevent confiscation of

the uncompleted manuscript of *Don Quixote,* Cervantes and his man-servant play out the story before a kangaroo court of fellow prisoners, who participate, taking various roles. Romantic and stirring; very popular.

Weidman, Jerome, and Abbott, George. *Fiorello!* (1959) Lyrics by Sheldon Harnick. Music by Jerry Bock. 7 interiors, 8 exteriors. 30m. 7w. extras. Tams-Witmark. Terms quoted on application.
The story of the budding political career of the scrappy young lawyer, Fiorello LaGuardia, up to his election as mayor of New York during the 1930s. An energetic study of a great man in a time of political corruption, with ample opportunity for humor and chorus numbers. For all groups. Ethnic interest: Jewish-American, Italian-American.

Willson, Meredith. *The Music Man.* (1957) Based on a story by Meredith Willson and Franklin Lacey. Lyrics and music by Meredith Willson. 6 exteriors, 3 interiors. 18m. 9w. extras. Music Theatre International. Terms quoted on application.
During his one-week stay in River City, Iowa, Prof. Hill convinces the townspeople that they need a big brass band. He is a charlatan who cannot read a note of music nor play any instrument, but while fleecing his customers he transforms a dull town into a singing and dancing community. Completely charming all the young ladies, the professor is himself charmed by Marian the librarian, and their relationship subtly transforms him into a reliable citizen. Within range of all groups.

Wilson, Sandy. *The Boy Friend.* (1954) Lyrics and music by Sandy Wilson. 1 interior, 2 exteriors. 12m. 13w. Music Theatre International. Terms quoted on application.
A British view of life in the twenties at a girls' finishing school in Paris. Polly, a millionaire's daughter, falls in love with Tony, a delivery boy who, of course, is really the son of Lord Brockhurst. To hold his interest, Polly pretends she is a working girl. An excellent satire of the times and of the musicals of the period. Especially good for high school.

Yellen, Sherman. *The Rothschilds.* Based on the book by Frederic Morton. Lyrics by Sheldon Harnick. Music by Jerry Bock. 29m. 4w. extras. French, manuscript. Terms quoted on application.
The role of the Jewish banking family, the Rothschilds, in world events during the time of Napoleon and the wars between the French and English. Needs mature performers.

Television Plays

Television, the major source of entertainment and news information for most American families, has had a major impact on most American lives, greatly affecting attendance at motion pictures and other theatrical events. The television industry is constantly searching for writers to meet the pressures and to fulfill the promises of ongoing daily programming.

In the late 1940s and through the mid-1950s, a series of programs broke on the networks which were to single out some new and exciting dramatists. These writers demonstrated exceptional talents in coping with the limitations of the small screen, the use of small casts, problems of planning for regular commercial breaks, specific time handicaps, etc. Shows such as *Omnibus, Studio One, Kraft Theatre, Philco-Goodyear Playhouse, Playhouse 90, Hallmark Hall of Fame,* among others, offered a format and great opportunities for writers such as Tad Mosel, Horton Foote, Alvin Sapinsley, Rod Serling, Reginald Rose, and Paddy Chayefsky. For the most part, television writers were adapting classics, contemporary novels, and short stories into television scripts; however, several writers, including those listed above, saw new possibilities for conveying dramatic situations by means of television to mass audiences.

Although very few articles can be found which deal with the development of television drama, publishers are printing scripts of television plays. These are available for personal reading and for study. More and more schools are offering courses dealing with media, and television drama is a major section of any such curriculum.

As the years have gone by, television has continued to display new possibilities, new dimensions, new talents. Each year's Emmy Awards presentations pay recognition to the many writers and skilled artists and technicians who are attempting to make television better. *Masterpiece Theatre* is one of the recent rewards of such efforts.

It is therefore only natural that some of the outstanding plays of television be included in this guide. It is hoped that the list will grow in quality as well as quantity.

Bibliography

Allen, Don. *The Electric Humanities: Patterns for Teaching Mass Media and Popular Culture.* Dayton: Pflaum-Standard, 1971.

Barrett, Marvin. *The Politics of Broadcasting.* New York: T. Y. Crowell, 1973.

Gettagno, Caleb. *Towards a Visual Culture: Educating through Television.* New York: Avon Books, 1971, out of print.

Hazard, Patrick D., ed. *TV as Art: Some Essays on Criticism.* Urbana, Ill.: National Council of Teachers of English, 1966, out of print.

Kirschner, Allen, and Kirschner, Linda, eds. *Radio and Television: Readings in the Mass Media.* New York: Odyssey Press, 1971.

Larsen, Otto N., ed. *Violence and the Mass Media.* New York: Harper and Row, 1968.

McLuhan, Marshall. *Understanding Media: The Extensions of Man.* New York: New American Library, 1964.

Roberts, Edward Barry. *Television Writing and Selling.* 5th ed. Boston: The Writer, Inc., 1967.

Postman, Neil, and the Committee on the Study of Television of the National Council of Teachers of English. *Television and the Teaching of English.* New York: Appleton-Century-Crofts, 1961, out of print.

Sarson, Evelyn, ed. *Action for Children's Television.* New York: Avon Books, 1971.

Skornia, Harry J. *Television and Society: An Inquest and Agenda for Improvement.* New York: McGraw-Hill, 1965.

Trapnell, Coles. *Teleplay: An Introduction to TV Writing.* Rev. ed. New York: Hawthorn Books, 1974.

Wylie, Max. *Writing for Television.* New York: Cowles Book Co., 1970.

Summaries of Plays

Note: A number of television plays have been adapted for production on the stage. In these cases, the availability of a stage adaptation has been noted in addition to the source of the original television version. Information concerning sets, book prices, and royalties pertain to stage versions.

Aurthur, Robert Alan. *Man on the Mountaintop.* 5m. 2w. In *Best Television Plays,* ed. by Gore Vidal.

A child prodigy who feels like a freak is reclaimed by a girl who has patience and loves him. She cannot secure reconciliation with his father, who never forgave him for the death of his mother in childbirth.

Baker, Elliott. *The Delinquent.* Drama in 1 act. 5m. 1w. Bethany Press $1.50 (in *The Delinquent, The Hipster, and The Square,* ed. by Alva I. Cox). Royalty to Bethany Press.

Three different members of the beat generation depict the pressures of the times. Modern jazz.

————. *The Hipster.* Drama in 1 act. 5m. 1w. Bethany Press $1.50 (in *The Delinquent, The Hipster, and The Square,* ed. by Alva I. Cox). Royalty to Bethany Press.

A group of hipsters who rebel against mass thinking and mass behavior use escape from involvement in life as their solution. Modern jazz.

————. *The Square.* Drama in 1 act. 6m. 1w. Bethany Press $1.50 (in *The Delinquent, The Hipster, and The Square,* ed. by Alva I. Cox). Royalty to Bethany Press.

Not wishing to risk examining the frustrations of life, the square protects himself with a college degree in suburbia.

Berg, Gertrude. *The Goldbergs (Rosie's Hair)*. Domestic comedy. 5m. 6w. 1 girl. In *The Best Television Plays, 1950–1951*, ed. by William I. Kaufman.

The Goldberg family faces the problem of an adolescent daughter's growing up and demonstrates, in its support of Rosie, that a family need not be rich to be strong. Ethnic interest: Jewish-American.

Chayefsky, Paddy. *The Bachelor Party*. 7m. 4w. In *Television Plays*, by Paddy Chayefsky.

With his wife pregnant, Charlie is bored. A bachelor party for a groom in his office provides the illusion of freedom. But the married men become more bored than ever by the monotony of bar after bar. The fascinating bachelor party seems hectic, and the groom becomes so drunk he almost calls off his wedding. Charlie is glad to come home.

———. *The Big Deal*. 9m. 2w. In *Great Television Plays*, ed. by William I. Kaufman.

Joe Manx, once a successful builder, lives on dreams of recouping his fortune. He tries to borrow $4,000 to buy marshland to build houses, but nobody will lend it to him. Harry Gerber offers him a job as building inspector at $3,600 per year, and he rejects it. Joe asks his daughter to lend him the $5,000 she had inherited and on which she hopes to marry a doctor who has not finished his education. When she agrees, Joe crumples and decides to take the job.

———. *Holiday Song*. 7m. 4w. In *Television Plays*, by Paddy Chayefsky.

A Jewish cantor, oppressed by the evils of the world, loses faith in God. His friends send him to see Rabbi Marcus. En route, he is put on the wrong subway train by a mysterious guard. First he meets a despairing Dutch girl; then he meets her lost husband. He reunites them and thus finds renewed faith—and a husband for his unwed niece. Ethnic interest: Jewish-American.

———. *Marty*. 7m. 7w. In *Television Plays*, by Paddy Chayefsky.

Marty, an Italian-American bachelor, is long past marrying age. His cousins ask his mother to take his aunt, with whom they cannot get along, into his house, and she agrees. They suggest that Marty go to the Waverly Ballroom, where he meets a schoolteacher, a plain girl not of his heritage. They like each other and, despite his aunt's and mother's selfish fears and his friend's disapproval, decide to marry. Ethnic interest: Italian-American.

————. *The Mother.* 2m. 8w. In *Television Plays*, by Paddy Chayefsky.

An elderly mother, who had lost her husband a month before, is desperate for something to do. Her daughter wants to take her into her home and prevent her from working because she is not well, but mother persists, although she loses every job she gets.

————. *Printer's Measure.* 11m. 6w. 3 boys, 1 girl. In *Television Plays*, by Paddy Chayefsky.

Because Mr. Healy takes pride in his craft of hand-setting type, he tries to inspire a boy in his shop. When the boss brings in a linotype machine, Healy is afraid of being fired and attempts to smash the machine. When the boy, whose father has just died, decides there is more of a future in learning linotype operation, Healy retires.

Costigan, James. *Little Moon of Alban.* In *Little Moon of Alban and A Wind from the South,* by James Costigan. Drama in 3 acts. Unit set, or cyclorama and drapes. 10m. 8w. French $1.75. Royalty $50—$25.

Set in Ireland during the political troubles of the 1920s. When Brigid Mary's fiancé is killed by an English lieutenant, she becomes a volunteer nurse in a religious order. Finding herself assigned to care for her fiancé's wounded killer, she is torn between her vows and her desire for revenge. This dilemma is made doubly poignant when the lieutenant unwillingly falls in love with her.

————. *A Wind from the South.* 5m. 4w. extras. In *Little Moon of Alban and A Wind from the South,* by James Costigan.

A girl whose brother runs a hotel in Ireland has a brief romance with an unhappily married American summer tourist.

Davis, Luther. *Run for Your Life (or, The Committee for the 25th).* In *Writing for Television,* by Max Wylie.

This play makes a plea for the control of Las Vegas gambling, or a true "25th Amendment," as author Davis envisions it, one that would outlaw gambling in all fifty states. Cappi, a gangster, gets Sarah Sinclair, an impressionable young woman, onto drugs. Paul Byron, a lawyer friend of the family, and Sinclair, her father and a former big city mayor, struggle heroically to save her.

Foote, Horton. *The Dancers.* In *Harrison, Texas: Eight Television Plays,* by Horton Foote. Comedy in 1 act. 1 hour. Modern costumes. 3m. 7w. Dramatists Play Service $1.75 (in volume). Royalty $15.

Horace's sister has arranged a dancing date for him with Emily, the most popular girl in town. Horace goes to her home, nervous because he can't dance very well, but discovers that she is being forced to go by her parents. Humiliated, he leaves. At a soda fountain he meets Mary

Catherine. She also lacks confidence, and despite the fact that Emily now wants to go with him, Horace takes Mary Catherine. Admitting their fears of not being good dancers, they find confidence in the knowledge of one another's liking and respect. Sensitive picture of teenage loneliness.

————. *Death of the Old Man*. In *Harrison, Texas: Eight Television Plays,* by Horton Foote. Drama in 1 act. 30 minutes. Interior. 19th century costumes. 4m. 3w. Dramatists Play Service $1.75 (in volume). Royalty $10.
An old man lies dying, worrying about what will happen to his spinster daughter Rosa, who has cared for him, and an old black servant. He lies powerless as he watches how his sons try to evade responsibility, but is gratified to see cousin Lyd offer his daughter and the servant a home.

————. *Old Man*. Based on a story by William Faulkner. 17m. 1w. extras. In *Three Plays,* by Horton Foote.
The story centers on the fate of two convicts released to help rescue people stranded during a violent flood of the Mississippi River (called the "Old Man"). Ironically, the so-called "Tall Convict," a man of strong moral convictions who rescues a pregnant woman, helps deliver her baby, and brings her back to safety, suffers a fate entirely out of proportion to his act of valor.

————. *Roots in a Parched Ground*. Originally entitled *The Night of the Storm*. In *Three Plays,* by Horton Foote. Drama in 3 acts. Unit set. 9m. 5w. 1 boy, 1 girl. Dramatists Play Service $1.75. Royalty $35—$25.
The story of a young boy, product of a broken marriage, and the conflicts in his life. The work depicts his mother's desperate attempts to survive in a serious economic recession, the boy's thirst for an education which she cannot afford, his attempts to escape from family tensions, and his eventual return home. The work closes with his mother's remarriage, her forced abandonment of her son, and the boy's uncertain fate as he faces a bleak and practically hopeless future.

————. *The Tears of My Sister*. 2m. 4w. In *Harrison, Texas: Eight Television Plays,* by Horton Foote.
Cecilia is upset by the nightly weeping of her lovely sister. Bessie, 18, is being persuaded by her mother to marry Stacy, 34, who is wealthy. Although Bessie loves Syd Davis, she yields to her mother's importunities.

————. *Tomorrow*. Based on the story by William Faulkner. In *Three Plays,* by Horton Foote. Drama in 3 acts. Unit set. 15m. (many bits) 3w. Dramatists Play Service $1.75. Royalty $50—$25.
A young lawyer who has just lost his first case arrives in a rural area in

the South. His client had killed a wild and brutal young man, and though the killing seemed justified, the jury was hung by one man—Jackson Fentry. From Fentry's neighbors the lawyer learns the story of a deserted woman's death and the man who sheltered her baby, who grew up to become the wild and brutal man his client had killed.

————. *A Young Lady of Property.* In *Best Television Plays,* ed. by Gore Vidal. Drama in 1 act. 1 hour. 3m. 6w. Dramatists Play Service $1.75 (in volume). Royalty $15.

Wilma, 15, was willed the family house by her mother. Her happy realization that her real purpose in life is to raise a family in the house she loves is shattered by the news that her father is going to marry Mrs. Leighton—a woman of whom the town disapproves—and plans to sell the house. She meets Mrs. Leighton, who she discovers is warm and sympathetic, and becomes reconciled to the marriage. Mrs. Leighton saves Wilma's house for her, but it is not the house which is important, Wilma finds, but the life in it.

Ford, Jesse Hill. *The Conversion of Buster Drumwright.* Unit set. 7m. 1w. extras. Vanderbilt University Press $3.50 (television and stage scripts). Royalty: contact publisher.

Ocie Hedgepath, one of a family of mountain people in east Tennessee, undertakes to avenge the murder of his sister and her child by Buster Drumwright, a killer with a record of the death of seventeen people. Drumwright has been captured and faces the prospect of lynching by an infuriated mob. Ocie's task, at the behest of his family, is to get to Drumwright and personally kill him before the mob does. Torn between his basic humanity and his family's demand, Ocie attempts to carry out his mission until he is faced with a crucial decision.

Gardner, Kirk. *A Trip to Czardis.* Based on the story by Edwin Granberry. 6m. 1w. extras. In *Writing for Television,* by Max Wylie.

Dramatizes the trip of a family to see their father who, unknown to them, is to be executed that very day for a crime the nature of which is never revealed. A poignant, powerful, and eloquent adaptation of an award-winning story.

MacLeish, Archibald. *The Secret of Freedom.* Drama in 1 act. 7m. 1w. 2 boys; extras if desired. Dramatists Play Service $1.75 (in *Three Short Plays,* by Archibald MacLeish). Royalty $15.

After the defeat of a badly needed school bond referendum, Joe and Jill, who had fought for its passage, begin to question the attitudes of people that would allow this to happen. They confront many attitudes in their search for the answer, but the town librarian comes closest to enlightening them. He sees the secret of freedom as "each man's cour-

age to believe . . . in himself, his town . . . the future of the country."
Strengthened, Joe and Jill resolve to win the next school bond vote.

Mercer, David. *The Generations.* A trilogy of plays. London: Calder
and Boyars, 1964.
Where the Difference Begins. Treats the nature and consequences of
political commitment. Conflict arises from the differing political faiths
of the two sons of Wilt Crowther, a Yorkshire workingman who has
toiled all his life to educate the boys. Edgar, the elder, is impressed by
his father's faith in socialism, but through education has absorbed
many middle class values. Richard, the younger, a political idealist,
respects his father's beliefs but is overwhelmed by the impossibility of
making any vital improvements in the wretched political, social, and
economic conditions that characterize postwar England.
A Climate of Fear. Centers on the threat to civilization of growing
nuclear power. Again, there is division in the families regarding the
bomb. Important characters are the Waring family—Leonard Waring,
a nuclear scientist, his wife Frieda, and their two children, Colin and
Frances.
The Birth of a Private Man. Continues the story of the two Waring
children of the previous play, dramatizing the later fortunes of Colin
Waring, now a confirmed revolutionary, his sister Frances, and the
militant Communist Jurek, whom she marries. Part of the play takes
place in Poland. The trilogy ends with the disillusioned Colin's tragic
death on the Berlin wall when he is caught in the crossfire of East
and West guards.

Miller, J. P. *The Rabbit Trap.* 5m. 2w. 1 boy. In *Best Television Plays,*
ed. by Gore Vidal. Stage version forthcoming from Dramatists Play
Service.
A man, influenced by his family, stands up to his boss despite the fact
that it costs him his job.

Monash, Paul. *Judd for the Defense.* In *Writing for Television,* by
Max Wylie.
This is a portrait of a black man, Jessie Aarons, "vengeful, primitive,
dangerous," and his defense by a dedicated lawyer, Clinton Judd, determined to see that Aarons receives proper justice.

Mosel, Tad. *Ernie Barger Is Fifty.* 7m. 2w. In *Other People's Houses,*
by Tad Mosel.
Ernie Barger leaves his ailing wife to go to his son's graduation. His
son shows that he no longer needs him and goes off to be married. His
business partner tells him he has not kept up to date and approves
designs without him. Barger breaks down, finding solace in his wife's
love.

————. *The Five Dollar Bill.* 3m. 2w. In *Best Television Plays, 1957,* ed. by William I. Kaufman.
Rebelling against his father's lack of understanding, a teenage boy turns to stealing.

————. *The Haven.* 3m. 1w. 1 boy, 1 girl. In *Other People's Houses,* by Tad Mosel.
Restless about his family life, Howie tries to break the monotony by selling his lakeside cabin. He is unsuccessful, and his wife promises to change her ways if they can return there. When they arrive, she finds the cabin cleaner than she left it. Other evidence tells her that Howie had been there that winter with another woman. When Howie tells her that the woman killed herself because he still loved his wife, they are reconciled.

————. *My Lost Saints.* 1m. 3w. 1 girl. In *Other People's Houses,* by Tad Mosel.
Kate has been a happy maid to the Hallets for eighteen years, idolizing them. Her mother loses her farm and stops in to see her on her way to Minneapolis. She falls and stays in bed unnecessarily for weeks, trying to get Kate to go with her and disorganizing the house. Eventually Mr. Hallet objects. When Mama gets Kate to agree to leave with her, she gets well in ten minutes. Kate is disillusioned, sends Mama to Minneapolis, and stays with the Hallets.

————. *Other People's Houses.* 3m. 2w. In *Other People's Houses,* by Tad Mosel.
Senile Dad causes Rena and Ralph so much trouble that they decide to ask Rena's sister Inez to put him in an old people's home. Inez objects, but she cannot find a solution and so realizes she must be unkind to her father. After she takes him to the home, Inez realizes that Rena has grown in independence and industry.

————. *Stars in the Summer Night.* 9m. 4w. In *Other People's Houses,* by Tad Mosel.
Miss Girard, 68, once a star of musical comedy, loses her job and tries to secure friends by giving away her possessions. She has no money, and her friend and maid leave her. When she is near the breaking point, she tells a policeman that she still has her last job. He takes her there, and she is reinstated at half salary and under humiliating conditions.

————. *The Waiting Place.* 1m. 2w. 1 boy, 1 girl. In *Other People's Houses,* by Tad Mosel.
A 14-year-old motherless girl, enamoured of her father and with a mind filled with adolescent fancies, uses a lonely ravine as her refuge. Her father cannot understand her. He misses her mother, but finds himself

attracted to the woman who does his housework. To destroy this attachment the girl remains in the ravine a whole evening. When her father does not come for her, she is forced to see things in their proper perspective and to approve of her father's forthcoming marriage.

Moser, James E. *Question: What Is Truth?* 13m. 3w. extras. In *Teleplay: An Introduction to TV Writing,* by Coles Trapnell (New York: Hawthorn Books, 1974).

The pilot teleplay for Moser's TV series *Slattery's People.* Slattery is a state representative in an unidentified capital closely resembling Sacramento. Slattery is shown working with his colleagues, launching an explosive investigation (it is his intimation that an important bill has been tampered with), clashing with the majority floor leader, and pursuing his fight against corruption regardless of who is involved. His final victory is achieved in an exposé of the guilty individuals.

Ribman, Ronald. *The Final War of Olly Winter.* 14m. 8w. 1 boy, extras. In *Great Television Plays,* ed. by William I. Kaufman.

The story of a black soldier in Vietnam. Flashbacks.

Rose, Reginald. *An Almanac of Liberty.* 15m. 7w. 1 boy, 1 girl, extras. In *Six Television Plays,* by Reginald Rose.

John Carter has been beaten by a gang. On the anniversary of the approval of the Bill of Rights by Congress, everyone assembles at Ridgeville Town Hall at 10:24 for an unknown reason. Out of the silence grows a revelation of antagonism toward Carter, who had said some unpopular things. Some come to Carter's support, and all realize they have violated the Bill of Rights.

————. *Crime in the Streets.* 4m. 1w. 7 boys. In *Six Television Plays,* by Reginald Rose.

Frankie is the leader of a gang of toughs. His father has abandoned the family, his mother works hard, and his little brother Richie gets all the attention. Ben, a social worker, tries to gain their confidence. The gang plans to kill McAllister, who informed on a member. Ben tells Frankie he needs love. At the moment of the killing, Richie intervenes, and Frankie's tough front breaks.

————. *Dino.* Stage adaptation by Kristin Sergel. Drama in 3 acts. 1 set. 7m. 11w. extras. Dramatic Publishing Co. $1.25. Royalty $35.

A play about the very serious problems of rehabilitating a juvenile delinquent. At the age of seventeen, Dino has already spent four years behind bars. Upon his release, he presents a serious difficulty to his family, to his girlfriend, to his neighborhood, and to himself. Dino's parole officer, competent but kind, launches his charge on the path to self-understanding. A disturbing play relevant to the lives of young people. For all groups. Ethnic interest: Italian-American.

————. *The Incredible World of Horace Ford.* 8m. 5w. 4 boys. In *Six Television Plays,* by Reginald Rose.

A psychological fantasy about a man's preoccupation with his childhood memories.

————. *The Remarkable Incident at Carson Corners.* In *Six Television Plays,* by Reginald Rose. Stage adaptation by Kristin Sergel. Drama. No scenery, minimum of props. 13m. 13w. extras. Dramatic Publishing Co. $1.75. Royalty $35.

The students put Mr. Kovalsky, the janitor of their school, on trial for the murder of a boy who fell to his death when the fire escape railing gave way. Eventually the entire town is proved to be responsible.

————. *Thunder on Sycamore Street.* In *Best Television Plays,* ed. by Gore Vidal. Stage adaptation by Kristin Sergel. Drama. 8m. 10w. extras. Dramatic Publishing Co. $1.75. Royalty $35.

All Sycamore Street is incensed when Joe Blake, an ex-convict (he had killed a man in an automobile accident), moves into their street. They march on his house, tell him to get out, and are near a riot. Joe stands up to them and is finally joined by Arthur, who is usually meek. The mob becomes ashamed and disperses.

————. *Twelve Angry Men.* In *Great Television Plays,* ed. by William I. Kaufman. Stage adaptation by Kristin Sergel. Drama. Jury room, jury box. Modern costumes. 15m. Dramatic Publishing Co. $1.75. Eldridge $1.75. Royalty $50.

A nineteen-year-old man has just stood trial for the fatal stabbing of his father. All the men in the jury are for his conviction, with one exception. Eventually he is able to interpret the evidence in such a way that he proves the accused is innocent. This, despite the overwhelming prejudice of some of the jurors, results in exoneration. A powerful play with a great deal of tension.

Sapinsley, Alvin. *Lee at Gettysburg.* 16m. In *Great Television Plays,* ed. by William I. Kaufman.

Robert E. Lee's plan for the battle of Gettysburg is thwarted by the deliberate delay of Generals Longstreet and Stuart in obeying his orders.

Serling, Rod. *The Lonely.* In *Writing for Television,* by Max Wylie.

In this play, one of the well-known TV suspense series, *The Twilight Zone,* prisoners sentenced to life incarceration are transported to satellites. The drama concerns the fate of Corry, one of the prisoners, and Alicia, a machine in the form of a woman which has been created by a compassionate space scientist to help him overcome his loneliness.

————. *Noon on Doomsday.* 7m. 4w. In *Television Plays for Writers,* ed. by A. S. Burack.

A freed killer and the townspeople are forced to face their guilt after a prejudiced trial.

————. *Requiem for a Heavyweight.* 17m. 2w. 1 boy, extras. In *Great Television Plays,* ed. by William I. Kaufman.

An injured prizefighter who "might have been champion" is saved from becoming a derelict by a young woman in an employment agency.

————. *The Strike.* 27m. In *Best Television Plays,* ed. by Gore Vidal.

An American Army officer has to decide between saving the remnant of five hundred men in his command or a twenty-man patrol marooned in enemy territory. Set during the Korean War.

Shaw, David. *Native Dancer.* 2m. 3w. In *Top TV Shows of the Year, 1954–1955,* ed. by Irving Settel.

A young girl is torn between marriage and a career as a dancer.

Simmons, Richard Alan. *The Price of Tomatoes.* In *Writing for Television,* by Max Wylie.

Fresco, an enterprising tomato farmer, races to beat his competitors to market with a heavy load of produce. On the way he encounters Anna, a pregnant woman who is about to give birth. Fresco's basic humanity prevails over his competitive instincts as he struggles through all sorts of obstacles to obtain aid to deliver her child. He finally succeeds in his determination to help her in her plight. He also triumphs over his competitors, getting to market before them.

Trewin, J. C., ed. *Elizabeth R.* Historical drama in 6 parts. New York: Frederick Ungar, 1972.

The Lion's Cub, by John Hale, 19m. 6w. extras. Traces Elizabeth's early years, describes the various court machinations during her growth to young womanhood, and ends with Mary Tudor's death and Elizabeth's ascension to the throne at the age of 25.

The Marriage Game, by Rosemary Anne Sisson, 9m. 6w. extras. Describes the attempts on the part of influential courtiers to prevail on Elizabeth to marry to provide an heir to the throne. Though Elizabeth bestows her favors lavishly on Robert Dudley, whom she makes an earl, she resists the various suitors and remains unmarried.

Shadow in the Sun, by Julian Mitchell, 12m. 5w. extras. Elizabeth, on the verge of a marriage to Alençon, the younger brother of the King of France, meets him and goes through a period of courtship with him. Dudley, Earl of Leicester, objects, is threatened with commitment to the Tower, but is saved by Sussex's interest. At the last minute Elizabeth changes her mind about her marriage to Alençon and through her Council buys him off.

Horrible Conspiracies, by Hugh Whitemore, 13m. 2w. extras. Dramatizes the tense emotional conflict between Mary, Queen of Scotland, Elizabeth's cousin, accused of conspiring against Elizabeth. The play ends with Mary's execution.

The Enterprise of England, by John Prebble, 18m. 1w. extras. Dramatizes the struggle with Philip II of Spain and his attempt to invade England with the Armada to avenge the death of Mary. His plan fails and Elizabeth triumphs. The play closes with news of the death of Dudley, Elizabeth's former lover.

Sweet England's Pride, by Ian Rodger, 18m. 5w. extras. Centers on the Irish Rebellion, highlighting the role of the Earl of Essex, sent to quell the revolt, his return and challenge to Elizabeth's power, and his imprisonment and execution. The play ends with the death of Elizabeth and the ascension of James VI of Scotland to the English throne.

————. *The Six Wives of Henry VIII.* Historical drama in 6 parts. New York: Frederick Ungar, 1972. Stage adaptations by Herbert Martin. Bare stage, minimum of props. 16th century English costumes. *Catherine of Aragon,* by Rosemary Anne Sisson, 9m. 5w.; *Anne Boleyn,* by Nick McCarty, 7m. 3w.; *Jane Seymour,* by Ian Thorne, 6m. 4w.; *Anne of Cleves,* by Jean Morris, 10m. 2w.; *Catherine Howard,* by Beverly Cross, 6m. 4w.; *Catherine Parr,* by John Prebble, 8m. 2w. Dramatic Publishing Co. $1.00 each. Royalty $20 each.

King Henry VIII is shown in this composite biography as a complex personality, viewed through his own actions and the light cast upon him by his six wives, in their dealings with and reactions to him. Each script illuminates the king's personality and character in cumulative fashion, from the time he succeeded to the English throne at the age of eighteen to his death at fifty-five.

Vidal, Gore. *Barn Burning.* Based on a story by William Faulkner. 3m. 1w. 1 boy, extras. In *Visit to a Small Planet and Other Television Plays,* by Gore Vidal.

A vengeful sharecropper who deliberately sets barns afire is found out by his small son's disclosure.

————. *A Sense of Justice.* 5m. 2w. extras. In *Visit to a Small Planet and Other Television Plays,* by Gore Vidal.

A supposedly disinterested man, seeking justice, fails to kill a ruthless politician. The man suddenly realizes that he does have an interest in life after all.

————. *Smoke.* Based on a story by William Faulkner. 6m. extras. In *Visit to a Small Planet and Other Television Plays,* by Gore Vidal.

After an evil father is mysteriously murdered, his sons fall out with one another over the inheritance of the land.

————. *The Turn of the Screw*. Based on the story by Henry James. 1m. 2w. 1 boy, 1 girl. In *Visit to a Small Planet and Other Television Plays,* by Gore Vidal.

The evil spirits of former servants haunt two children who are protected by a loyal governess.

————. *Visit to a Small Planet*. In *Visit to a Small Planet and Other Television Plays,* by Gore Vidal. Comedy. Interior. 8m. 2w. Dramatists Play Service $1.75. Royalty $50—$25.

Kreton, who comes from the future and another planet, lands on earth, thinking he has arrived in time to see the Civil War. But he has misjudged and arrives in 1957 in an average community whose population includes a general, a boy and girl in love, a TV newscaster, and a Siamese cat. Just as he is about to entertain himself with a war, a compatriot comes to take him back.

Violett, Ellen. *The Lottery*. Based on the story by Shirley Jackson. 6m. 2w. 1 boy, extras. In *The Best Television Plays, 1950–1951,* ed. by William I. Kaufman.

The citizens of a small town participate in an outrageous lottery because it is customary to do so.

Wasserman, Dale, and Balch, Jack. *Elisha and the Long Knives*. 8m. 1w. In *Top TV Shows of the Year, 1954–1955,* ed. by Irving Settel.

The story of an orphan boy on the Santa Fe Trail in the 1840s.

Appendixes

Play Publishers and Agents

This directory lists publishers, distributors, or agents controlling amateur performance rights to plays described in the *Guide to Play Selection*. Addresses of authors representing their own works, if known, are also given. Publishers of the anthologies and collections described in the next section, or of plays in general, have not been listed.

The American Place Theatre, 111 West 46th Street, New York, New York 10036.

The Anchorage Press, Inc., Anchorage, Kentucky 40223.

Theodore Apstein, c/o Mel Bloom & Associates, 8693 Wilshire Boulevard, Beverly Hills, California 90211.

Associated Publishers, Inc., 1407 14th Street N.W., Washington, D.C. 20005.

Baker's Plays, 100 Chauncy Street, Boston, Massachusetts 02111.

Kingsley B. Bass, Jr., c/o Donald C. Farber, 800 Third Avenue, New York, New York 10022.

The Bethany Press, Box 179, Saint Louis, Missouri 63166. No royalty charged to groups using plays educationally if no admission fee is charged and if one copy of book is purchased for each speaking part.

James W. Butcher, c/o College of Fine Arts, Howard University, Washington, D.C. 20059.

Ben Caldwell, P.O. Box 656, Morningside Station, Harlem, New York 10026.

I. E. Clark, Box 246, Schulenburg, Texas 78956.

N. R. Davidson, address not known.

Dodd, Mead and Company, 79 Madison Avenue, New York, New York 10016.

Owen Dodson, 350 West 51st Street, Apt. 17-B, New York, New York 10019.

The Drama Review, 51 West 4th Street, Room 300, New York, New York 10012.

The Dramatic Publishing Company, 86 East Randolph Street, Chicago, Illinois 60601.

Dramatists Play Service, Inc., 440 Park Avenue South, New York, New York 10016.

Randolph Edmonds, P.O. Box 765, Lawrenceville, Virginia 23868.

Eldridge Publishing Company, P.O. Drawer 209, Franklin, Ohio 45005.

Exposition Press, Inc., 900 South Oyster Bay Road, Hicksville, New York 11801.

Samuel French, Inc., 25 West 45th Street, New York, New York 10036; western states: 7623 Sunset Boulevard, Hollywood, California 90046; Canada: 27 Grenville Street, Toronto, Ontario M4Y IAI.

Jimmie Garrett, address not known.

Raven Hail, 3061 Cridelle, Dallas, Texas 75220.

Hatch-Billops Studio, 736 Broadway, New York, New York 10003.

Ronald Hobbs Literary Agency, 211 East 43rd Street, New York, New York 10017.

Ninon Karlweis, 250 East 65th Street, New York, New York 10021.

The Sterling Lord Agency, Inc., 660 Madison Avenue, New York, New York 10021.

René Marqués, P.O. Box 432, San Juan, Puerto Rico 00902.

David McKay Company, Inc., Play Department, 750 Third Avenue, New York, New York 10017.

May Miller (Sullivan), 1632 S. Street N.W., Washington, D.C. 20009.

Ronald Milner, c/o Lewis, White, Lee, Clay & Graves, 409 Griswold, 8th floor, Detroit, Michigan 48226.

El Muhajir (Marvin X), c/o Black Educational Theatre, Inc., P.O. Box 6536, San Francisco, California 94101.

Music Theatre International, 119 West 57th Street, New York, New York 10019.

The New Dramatists, Inc., 424 West 44th Street, New York, New York 10036.

Harold Ober Associates, Inc., 40 East 49th Street, New York, New York 10017.

The O'Neill Memorial Theater Center, Inc., 305 Great Neck Road, Waterford, Connecticut 06385.

Charles Patterson, 1299 California, #20, San Francisco, California 94109.

Pioneer Drama Service, 2172 South Colorado Boulevard, Denver, Colorado 80222.

Plays, Inc., 8 Arlington Street, Boston, Massachusetts 02116.

Theodore Pratt, estate of, Route 1, Delray Beach, Florida 33444.

Willis Richardson, 2023 13th Street N.W., Washington, D.C. 20009. Royalty for each performance of a play by a high school: $10; college: $15; community group: $20 (per letter of 17 December 1974).

Flora Roberts, Inc., 116 East 59th Street, New York, New York 10022.

The Rodgers and Hammerstein Library, 598 Madison Avenue, New York, New York 10022.

Sonia Sanchez, address not known.

Tams-Witmark Music Library, Inc., 757 Third Avenue, New York, New York 10017.

Theatre Maximus, 1650 Broadway, Suite 501, New York, New York 10019.

Trucha Publications, Inc., Box 5223, Lubbock, Texas 79417.

Luis Valdez, Cucaracha Publications, P.O. Box 1278, San Juan Bautista, California 95045.

Vanderbilt University Press, Nashville, Tennessee 37235.

Anthologies and Collections of Plays

This bibliography lists the contents of anthologies and collections containing plays described in the *Guide to Play Selection*. Each anthology or collection is assigned a number, which is cross-referenced in the title index. Consultation of the title index will reveal the number of an anthology or collection in which a play may be found. With the few exceptions noted, the list is restricted to books in print at the time of this compilation and, in the main, to publishers within the United States. Some titles have been included as useful references though they do not contain any plays described in this guide.

1. *Absurd Drama*. Harmondsworth: Penguin Books, 1965.
Amádée, Professor Tatanne, Two Executioners, The Zoo Story.

2. Albee, Edward. *The Zoo Story, The Death of Bessie Smith, The Sandbox*. New York: G. P. Putnam's Sons, 1960.

3. Allison, Alexander W., et al., eds. *Masterpieces of the Drama*. 3rd ed. New York: Macmillan Co., 1974.
Oedipus Rex, Volpone, The Miser, The Rivals, Hedda Gabler, The Cherry Orchard, Riders to the Sea, Juno and the Paycock, The House of Bernarda Alba, The Madwoman of Chaillot, The Caucasian Chalk Circle, All That Fall, Act without Words.

4. Anderson, Maxwell. *Three Plays by Maxwell Anderson*. Ed. George Freedley. New York: Simon and Schuster, 1962.
Joan of Lorraine, Journey to Jerusalem, Valley Forge.

5. Anouilh, Jean. *Five Plays*. Vol. 1. New York: Hill and Wang, 1958.
Romeo and Jeanette, The Rehearsal, The Ermine, Antigone, Eurydice.

6. ———. *Five Plays*. Vol. 2. New York: Hill and Wang, 1959.
Ardèle, Time Remembered, Mademoiselle Colombe, The Restless Heart, The Lark.

7. ———. *Seven Plays*. Vol. 3. New York: Hill and Wang, 1967.
Thieves' Carnival, Medea, Cécile, or, The School for Fathers, Traveler without Luggage, The Orchestra, Episode in the Life of an Author, Catch as Catch Can.

8. Arden, John. *Three Plays*. New York: Grove Press, 1966.
Live like Pigs, The Waters of Babylon, The Happy Haven.

9. Ardrey, Robert. *Plays of Three Decades*. New York: Atheneum Publishers, 1968.
Thunder Rock, Jeb, The Shadow of Heroes.

10. Arrabal, Fernando. *Guernica and Other Plays*. New York: Grove Press, 1969.

The Labyrinth, The Tricycle, Picnic on the Battlefield, Guernica.

11. Atkinson, Brooks, ed. *New Voices in the American Theatre*. New York: Modern Library, 1955.

A Streetcar Named Desire, Death of a Salesman, Come Back, Little Sheba, The Seven Year Itch, Tea and Sympathy, The Caine Mutiny Court-Martial.

12. Bailey, J. Q., ed. *British Plays of the Nineteenth Century*. New York: Odyssey Press, 1966.

Bertram, or, The Castle of St. Aldobrand, Richelieu, The Patrician's Daughter, London Assurance, Our American Cousin, Tale of Mystery, Luke the Labourer, The Rent-Day, After Dark, East Lynne, The Silver King, Caste, Engaged, Widowers' Houses, The Masqueraders, The Notorious Mrs. Ebbsmith.

13. Ballet, Arthur H., ed. *Playwrights for Tomorrow*. 11 vols. Minneapolis: University of Minnesota Press, 1966–73.

Vol. 1: The Space Fan, The Master, Ex-Miss Copper Queen on a Set of Pills, A Bad Play for an Old Lady, And Things That Go Bump in the Night.

Vol. 2: Tango Palace, The Successful Life of Three, A Skit for Vaudeville, Shelter Area, The Boy Who Came to Leave.

Vol. 3: Five Easy Payments, Where Is the Queen?, The Great Git-Away, With Malice Aforethought, I, Elizabeth Otis, Being of Sound Mind.

Vol. 4: The World Tipped Over, and Laying on Its Side, Visions of Sugar Plums, The Strangler, The Long War.

Vol. 5: Fair Beckoning One, The New Chautauqua.

Vol. 6: The Thing Itself, The Marriage Test, The End of the World, or, Fragments from a Work in Progress.

Vol. 7: Grace and George and God, Assassin!, Freddie the Pigeon, Rags, The Orientals, Drive-In.

Vol. 8: A Gun Play, Anniversary on Weedy Hill, The Nihilist.

Vol. 9: Encore, Madame Popov, Children of the Kingdom, Psalms of Two Davids.

Vol. 10: The Unknown Chinaman, Fox, Hound, and Huntress, Escape by Balloon, Stops, Three Miles to Poley.

Vol. 11: Boxes, Canvas, Bierce Takes On the Railroad!, Chamber Piece.

14. Baraka, Imamu Amiri (LeRoi Jones). *The Baptism and The Toilet*. New York: Grove Press, 1966.

15. ———. *Dutchman and The Slave.* New York: William Morrow and Co., 1964.

16. ———. *Four Black Revolutionary Plays.* Indianapolis: Bobbs-Merrill, 1969.
Experimental Death Unit #1, A Black Mass, Great Goodness of Life: A Coon Show, Manheart.

17. Barnes, Clive, ed. *Fifty Best Plays of the American Theatre.* Vols. 1–4. New York: Crown Publishers, 1969.
Vol. 1: The Contrast, Salvation Nell, Rain, Porgy, Street Scene, Men in White, Uncle Tom's Cabin, The Hairy Ape, Desire under the Elms, The Front Page, Green Pastures, Tobacco Road.
Vol. 2: The Children's Hour, Ethan Frome, You Can't Take It with You, Abe Lincoln in Illinois, The Man Who Came to Dinner, Awake and Sing!, Bury the Dead, High Tor, Golden Boy, On Borrowed Time, The Matchmaker, The Philadelphia Story, Life with Father.
Vol. 3: The Time of Your Life, Arsenic and Old Lace, The Glass Menagerie, A Streetcar Named Desire, State of the Union, Harvey, Dream Girl, Born Yesterday, Medea, Death of a Salesman, The Member of the Wedding, Mister Roberts.
Vol. 4: Come Back, Little Sheba, The Seven Year Itch, Tea and Sympathy, The Diary of Anne Frank, Two for the Seesaw, Who's Afraid of Virginia Woolf?, The Fourposter, The Crucible, The Teahouse of the August Moon, Look Homeward Angel, Oh Dad Poor Dad . . . , The Odd Couple, Fiddler on the Roof.

18. ———. *John Gassner's Best American Plays—Seventh Series, 1967–73.* New York: Crown Publishers, 1974.
Ceremonies in Dark Old Men, Scuba Duba, The Price, The House of Blue Leaves, Sticks and Bones, 1776, Lemon Sky, Indians, Subject to Fits, Tom Paine, Little Murders, Play It Again, Sam, The Prisoner of Second Avenue, The Great White Hope, The Boys in the Band, Morning, Noon, and Night.

19. Barnet, Sylvan, Berman, Morton, and Burto, William, eds. *Tragedy and Comedy: An Anthology of Drama.* Boston: Little, Brown and Co., 1967.
Oedipus the King, The Birds, Othello, Hedda Gabler, As You Like It, The Misanthrope, Henry IV, Major Barbara, A Streetcar Named Desire, The Matchmaker.

20. Barrie, James M. *The Plays.* New York: Charles Scribner's Sons, 1952.
Peter Pan, or, The Boy Who Would Not Grow Up, Quality Street, The Admirable Crichton, Alice Sit-by-the-Fire, What Every Woman Knows,

A Kiss for Cinderella, Dear Brutus, Mary Rose, Pantaloon, Half an Hour, Seven Women, Old Friends, Rosalind, The Will, The Twelve-Pound Look, The New Word, A Well-Remembered Voice, Barbara's Wedding, The Old Lady Shows Her Medals, Shall We Join the Ladies?

21. Bauer, Wolfgang. *Change and Other Plays*. Tr. Martin Esslin, et al. New York: Hill and Wang, 1973.
Change, Party for Six, Magic Afternoon.

22. Bauland, Peter, and Ingram, William, eds. *The Tradition of the Theatre*. Boston: Allyn and Bacon, 1971.
Antigone, The Second Shepherds' Play, The Duchess of Malfi, The Would-Be Gentleman, The Country Wife, Hedda Gabler, The Devil's Disciple, A Dream Play, The Cherry Orchard, The Caucasian Chalk Circle, The Crucible, The Visit.

23. Beckett, Samuel. *Cascando and Other Short Dramatic Pieces*. New York: Grove Press, 1969.
Cascando, Words and Music, Film, Play, Come and Go, Eh Joe.

24. ———. *Krapp's Last Tape and Other Dramatic Pieces*. New York: Grove Press, 1960.
Krapp's Last Tape, All That Fall, Embers, Act without Words I, Act without Words II.

25. Behan, Brendan. *The Quare Fellow and The Hostage: Two Plays*. New York: Grove Press, 1965.

26. Benedikt, Michael, ed. *A Theatre Experiment: An Anthology of American Plays*. Garden City: Doubleday and Co., 1967.
The Long Christmas Dinner, The Ping-Pong Players, The Tridget of Greva, Abend di Anni Nouveau, Three Travelers Watch a Sunrise, Santa Claus, The Birthday, Benito Cereno, George Washington Crossing the Delaware, Hot Buttered Roll, Gallows Humor, The Falling Sickness, Poem-Plays, What Happened, Flower, Meat Joy, Gas.

27. Benedikt, Michael, and Wellwarth, George E., eds. *Modern French Theatre*. New York: E. P. Dutton and Co., 1964.
Ubu Roi, The Breasts of Tiresias, Wedding at the Eiffel Tower, The Pelicans, The Gas Heart, If You Please, The Mirror Wardrobe, One Fine Evening, Circus Story, Jet of Blood, En G-g-g-g-garrde, Odyssey of Ulysses Palmiped, Mysteries of Love, Humulus the Mute, La Place de L'Étoile, One Way for Another, Architruc, The Painting.

28. ———. *Modern Spanish Theatre*. New York: E. P. Dutton and Co., 1968.
Divine Words, The Shoemaker's Prodigious Wife, Three Top Hats,

Night and War in the Prado Museum, Suicide Prohibited in Springtime, First Communion, The New Item, Football.

29. ———. *Postwar German Theatre*. New York: E. P. Dutton and Co., 1968.

Raft of the Medusa, The Outsider, Dr. Korczaki and the Children, Incident at Twilight, Great Fury of Phillip Hotz, Freedom for Clemens, Let's Eat Hair, The Chinese Icebox, Rocking Back and Forth, Nightpiece, The Tower.

30. Bentley, Eric, ed. *From the Modern Repertoire, Series 1–3*. Bloomington: Indiana University Press, 1949–56.

Series 1: Fantasio, Danton's Death, La Parisienne, Round Dance, The Snob, Sweeney Agonistes, The Threepenny Opera, The Love of Don Perlimplin and Belisa in the Garden, The Infernal Machine, A Full Moon in March.

Series 2: Jest, Satire, Irony and Deeper Significance, Easy Money, The Epidemic, The Marquis of Keith, Him, Venus and Adonis, Electra, The King and the Duke, The Dark Tower, Galileo.

Series 3: Leonce and Lena, A Door Should Be Either Open or Shut, Thérèse Raquin, The Magistrate, Anatole, Dr. Knock, Saint Joan of the Stockyards, Intimate Relations, Cécile, or, The School for Fathers, The Cretan Woman.

31. ———. *Let's Get a Divorce and Other Plays*. New York: Hill and Wang, 1958.

A Trip Abroad, Célimaré, Let's Get a Divorce!, These Corn Fields, Keep an Eye on Amelie!, A United Family.

32. ———. *The Modern Theatre*. Vols. 1–6. Garden City: Doubleday and Co., 1955–57.

Vol. 1: Woyzeck, Cavalleria Rusticana, Woman of Paris, The Threepenny Opera, Electra.

Vol. 2: Fantasio, Diary of a Scoundrel, La Ronde, Purgatory, Mother Courage and Her Children.

Vol. 3: The Gamblers, Italian Straw Hat, One Day More, Judith, Thieves' Carnival.

Vol. 4: From the American Drama: Guys and Dolls, Captain Jinks of the Horse Marines, New York Idea, Pullman Car Hiawatha, The Man with His Heart in the Highlands.

Vol. 5: Danton's Death, The Marriage, Escurial, Medea, Cock-a-Doodle Dandy.

Vol. 6: Lorenzaccio, Spring's Awakening, Underpants, Social Success, Measures Taken.

33. Bernard, Kenneth. *Night Club and Other Plays*. New York: Drama Book Specialists, 1973.
Night Club, The Moke-Eater, The Lovers, Mary Jane, The Monkeys of the Organ Grinder, The Giants in the Earth.

34. Bertin, Charles. *Two Plays by Charles Bertin*. Tr. William J. Smith. Minneapolis: University of Minnesota Press, 1970.
Christopher Columbus, Don Juan.

35. Betti, Ugo. *Three Plays*. Tr. Henry Reed. New York: Grove Press, 1958.
The Queen and the Rebels, The Burnt Flower-Bed, Summertime.

36. Birner, William B., ed. *Twenty Plays for Young People*. Anchorage, Ky.: Anchorage Press, 1967.
Jack and the Beanstalk, Tom Sawyer, The Indian Captive, The Ghost of Mr. Penny, Rumpelstiltskin, Peter, Peter, Pumpkin Eater, The Land of the Dragon, Huckleberry Finn, Arthur and the Magic Sword, Niccolo and Nicolette, Reynard the Fox, Johnny Moonbeam and the Silver Arrow, Abe Lincoln of Pigeon Creek, The Man Who Killed Time, Androcles and the Lion, Two Pails of Water, Rags to Riches, The Great Cross-Country Race, Trudi and the Minstrel, Don Quixote of La Mancha.

37. *Black Quartet*. New York: New American Library, 1970.
Prayer Meeting, or, The First Militant Minister, The Warning, The Gentleman Caller, Great Goodness of Life: A Coon Show.

38. Block, Haskell M., and Shedd, Robert G., eds. *Masters of Modern Drama*. New York: Random House, 1962.
Peer Gynt, Ghosts, Miss Julie, The Ghost Sonata, The Weavers, The Intruder, Death and the Fool, The Sea Gull, The Cherry Orchard, The Lower Depths, La Ronde, The Marquis of Keith, Man and Superman, Major Barbara, Riders to the Sea, The Playboy of the Western World, At the Hawks Well, Juno and the Paycock, Cock-a-Doodle Dandy, From Morn to Midnight, Henry IV, Orphée, Blood Wedding, The Emperor Jones, The Iceman Cometh, Awake and Sing, The Time of Your Life, Electra, The Madwoman of Chaillot, Thieves' Carnival, Antigone, No Exit, Caligula, Mother Courage and Her Children, The Good Woman of Setzuan, The Devil's General, The Matchmaker, The Glass Menagerie, Death of a Salesman, Marty, Look Back in Anger, Endgame, The Bald Soprano, The Visit, Biedermann and the Firebugs.

39. Bloomfield, Morton W., and Elliott, Robert C., eds. *Great Plays: Sophocles to Brecht*. Rev. ed. New York: Holt, Rinehart and Winston, 1965.

Antigone, Othello, The Misanthrope, The Way of the World, Miss Julie, Hedda Gabler, Arms and the Man, The Three Sisters, The Hairy Ape, The Glass Menagerie, The Caucasian Chalk Circle.

40. Booth, Michael R., ed. *English Plays of the Nineteenth Century.* Vols. 2–4. New York: Oxford University Press, 1969–73.
Vol. 2: Dramas 1850–1900: The Corsican Brothers, The Ticket-of-Leave Man, The Shaughraun, The Second Mrs. Tanqueray, Mrs. Dane's Defence.
Vol. 3: Comedies: John Bull, Money, New Men and Old Acres, Engaged, The Tyranny of Tears.
Vol. 4: Farces: Raising the Wind, Mr. Paul Pry, Patter versus Clatter, Diamond Cut Diamond, How to Settle Accounts with Your Laundress, Box and Cox, The Area Belle, Tom Cobb, The Magistrate.

41. Bradbury, Ray. *The Wonderful Ice Cream Suit and Other Plays.* New York: Bantam Books, 1972.
The Wonderful Ice Cream Suit, The Veldt, To the Chicago Abyss.

42. Brasmer, William, and Consolo, Dominick, eds. *Black Drama: An Anthology.* Columbus: Charles E. Merrill Publishing Co., 1970.
Contribution, Native Son, Day of Absence, Happy Ending, Funny-house of a Negro, Purlie Victorious.

43. Brecht, Bertolt. *Collected Plays.* Vol. 1. Eds. Ralph Manheim and John Willett. New York: Random House, 1971.
Baal, Drums in the Night, In the Jungle of Cities, The Life of Edward the Second of England, The Beggar, or, The Dead Dog, The Catch, He Drives Out a Devil, Lux in Tenebris, The Wedding.

44. ————. *Collected Plays.* Vol. 5. Eds. Ralph Manheim and John Willett. New York: Random House, 1972.
The Life of Galileo, The Trial of Lucullus, Mother Courage and Her Children.

45. ————. *Collected Plays.* Vol. 7. Eds. Ralph Manheim and John Willett. New York: Random House, 1975.
The Visions of Simone Machard, Schweyk in the Second World War, The Caucasian Chalk Circle, The Duchess of Malfi.

46. ————. *Collected Plays.* Vol. 9. Eds. Ralph Manheim and John Willett. New York: Random House, 1973.
The Tutor, Coriolanus, The Trial of Joan of Arc at Rouen, 1431, Trumpets and Drums.

47. ————. *The Jewish Wife and Other Short Plays.* Tr. Eric Bentley. New York: Grove Press, 1965.

The Jewish Wife, In Search of Justice, The Informer, The Elephant Calf, The Measures Taken, The Exception and the Rule, Salzburg Dance of Death.

48. ———. *Jungle of Cities and Other Plays.* Tr. Eric Bentley. New York: Grove Press, 1965.
In the Jungle of Cities, Drums in the Night, Roundheads and Peakheads.

49. ———. *Seven Plays.* Tr. Eric Bentley. New York: Grove Press, 1961.
Galileo, Saint Joan of the Stockyards, In the Swamp, A Man's a Man, Mother Courage and Her Children. The Good Woman of Setzuan, The Caucasian Chalk Circle.

50. Brockett, Oscar, and Brockett, Lenyth, eds. *Plays for the Theatre: An Anthology of World Drama.* 2nd ed. New York: Holt, Rinehart and Winston, 1974.
The School for Scandal, Oedipus Rex, The Menaechmi, The Second Shepherds' Play, King Lear, Tartuffe, The Wild Duck, From Morn to Midnight, The Good Woman of Setzuan, The Death of a Salesman, The New Tenant, Sticks and Bones.

51. Bulgakov, Mikhail. *The Early Plays of Mikhail Bulgakov.* Tr. Carl and Ellendea Proffer, et al. Bloomington: Indiana University Press, 1972.
The Days of the Turbins, Zoga's Apartment, Flight, The Crimson Island, A Cabal of Hypocrites.

52. Bullins, Ed. *Five Plays.* Indianapolis: Bobbs-Merrill, 1969.
Goin' a Buffalo, In the Wine Time, A Son, Come Home, The Electronic Nigger, Clara's Ole Man.

53. ———. *Four Dynamite Plays.* New York: William Morrow and Co., 1972.
It Bees Dat Way, Death List, The Pig Pen, Night of the Beat.

54. Bullins, Ed, ed. *The New Lafayette Theater Presents the Complete Plays and Aesthetic Comments by Six Black Playwrights.* Garden City: Doubleday and Co., 1974.
The Fabulous Miss Marie, What If It Had Turned Up Heads, On Being Hit, His First Step, Uh, Uh, But How Do It Free Us?, Black Terror.

55. ———. *New Plays from the Black Theatre.* New York: Bantam Books, 1969.
The Death of Malcolm X, The Rise, In New England Winter, El Hajj Malik, Family Portrait, Growin' into Blackness, Sister Son/Ji, The

King of Soul, The Man Who Trusted the Devil Twice, The Black Bird, We Righteous Bombers.

56. Burack, A. S., ed. *Prize Contest Plays for Young People*. Rev. ed. Boston: Plays, Inc., 1969.
Orchids for Margaret, N for Nuisance, Mind over Matter, The Cuckoo, Cry Witch, Sticks and Stones, Minority of Millions, All This and Alan Too, The Ten-Penny Tragedy, The Nerve of Napoleon, Society Page, Jimmy Six, Runaway, The Straw Boy.

57. ———. *Television Plays for Writers*. Boston: The Writer, Inc., 1957.
The Narrow Man, A Real Fine Cutting Edge, Flight, Mock Trial, The Out-of-Towners, Tragedy in a Temporary Town, Noon on Dooms-day, Honor.

58. Camus, Albert. *Caligula and Three Other Plays*. New York: Vintage Books, 1962.
Caligula, The Misunderstanding, State of Siege, The Just Assassins.

59. Capote, Truman, Perry, Eleanor, and Perry, Frank, eds. *Trilogy: An Experiment in Multimedia*. New York: Macmillan Co., 1971.
A Christmas Memory, Miriam, Among the Paths to Eden.

60. Caputi, Anthony, ed. *Masterworks of World Drama: Romanticism and Realism*. Vol. 6. Lexington: D. C. Heath and Co., 1968.
Prince Friedrich of Hamburg, The Inspector General, Danton's Death, The Cenci, A Month in the Country.

61. ———. *Modern Drama: Annotated Texts with Critical Essays*. New York: W. W. Norton and Co., 1966.
The Wild Duck, The Three Sisters, The Devil's Disciple, A Dream Play, Desire under the Elms, Henry IV.

62. Cassell, Richard A., and Knepler, Henry, eds. *What Is the Play?* Glenview, Ill.: Scott, Foresman and Co., 1967.
Hughie, Arms and the Man, King Henry IV (Part I), An Enemy of the People, The Matchmaker, Scapin, The Alchemist, My Kinsman, Major Molineux, Antigone, The Visit, Christopher Columbus.

63. Cerf, Bennett, ed. *Four Contemporary American Plays*. New York: Vintage Books, 1961.
The Tenth Man, A Raisin in the Sun, Toys in the Attic, The Andersonville Trial.

64. ———. *Plays of Our Time*. New York: Random House, 1967.
The Iceman Cometh, A Streetcar Named Desire, Death of a Salesman,

Mister Roberts, Come Back, Little Sheba, Look Back in Anger, A Raisin in the Sun, A Man for All Seasons, Luv.

65. ——. *Six American Plays for Today.* New York: Modern Library, 1961.
Camino Real, The Dark at the Top of the Stairs, Sunrise at Campobello, A Raisin in the Sun, The Tenth Man, Toys in the Attic.

66. Cerf, Bennett, and Cartmell, Van H., eds. *Sixteen Famous American Plays.* New York: Modern Library, 1941.
They Knew What They Wanted, The Front Page, The Green Pastures, Biography, Ah, Wilderness!, The Petrified Forest, Waiting for Lefty, Dead End, Boy Meets Girl, The Women, Having Wonderful Time, Our Town, The Little Foxes, The Man Who Came to Dinner, The Time of Your Life, Life with Father.

67. ——. *Sixteen Famous British Plays.* New York: Modern Library, 1942.
The Green Goddess, What Every Woman Knows, Milestones, The Barretts of Wimpole Street, Cavalcade, Loyalties, Victoria Regina, The Circle, Mr. Pim Passes By, The Second Mrs. Tanqueray, Dangerous Corner, The Green Bay Tree, Journey's End, Outward Bound, The Importance of Being Earnest, The Corn Is Green.

68. ——. *Sixteen Famous European Plays.* New York: Modern Library, 1943.
The Wild Duck, The Weavers, The Sea Gull, The Lower Depths, The Dybbuk, Cyrano de Bergerac, Tovarich, Amphitryon, The Cradle Song, Six Characters in Search of an Author, Anatol, R.U.R., Liliom, Grand Hotel, The Playboy of the Western World, Shadow and Substance.

69. ——. *Thirty Famous One-Act Plays.* New York: Modern Library, 1949.
The Man Who Married a Dumb Wife, Miss Julie, Salomé, The Rising of the Moon, The Boor, The Twelve-Pound Look, The Green Cockatoo, A Miracle of St. Anthony, The Monkey's Paw, The Little Man, Riders to the Sea, A Sunny Morning, A Night at an Inn, The Dear Departed, The Drums of Oude, Helena's Husband, Suppressed Desires, The Game of Chess, Lithuania, The Valiant, In the Zone, If Men Played Cards as Women Do, Another Way Out, The Clod, Aria da Capo, Overtones, Fumed Oak, Waiting for Lefty, Hello Out There, Bury the Dead.

70. ——. *Twenty-Four Favorite One-Act Plays.* Garden City: Doubleday and Co., 1958.
A Memory of Two Mondays, The Browning Version, Twenty-Seven Wagons Full of Cotton, Sorry, Wrong Number, Glory in the Flower, Hands across the Sea, The Devil and Daniel Webster, The Happy

Journey, Here We Are, The Traveler, The Still Alarm, The Moon of the Caribbees, The Maker of Dreams, The Flattering Word, The Tridget of Greva, The Apollo of Bellac, Trifles, The Ugly Duckling, The Jest of Hahalaba, In the Shadow of the Glen, Cathleen ni Houlihan, A Marriage Proposal, Spreading the News, A Florentine Tragedy.

71. Chayefsky, Paddy. *Television Plays.* New York: Simon and Schuster, 1955, out of print.

Holiday Song, Printer's Measure, The Big Deal, Marty, The Mother, The Bachelor Party.

72. Chekhov, Anton. *Best Plays by Anton Chekhov.* Tr. Stark Young. New York: Modern Library, 1956.

The Sea Gull, Uncle Vanya, The Three Sisters, The Cherry Orchard.

73. ———. *The Brute and Other Farces.* Tr. Eric Bentley, et al. New York: Grove Press, 1958.

The Brute, The Harmfulness of Tobacco, Swan Song, The Marriage Proposal, Summer in the Country, A Wedding, The Celebration.

74. ———. *Four Plays.* Tr. David Magarshack. New York: Hill and Wang, 1969.

The Seagull, Uncle Vanya, The Cherry Orchard, The Three Sisters.

75. Clark, Barrett H., and Davenport, William H. *Nine Modern Plays.* New York: Appleton-Century-Crofts, 1951.

The Hairy Ape, Street Scene, Green Grow the Lilacs, High Tor, Stage Door, You Can't Take It with You, Abe Lincoln in Illinois, The Glass Menagerie, Command Decision.

76. *Classic Irish Drama.* Harmondsworth: Penguin Books, 1964.

Countess Cathleen, The Playboy of the Western World, Cock-a-Doodle Dandy.

77. Clayes, Stanley A., ed. *Drama and Discussion.* New York: Appleton-Century-Crofts, 1967.

The Libation Bearers, Electra (Sophocles), Hamlet, The Trojan Women, Tiger at the Gates, Riders to the Sea, Blood Wedding, Mother Courage and Her Children, Saint Joan, The Lark, Ghosts, The Cherry Orchard, A Streetcar Named Desire, All That Fall.

78. Clayes, Stanley, and Spencer, David, eds. *Contemporary Drama: Thirteen Plays.* 2nd ed. New York: Charles Scribner's Sons, 1970.

The Wild Duck, Uncle Vanya, Miss Julie, The House of Bernarda Alba, Ondine, The Caucasian Chalk Circle, The Devil's Disciple, Juno and the Paycock, The Country Girl, The Rose Tattoo, A View from the Bridge, America Hurrah, A Son, Come Home.

79. Clurman, Harold, ed. *Famous American Plays of the Nineteen Sixties.* New York: Dell Publications, 1972.
We Bombed in New Haven, The Boys in the Band, Hogan's Goat, Benito Cereno, The Indian Wants the Bronx.

80. ———. *Famous American Plays of the Nineteen Thirties.* New York: Dell Publications, 1959.
Awake and Sing, End of Summer, Idiot's Delight, Of Mice and Men, Time of Your Life.

81. ———. *Seven Plays of the Modern Theatre.* New York: Grove Press, 1962.
Waiting for Godot, The Quare Fellow, Taste of Honey, The Connection, The Balcony, Rhinoceros, The Birthday Party.

82. Cocteau, Jean. *Five Plays.* New York: Hill and Wang, 1961.
The Eagle with Two Heads, Antigone, Orphée, The Holy Terrors, Intimate Relations.

83. ———. *The Infernal Machine and Other Plays.* Tr. W. H. Auden, et al. New York: New Directions, 1967.
Orpheus, The Infernal Machine, The Knights of the Round Table, Bacchus, The Eiffel Tower Wedding Party, Oedipus Rex.

84. Cohen, Helen Louise, ed. *One-Act Plays by Modern Authors.* New York: Harcourt Brace Jovanovich, 1968.
Beauty and the Jacobin, Pierrot of the Minute, The Maker of Dreams, Gettysburg, Wurzel-Flummery, Maid of France, Spreading the News, Welsh Honeymoon, Boy Will, Riders to the Sea, A Night at an Inn, Twilight Saint, Masque of Two Strangers, The Intruder, Fortune and Men's Eyes, Little Man.

85. Cohn, Ruby, and Dukore, Bernard, eds. *Twentieth Century Drama.* New York: Random House, 1966.
Juno and the Paycock, Major Barbara, The Playboy of the Western World, The Only Jealousy of Elmer, Murder in the Cathedral, Awake and Sing.

86. Collins, Margaret, and Collins, Fletcher Jr., eds. *Theatre Wagon: Plays of Place and Any Place.* Charlottesville: University of Virginia Press, 1973.
Love Is a Daisy, Birdwatchers, A Merry Death, On the Corner of Cherry and Elsewhere, Sandcastle, Three Filosofers in a Firetower, Styopik and Manya.

87. Congdon, S. P., ed. *Drama Reader: Full-length Plays for the Secondary School.* 2nd ed. New York: Odyssey Press, 1962.

Seven Keys to Baldpate, Dulcy, R.U.R., Antigone, Richard III.

88. Coover, Robert. *A Theological Position: Four Plays*. New York: E. P. Dutton and Co., 1972.

The Kid, Love Scene, Rip Awake, A Theological Position.

89. Corbin, Richard, and Balf, Miriam, eds. *Twelve American Plays*. Alt. ed. New York: Charles Scribner's Sons, 1973.

Arsenic and Old Lace, The Little Foxes, The Rainmaker, Our Town, The Teahouse of the August Moon, There Shall Be No Night, The King and I, Requiem for a Heavyweight, Harvey, The Glass Menagerie, Day of Absence.

90. Corrigan, Robert, ed. *Comedy: A Critical Anthology*. Boston: Houghton Mifflin Co., 1971.

Lysistrata, Twelfth Night, Volpone, Tartuffe, The School for Scandal, The Importance of Being Earnest, The Cherry Orchard, The Playboy of the Western World, The Madwoman of Chaillot, Puntilla and His Hired Hand, The Last Analysis.

91. ———. *Masterpieces of the Modern Central European Theatre*. New York: Macmillan Co., 1967.

Game of Love, La Ronde, Electra, R.U.R., The Play's the Thing.

92. ———. *Masterpieces of the Modern Theatre*. Vols. 1–8. New York: Macmillan Co., 1967.

Vol. 1: English: The Importance of Being Earnest, Major Barbara, Loyalties, Dear Brutus, Enter Sally Gold.

Vol. 2: French: The Parisian Woman, Christopher Columbus, Electra, Eurydice, Queen after Death, Improvisation of the Shepherd's Chameleon.

Vol. 3: German: Woyzeck, Maria Magdalena, The Weavers, The Marquis of Keith, The Caucasian Chalk Circle.

Vol. 4: Irish: The Countess Cathleen, The Playboy of the Western World, Riders to the Sea, The Silver Tassie, Cock-a-Doodle Dandy.

Vol. 5: Italian: Six Characters in Search of an Author, The Pleasure of Honesty, Crime on Goat Island, Filumena Marturano, The Academy, The Return.

Vol. 6: Russian: A Month in the Country, Uncle Vanya, The Cherry Orchard, The Lower Depths, The Bedbug.

Vol. 7: Scandinavian: Hedda Gabler, Miss Julie, The Ghost Sonata, The Difficult Hour, The Defeat, Anna Sophie Hedvig.

Vol. 8: Spanish: The Witches' Sabbath, The Cradle Song, The Love of Don Perlimplin and Belisa in the Garden, The Dream Weaver, Death Thrust.

93. ———. *The Modern Theatre.* New York: Macmillan Co., 1964. Woyzeck, Maria Magdalene, The Weavers, La Ronde, The Marquis of Keith, Electra (Hofmannsthal), The Caucasian Chalk Circle, The Chinese Wall, The Visit, The Wild 'Duck, Hedda Gabler, Miss Julie, The Ghost Sonata, Uncle Vanya, The Lower Depths, Six Characters in Search of an Author, The Queen and the Rebels, Yerma, Anna Kleiber, Electra (Giraudoux), Eurydice, The Victors, Deathwatch, The Chairs, Endgame, On Baile's Strand, The Playboy of the Western World, The Plough and the Stars, Major Barbara, Murder in the Cathedral, A Sleep of Prisoners, Desire under the Elms, The Little Foxes, The Time of Your Life, The Skin of Our Teeth, The Glass Menagerie, A View from the Bridge.

94. ———. *New American Plays.* Vol. 1. New York: Hill and Wang, 1965. The Death and Life of Sneaky Fitch, Socrates Wounded, Constantinople Smith, The Hundred and First, Ginger Anne, Pigeons, The Golden Bull of Boredom, Blood Money, Mr. Briggs, A Summer Ghost.

95. ———. *New Theatre of Europe.* Vols. 1–3. New York: Dell Publications, 1962–68. Vol. 1: A Man for All Seasons, Anna Kleiber, Masks of Angels, Pantagleize, Corruption in the Palace of Justice. Vol. 2: Mother Courage and Her Children, The Cage, The Suicide, The Wicked Cooks, Vasco. Vol. 3: Inadmissible Evidence, The Sunday Promenade, The Curve, The Laundry.

96. ———. *The Twentieth Century: British Drama.* New York: Dell Publications, 1965. Heartbreak House, Loyalties, Private Lives, The Chalk Garden, A Man for All Seasons, The Knack.

97. Costigan, James. *Little Moon of Alban and A Wind from the South.* New York: Simon and Schuster, 1959, out of print.

98. Couch, William Jr., ed. *New Black Playwrights.* New York: Avon Books, 1970. Happy Ending, Day of Absence, A Rat's Mass, Ceremonies in Dark Old Men, Goin' a Buffalo, Family Meeting.

99. Courteline, Georges. *Plays of Courteline.* Vol. 1. Tr. Albert Bermel, et al. New York: Theatre Arts, 1961. Article Three Hundred and Thirty, Badiñ the Bold, Hold On, Hortense, Afraid to Fight, Boubouroche.

100. Cox, Alva I., ed. *The Delinquent, The Hipster, and The Square,* by Elliott Baker. St. Louis: Bethany Press, 1962.

101. Cox, R. David, and Cox, Shirley S., eds. *Themes in the One-Act Play.* New York: McGraw-Hill Book Co., 1971.
The Long Fall, The Rope, Crawling Arnold, The Bridge, Here We Are, Pyramus and Thisbe, The Golden Axe, Sunday Costs Five Pesos, The Beer Can Tree, Something Unspoken, Waiting for the Bus, The Governor's Lady, Sorry, Wrong Number, Hello Out There, Pullman Car Hiawatha, Riders to the Sea.

102. Cubeta, Paul, ed. *Modern Drama for Analysis.* 3rd ed. New York: Holt, Rinehart and Winston, 1962.
The Glass Menagerie, The Cherry Orchard, The Devil's Disciple, Rosmersholm, Desire under the Elms, The Skin of Our Teeth, View from the Bridge, Becket, The Sandbox.

103. Dana, H. W. L., ed. *Seven Soviet Plays.* New York: Macmillan Co., 1946.
Field Marshall Kutuzov, The Orchards of Polovchansk, On the Eve, Smoke of the Fatherland, Engineer Sergeyev, The Russian People, The Front.

104. Dean, Leonard F., ed. *Twelve Great Plays.* New York: Harcourt Brace Jovanovich, 1970.
Agamemnon, Oedipus Rex, The Jew of Malta, Henry IV (Part I), The Alchemist, Tartuffe, Ghosts, The Cherry Orchard, Six Characters in Search of an Author, The Caucasian Chalk Circle, The Glass Menagerie, The House of Cowards.

105. Dean, Phillip Hayes. *The Sty of the Blind Pig and Other Plays.* Indianapolis: Bobbs-Merrill, 1973.
The Sty of the Blind Pig, American Night Cry (a trilogy).

106. De León, Nephtalí. *Five Plays.* Denver: Totínem Publications, 1972.
The Death of Ernesto Nerios, ¡Chicanos! The Living and the Dead!, Play Number 9, The Judging of Man, The Flies.

107. Dent, Anthony, ed. *International Modern Plays.* New York: E. P. Dutton and Co., 1950.
Life of the Insects, The Mask and the Face, The Infernal Machine, Hannele, Miss Julie.

108. Dias, Earl J., ed. *New Comedies for Teen-agers.* Boston: Plays, Inc., 1970.
Way, Way Down East, Feudin's Fun, The Sands of Time, Stop the

Presses, The Case of the Missing Pearls, Strong and Silent, Out of This
World, Stage Bare, The Natives are Restless Tonight, Abner Crane
from Hayseed Lane, The Face Is Familiar, What Ho!

109. ———. *One-Act Plays for Teen-agers*. Boston: Plays, Inc., 1961.
Landslide for Shakespeare, Printer's Devil, Hold Back the Redskins,
Bow-Wow Blues, The Beatnik and the Bard, The Cleanest Town in the
West, Treasure at Bentley Inn, The Gift of Laughter, Video Christ-
mas, Christmas Spirit, Dean Lottie, Cast Up by the Sea, The Little
Man Who Wasn't There, The Mantle, Madison Avenue Merry-Go-
Round.

110. Dickinson, Thomas H., ed. *Chief Contemporary Dramatists*. 3rd
series. Boston: Houghton Mifflin Co., 1930.
The Emperor Jones, In Abraham's Bosom, The Silver Cord, The Dover
Road, Juno and the Paycock, Such Is Life, From Morn to Midnight,
Electra, The Steamship Tenacity, Time Is a Dream, Naked, The Love
of Three Kings, Malvaloca, A Lily among Thorns, He Who Gets
Slapped, The Theatre of the Soul, Liliom, R.U.R., The Dybbuk,
Eyvind of the Hills.

111. Dietrick, R. F., Carpenter, William E., and Kerrane, Kevin, eds.
The Art of Modern Drama. New York: Holt, Rinehart and Winston,
1969.
The Wild Duck, Caesar and Cleopatra, The Cherry Orchard, A View
from the Bridge, The Glass Menagerie, The Caucasian Chalk Circle,
Luther, A Raisin in the Sun.

112. Dietz, Norman D., ed. *Fables and Vaudevilles and Plays*. Rich-
mond: John Knox Press, 1968.
The Apple Bit, Tilly Tutweiler's Silly Trip to the Moon, Deux ex
Machinist, Old Ymir's Clay Pot, Harry and the Angel, O to Be Living, O to Be Dying.

113. Dizenzo, Charles. *Big Mother and Other Plays*. New York: Grove
Press, 1970.
Big Mother, An Evening for Merlin Finch, The Last Straw.

114. Dodson, Daniel B., ed. *Twelve Modern Plays*. Belmont, Calif.:
Wadsworth Publishing Co., 1970.
The Wild Duck, Miss Julie, The Three Sisters, Henry IV, Heartbreak
House, The Playboy of the Western World, The House of Bernarda
Alba, The Good Woman of Setzuan, Tiger at the Gates, Antigone,
The Little Foxes, The Crucible.

115. Donleavy, J. P. *The Plays of J. P. Donleavy*. New York: Dela-
corte Press, 1972.

The Ginger Man, Fairy Tales of New York, A Singular Man, The Sad-
dest Summer of Samuel S.

116. Downer, Alan, ed. *Great World Theater: An Introduction to
Drama.* New York: Harper and Row, 1964.
The Bacchae, Antigone, The Little Ghost, The Toy Cart, Everyman,
The Duchess of Malfi, The Misanthrope, She Stoops to Conquer, Sol-
ness, The Master Builder, Three Sisters, Tiger at the Gates, The Skin
of Our Teeth, A View from the Bridge, Six Characters in Search of
an Author.

117. Dukore, Bernard, ed. *Drama and Revolution.* New York: Holt,
Rinehart and Winston, 1971.
Prometheus Bound, Master Olaf, My Kinsman, Major Milineux, Dan-
ton's Death, Saint Joan of the Stockyards, The Plough and the Stars,
The Long March, Commissioner, The Slave, Justice.

118. Dürrenmatt, Friedrich. *Four Plays.* New York: Grove Press, 1966.
Romulus the Great, The Marriage of Mr. Mississippi, An Angel Comes
to Babylon, The Physicists.

119. Edmonds, Randolph. *The Land of Cotton and Other Plays.* Washington: Associated Publishers, 1942, out of print. Reprinted by University Microfilms, 1970.
The Land of Cotton, Gangsters over Harlem, Yellow Death, Silas
Brown, The High Court of Historia.

120. ———. *Six Plays for a Negro Theater.* Boston: Baker's Plays,
1934, out of print. Reprinted by University Microfilms, 1970.
Bad Man, Bleeding Hearts, Breeders, Nat Turner, The New Window,
Old Man Pete.

121. Esslin, Martin, ed. *New Theatre of Europe.* Vol. 4. New York:
Dell Publications, 1970.
The Advertisement, Saved, The Raspberry Picker, Tomorrow from Any
Window, Self-Accusation.

122. Evreinov, Nikolai. *Life as Theater: Five Modern Plays by Nikolai
Evreinov.* Ann Arbor: Ardis Publications, 1973.
The Ship of the Righteous, The Main Thing, The Theater of the Soul,
A Merry Death, The Theater of Eternal War.

123. Eyen, Tom. *Sarah B. Divine and Other Plays.* New York: Drama
Book Specialists, 1973.
Why Hanna's Skirt Won't Stay Down, Who Killed My Bald Sister
Sophie?, What Is Making Gilda So Gray?, Sarah B. Divine!, Areatha
in the Ice Palace, The Kama Sutra, My Next Husband Will Be a

Beauty, The Death of Off Broadway, The White Whore and the Bit Player, Grand Tenement/November 22nd.

124. Felheim, Marvin, ed. *Comedy: Plays, Theory, and Criticism.* New York: Harcourt Brace Jovanovich, 1962.

The Birds, Twelfth Night, The Misanthrope, The Critic, A Wedding, The Man of Destiny, The Importance of Being Earnest, A Phoenix Too Frequent.

125. Feydeau, Georges. *Four Farces.* Tr. Norman R. Shapiro. Chicago: University of Chicago Press, 1970.

Wooed and Viewed, On the Merry-Go-Wrong, Not by Bed Alone, Going to Pot.

126. Fitzjohn, Donald. *English One-Act Plays of Today.* New York: Oxford University Press, 1962.

Lord Byron's Love Letter, The.Browning Version, A Phoenix Too Frequent, The Bespoke Overcoat, The Pen of My Aunt, Mother's Day, Trifles, Dock Brief.

127. *Five Great Modern Irish Plays.* New York: Modern Library, 1941.

The Playboy of the Western World, Juno and the Paycock, Riders to the Sea, Spreading the News, Shadow and Substance.

128. Foote, Horton. *Harrison, Texas: Eight Television Plays.* New York: Harcourt, Brace and World, 1956, out of print.

A Young Lady of Property, John Turner Davis, The Tears of My Sister, The Death of the Old Man, Expectant Relations, The Midnight Caller, The Dancers, The Trip to Bountiful.

129. ————. *Three Plays.* New York: Harcourt Brace Jovanovich, 1962.

Roots in a Parched Ground, Old Man, Tomorrow.

130. Fornés, Mariá Irene. *Promenade and Other Plays.* New York: Drama Book Specialists, 1973.

A Vietnamese Wedding, The Red Burning Light, Molly's Dream, Dr. Kheal, Tango Palace, The Successful Life of Three, Promenade.

131. Fowlie, Wallace, ed. *Four Modern French Comedies.* New York: G. P. Putnam's Sons, 1960.

Ubu Roi, Commissioner, Professor Tatanne, Clerambard.

132. Freedley, George, ed. *Three Plays about Crime and Criminals.* New York: Simon and Schuster, 1962.

Arsenic and Old Lace, Kind Lady, Detective Story.

133. Frisch, Max. *Three Plays*. Tr. James Rosenberg. New York: Hill and Wang, 1967.
Don Juan, or, The Love of Geometry, The Great Rage of Philip Hotz, When the War Was Over.

134. Fugard, Athol. *Three Port Elizabeth Plays*. New York: Viking Press, 1974.
The Blood Knot, Hello and Goodbye, Boesman and Lena.

135. Galsworthy, John. *Plays*. New York: Charles Scribner's Sons, 1928.
The Silver Box, Joy, Strife, The Eldest Son, Justice, The Little Dream, The Pigeon, The Fugitive, The Mob, A Bit o' Love, The Foundation, The Skin Game, A Family Man, Loyalties, Windows, The Forest, Old English, The Show, Escape; Six short plays: The First and Last, The Little Man, Hall-Marked, Deceit, The Sun, Punch and Go.

136. García Lorca, Federico. *Five Plays: Comedies and Tragedies*. Tr. James Graham-Luján and Richard L. O'Connell. New York: New Directions, 1963.
The Shoemaker's Prodigious Wife, Don Perlimplin, Doña Rosita the Spinster, The Butterfly's Evil Spell, The Billy-Club Puppets.

137. ———. *Three Tragedies*. Tr. James Graham-Luján and Richard L. O'Connell. New York: New Directions, 1955.
The House of Bernarda Alba, Blood Wedding, Yerma.

138. Gassner, John, ed. *Best American Plays: 1918–58*. New York: Crown Publishers, 1961.
Harvey, Ethan Frome, The Teahouse of the August Moon, On Borrowed Time, Men in White, Clarence, Biography, Awake and Sing, Yellow Jack, The Adding Machine, Rain, Children of Darkness, The Diary of Anne Frank, Green Grow the Lilacs, Here Come the Clowns, Morning's at Seven, The House of Connelly.

139. ———. *Best Plays of the Modern American Theatre: Second Series, 1939–46*. New York: Crown Publishers, 1947.
The Glass Menagerie, The Time of Your Life, I Remember Mama, Life with Father, Born Yesterday, The Voice of the Turtle, The Male Animal, The Man Who Came to Dinner, Dream Girl, The Philadelphia Story, Arsenic and Old Lace, The Hasty Heart, Home of the Brave, Tomorrow the World, Watch on the Rhine, The Patriots, Abe Lincoln in Illinois.

140. ———. *Best American Plays: Third Series, 1945–51*. New York: Crown Publishers, 1952.
Death of a Salesman, Medea, Detective Story, A Streetcar Named Desire, Billy Budd, The Member of the Wedding, State of the Union, The

Autumn Garden, The Iceman Cometh, Bell, Book and Candle, Mister
Roberts, Anne of the Thousand Days, Come Back, Little Sheba, All
My Sons, Darkness at Noon, The Moon Is Blue, Summer and Smoke.

141. ———. *Best American Plays: Fourth Series, 1952–57.* New York:
Crown Publishers, 1958.
I Am a Camera, Cat on a Hot Tin Roof, The Rose Tattoo, A Moon
for the Misbegotten, Tea and Sympathy, A View from the Bridge, The
Crucible, Inherit the Wind, The Caine Mutiny Court-Martial, The
Fourposter, The Seven Year Itch, The Matchmaker, No Time for
Sergeants, The Solid Gold Cadillac.

142. ———. *Best American Plays: Fifth Series, 1958–63.* New York:
Crown Publishers, 1963.
A Touch of the Poet, The Night of the Iguana, The Dark at the Top
of the Stairs, Who's Afraid of Virginia Woolf?, The Rope Dancers,
Look Homeward Angel, All the Way Home, Silent Night, Lonely
Night, Two for the Seesaw, Mary, Mary, A Thousand Clowns, The
Cave Dwellers, Oh Dad Poor Dad . . . , Orpheus Descending, Gideon,
J.B., The Best Man.

143. ———. *Best American Plays: Supplementary Volume, 1918–58.*
New York: Crown Publishers, 1961.
Clarence, Rain, The Adding Machine, Green Grow the Lilacs, The
House of Connelly, Children of Darkness, Biography, On Borrowed
Time, Morning's at Seven, Ethan Frome, Men in White, Yellow Jack,
Awake and Sing, Here Come the Clowns, Harvey, The Teahouse of
the August Moon, The Diary of Anne Frank.

144. ———. *A Treasury of the Theatre: From Aeschylus to Ostrovsky.*
New York: Simon and Schuster, 1967. Distributed by Holt, Rinehart
and Winston.
Agamemnon, Oedipus the King, The Searching Satyrs, The Trojan
Women, The Bacchae, The Frogs, The Menaechmi, The Brothers,
Thyestes, Shakuntala, Sotoba Komachi, Paphnutius, Abraham and Isaac,
The Second Shepherds' Play, The Death of Pilate, Everyman, The Por-
trait, The Cave of Salamanca, Fuente Ovejuna, Life Is a Dream, Doctor
Faustus, Hamlet, Volpone, The Vision of Delight, The Duchess of Malfi,
The Cid, The Misanthrope, Phaedra, The Way of the World, The
Beggar's Opera, The School for Scandal, Faust (Part I), Mary Stuart,
Danton's Death, Hernani, No Trifling with Love, The London Mer-
chant, Maria Magdalena, The Inspector, A Month in the Country, The
Thunderstorm.

145. ———. *A Treasury of the Theatre: From Ibsen to Sartre.* Vol. 2.
Rev. 3rd ed. New York: Simon and Schuster, 1963.
Ghosts, Hedda Gabler, The Father, The Vultures, The Weavers, The

Tenor, The Power of Darkness, The Cherry Orchard, The Lower Depths, The Intruder, Cyrano de Bergerac, There Are Crimes and Crimes, Liliom, Six Characters in Search of an Author, R.U.R., From the Private Life of the Master Race, The Flies.

146. ———. *A Treasury of the Theatre: From Wilde to Ionesco.* Vol. 3. Rev. 3rd ed. New York: Simon and Schuster, 1963.

The Importance of Being Earnest, Candida, The Admirable Crichton, Escape, The Workhouse Ward, Riders to the Sea, The Plough and the Stars, The Circle, Journey's End, Blithe Spirit, Anna Christie, The Hairy Ape, What Price Glory?, Elizabeth the Queen, Green Pastures, Our Town, Golden Boy, The Little Foxes, My Heart's in the Highlands, The Glass Menagerie, Death of a Salesman, A Dream Play, The Tidings Brought to Mary, The Madwoman of Chaillot, The Lark, The Maids, The Chairs.

147. ———. *Twenty Best European Plays on the American Stage.* New York: Crown Publishers, 1957.

Tiger at the Gates, The Lark, A Month in the Country, My Three Angels, Ondine, The Madwoman of Chaillot, No Exit, Jacobowsky and the Colonel, The Sea Gull, Noah, Volpone, The Late Christopher Bean, The Play's the Thing, As You Desire Me, The Good Hope, The World We Live In (The Insect Comedy), The Dybbuk, From Morn to Midnight, The Passion Flower, Redemption.

148. ———. *Twenty Best Plays of the Modern American Theatre.* New York: Crown Publishers, 1939.

Idiot's Delight, Of Mice and Men, Golden Boy, The Women, End of Summer, Green Pastures, Dead End, Yes, My Darling Daughter, The Fall of the City, Boy Meets Girl, Winterset, The Children's Hour, Johnny Johnson, Tobacco Road, Bury the Dead, You Can't Take It with You, Stage Door, Animal Kingdom, Three Men on a Horse, High Tor.

149. ———. *Twenty-Five Best Plays of the Modern American Theatre. Early Series.* New York: Crown Publishers, 1949.

The Hairy Ape, Desire under the Elms, What Price Glory?, They Knew What They Wanted, Beggar on Horseback, Craig's Wife, Broadway, Paris Bound, The Road to Rome, The Second Man, Saturday's Children, Porgy, The Front Page, Machinal, Gods of Lightning, Street Scene, Strictly Dishonorable, Berkeley Square, The Clod, Trifles, 'Ile, Aria da Capo, Poor Aubrey, White Dresses, Minnie Field.

150. Gassner, John, and Barnes, Clive, eds. *Best American Plays: Sixth Series, 1963–67.* New York: Crown Publishers, 1971.

Benito Cereno, Hogan's Goat, The Fantasticks, The Sign in Sidney Brustein's Window, You Know I Can't Hear You When the Water's

Running, The Lion in Winter, Tiny Alice, The Toilet, Hughie, Fiddler on the Roof, In White America, Slow Dance on the Killing Ground, The Owl and the Pussycat, The Odd Couple, The Subject Was Roses, Blues for Mr. Charlie, The Last Analysis.

151. ———. *Fifty Best Plays of the American Theatre: From 1787 to the Present.* Vols. 1–4. New York: Crown Publishers, 1970.

Vol. 1: The Contrast, Uncle Tom's Cabin, Salvation Nell, The Hairy Ape, Rain, Desire under the Elms, Porgy, The Front Page, Street Scene, Green Pastures, Men in White, Tobacco Road.

Vol. 2: The Children's Hour, Awake and Sing, Ethan Frome, Bury the Dead, You Can't Take It with You, High Tor, Golden Boy, On Borrowed Time, Abe Lincoln in Illinois, The Matchmaker, The Philadelphia Story, The Man Who Came to Dinner, Life with Father.

Vol. 3: The Time of Your Life, Arsenic and Old Lace, Harvey, The Glass Menagerie, A Streetcar Named Desire, State of the Union, Dream Girl, Born Yesterday, Medea, Mister Roberts, Death of a Salesman, The Member of the Wedding.

Vol. 4: Come Back, Little Sheba, The Fourposter, The Seven Year Itch, The Crucible, Tea and Sympathy, The Teahouse of the August Moon, The Diary of Anne Frank, Look Homeward Angel, Two for the Seesaw, Oh Dad Poor Dad . . . , Who's Afraid of Virginia Woolf?, The Odd Couple, Fiddler on the Roof.

152. Gassner, John, and Dukore, Bernard F., eds. *A Treasury of the Theatre: From Henrik Ibsen to Robert Lowell.* 4th ed. New York: Simon and Schuster, 1970. Distributed by Holt, Rinehart and Winston.

Ghosts, Hedda Gabler, The Vultures, The Power of Darkness, The Father, A Dream Play, The Intruder, The Weavers, The Importance of Being Earnest, Candida, Heartbreak House, Ubu the King, Cyrano de Bergerac, The Tenor, The Cherry Orchard, The Lower Depths, Riders to the Sea, The Playboy of the Western World, The Tidings Brought to Mary, The Circle, Six Characters in Search of an Author, The Cuttlefish, The Hairy Ape, A Moon for the Misbegotten, The Spurt of Blood, The Plough and the Stars, Elizabeth the Queen, Blood Wedding, Golden Boy, Our Town, Purgatory, Galileo, The Good Woman of Setzuan, My Heart's in the Highlands, The Little Foxes, The Madwoman of Chaillot, The Lark, The Flies, The Glass Menagerie, Death of a Salesman, Epitaph for George Dillon, A Slight Ache, Who's Afraid of Virginia Woolf?, Dutchman, Benito Cereno.

153. Gassner, John, and Gassner, Mollie, eds. *Best Plays of the Early American Theatre: From the Beginning to 1916.* New York: Crown Publishers, 1967.

The Contrast, Superstition, Charles the Second, Fashion, Uncle Tom's Cabin, The Octoroon, The Count of Monte Cristo, The Mouse-trap,

Secret Service, The Great Divide, The New York Idea, The Truth, The Witching Hour, Salvation Nell, The Easiest Way, The Scarecrow.

154. ———. *15 International One-Act Plays*. New York: Simon and Schuster, 1969.

The Warrior's Barrow, Trial by Jury, Cavalleria Rusticana, Mother-love, The Proposal, The Man of Destiny, Interior, The Tenor, Riders to the Sea, Love of One's Neighbor, The Apollo of Bellac, The Long Christmas Dinner, The Love of Don Perlimplin and Belisa in the Garden, The Man with His Heart in the Highlands, Sunday Costs Five Pesos.

155. Gassner, John, and Sweetkind, Morris, eds. *Introducing the Drama: An Anthology*. New York: Holt, Rinehart and Winston, 1963.

Antigone, Romeo and Juliet, An Enemy of the People, A Night at an Inn, The Barretts of Wimpole Street, The Glass Menagerie, Everyman, The Scarecrow, The Pretentious Ladies, The School for Scandal, Arms and the Man, Then and Now, The Late Christopher Bean, The Apollo of Bellac.

156. Genet, Jean. *The Maids and Deathwatch: Two Plays*. Tr. Bernard Frechtman. New York: Grove Press, 1954.

157. Gibson, William. *Dinny and the Witches and The Miracle Worker: Two Plays*. New York: Atheneum Publishers, 1960.

158. Ghelderode, Michel de. *Seven Plays*. Vols. 1–2. New York: Hill and Wang, 1960–64.

Vol. 1: Chronicles of Hell, Barabbas, The Woman at the Tomb, Pantagleize, The Blind Men, Three Actors and Their Drama, Lord Halewyn.

Vol. 2: Red Magic, Hop, Signor, The Death of Doctor Faust, Christopher Columbus, A Night of Pity, Piet Bouteilk, Miss Jairus.

159. Ghéon, Henri, and Brochet, Henri. *St. Anne and the Gouty Rector and Other Plays*. New York: David McKay Co., 1950.

St. Anne and the Gouty Rector, The Gardener Who Was Afraid of Death, The Sausage Maker's Interlude, The Poor Man Who Died because He Wore Gloves, Parade at the Devil's Bridge, Christmas at the Crossroads, St. Felix and His Potatoes.

160. Giraudoux, Jean. *Four Plays*. Vol. 1. Tr. Maurice Valency. New York: Hill and Wang, 1963.

Ondine, The Enchanted, The Madwoman of Chaillot, The Apollo of Bellac.

161. ———. *Three Plays*. Vol. 2. Tr. Phyllis La Farge, et al. New York: Hill and Wang, 1964.

Siegfried, Amphitryon 38, Electra.

162. Glenny, Michael. *Three Soviet Plays.* Harmondsworth: Penguin Books, 1966.
The Bedbug, Marya, The Dragon.

163. Goldstone, Richard H., and Lass, Abraham H., eds. *The Mentor Book of Short Plays.* New York: New American Library, 1969.
A Trip to Czardis, To Bobolink, for Her Spirit, Riders to the Sea, Visit to a Small Planet, The Mother, Thunder on Sycamore Street, The Rising of the Moon, The Happy Journey, Lord Byron's Love Letter, A Marriage Proposal, The Romancers, The Browning Version.

164. Goodman, Randolph, ed. *From Script to Stage: Eight Modern Plays.* New York: Holt, Rinehart and Winston, 1971.
Hedda Gabler, A Dream Play, The Seagull, The Apes Shall Inherit the Earth, Pygmalion, Desire under the Elms, Seven Deadly Sins of the Lower Middle Class, The Old Tune.

165. Gorky, Maxim. *The Lower Depths and Other Plays.* Tr. Alexander Bakshy, et al. New Haven: Yale University Press, 1968.
The Lower Depths, Barbarians, Enemies, Queer People, Vassa Zheleznova, Zykovs, Yegor Bulychov.

166. Green, Paul. *Five Plays of the South.* New York: Hill and Wang, 1963.
Johnny Johnson, In Abraham's Bosom, The House of Connelly, Hymn to the Rising Sun, White Dresses.

167. Griffith, Francis, and Mersand, Joseph, eds. *Eight American Ethnic Plays.* New York: Charles Scribner's Sons, 1974.
Hogan's Goat, I Remember Mama, The Tenth Man, Dino, A Raisin in the Sun, Day of Absence, The Oxcart, Wetback Run.

168. Griffith, Francis, Mersand, Joseph, and Maggio, Joseph B., eds. *One Act Plays for Our Times.* New York: Popular Library, 1973.
The Devil and Daniel Webster, The Man with His Heart in the Highlands, The Ugly Duckling, The Case of the Crushed Petunias, The Rocking Horse, Fortunata Writes a Letter, Dark Glasses, A Pound on Demand, The Final War of Olly Winter, Frederick Douglass, Dino, Gaucho.

169. Guare, John. *Cop Out, Muzeeka, Home Fires.* New York: Grove Press, 1969.

170. Halline, Allan G. *Six Modern American Plays.* New York: Modern Library, 1951.
The Emperor Jones, Winterset, The Man Who Came to Dinner, The Little Foxes, The Glass Menagerie, Mister Roberts.

171. Hammerstein, Oscar II. *Six Plays.* New York: Modern Library, 1959.

Oklahoma!, Carousel, Allegro, South Pacific, The King and I, Me and Juliet.

172. Handke, Peter. *Kaspar and Other Plays.* Tr. Michael Roloff. New York: Hill and Wang, 1970.

Kaspar, Offending the Audience, Self-Accusation.

173. Hanger, Eunice, ed. *Three Australian Plays.* Minneapolis: University of Minnesota Press, 1968.

Rusty Bugles, We Find the Bunyip, Well.

174. Hansberry, Lorraine. *Les Blancs: The Collected Last Plays of Lorraine Hansberry.* New York: Grove Press, 1973.

Les Blancs, The Drinking Gourd, What Use Are the Flowers?

175. ———. *A Raisin in the Sun and The Sign in Sidney Brustein's Window.* New York: New American Library, 1966.

176. Hatch, James V., and Shine, Ted, eds. *Black Theater, U.S.A.: 1843–1974.* New York: Free Press (Macmillan), 1974.

The Black Doctor, The Brown Overcoat, The Escape, or, A Leap for Freedom, Caleb the Degenerate, Appearances, Rachel, Mine Eyes Have Seen, They That Sit in Darkness, For Unborn Children, The Church Fight, Undertow, The Purple Flower, A Sunday Morning in the South, Balo, 'Cruiter, The Idle Head, Bad Man, Job Hunters, Don't You Want to Be Here?, Big White Fog, Divine Comedy, Graven Images, Natural Man, Flight of the Natives, Native Son, District of Columbia, Walk Hard, The Tumult and the Shouting, The Amen Corner, Take a Giant Step, In Splendid Error, Star of the Morning, Limitations of Life, Dry August, Fly Blackbird, Day of Absence, The Drinking Gourd, Wine in the Wilderness, The Owl Answers, Job Security, Little Ham, The Slave, Goin' a Buffalo, Herbert III, Black Love Song #1.

177. Hatlen, Theodore W., ed. *Drama: Principles and Plays.* New York: Appleton-Century-Crofts, 1967.

Antigone, Hamlet, The Miser, The School for Scandal, An Enemy of the People, Miss Julie, Major Barbara, Desire under the Elms, The Caucasian Chalk Circle, The Glass Menagerie, The Leader, Act without Words.

178. Haugen, Einar. *Fire and Ice: Three Icelandic Plays.* Madison: University of Wisconsin Press, 1967.

The Wish, The Golden Gate, Atoms and Madams.

179. Hawkes, John. *The Innocent Party*. New York: New Directions, 1967.
The Questions, The Innocent Party, The Undertaker, The Wax Museum.

180. Hayes, Richard, ed. *Port-Royal and Other Plays*. New York: Hill and Wang, 1962.
Port-Royal, Asmodée, Tobias and Sarah, Little Poor Man.

181. Hellman, Lillian. *The Collected Plays*. Boston: Little, Brown and Co., 1972.
The Children's Hour, Days to Come, The Little Foxes, Watch on the Rhine, Candide, Toys in the Attic, The Searching Wind, Another Part of the Forest, Montserrat, The Autumn Garden, The Lark, My Mother, My Father and Me.

182. Hewes, Henry, ed. *Famous American Plays of the Nineteen Forties*. New York: Dell Publications, 1968.
The Skin of Our Teeth, Home of the Brave, All My Sons, Lost in the Stars, The Member of the Wedding.

183. Hoffman, William M., ed. *New American Plays*. Vols. 2–4. New York: Hill and Wang, 1968–71.
Vol. 2: Futz, Until the Monkey Comes, A Message from Couger, French Grey, The Abstract Wife, Passacaglia, The White Whore and the Bit Player, The Owl Answers.
Vol. 3: The Electronic Nigger, The Poet's Papers, Always with Love, Thank You, Miss Victoria, The Golden Circle, An American Playground, Sampler, The King of Spain.
Vol. 4: Slaughterhouse Play, At War with the Mongols, Captain Jack's Revenge, African Medea, Icarus, Moby Tick.

184. Hogan, Robert, ed. *Seven Irish Plays*. Minneapolis: University of Minnesota Press, 1967.
The Visiting House, Design for a Headstone, Song of the Anvil, Copperfaced Jack, Sharon's Grave, Many Young Men of Twenty, The Ice Goddess.

185. Holt, Marion, ed. *The Modern Spanish Stage: Four Plays*. New York: Hill and Wang, 1970.
The Concert at Saint Ovide, Condemned Squad, The Blindfold, The Boat without a Fisherman.

186. *Homecoming and Other Plays, The*. New York: Scholastic Book Services, 1975.
The Homecoming, To All My Friends on Shore, The Dream Spinner, Printer's Measure, Big Deal in Laredo.

187. Houghton, Norris, ed. *Masterpieces of Continental Drama: Seeds of Modern Drama*. New York: Dell Publications, 1963.
Thérèse Raquin, An Enemy of the People, Miss Julie, The Weavers, The Sea Gull.

188. Hughes, Langston. *Five Plays by Langston Hughes*. Ed. Webster Smalley. Bloomington: Indiana University Press, 1963.
Tambourines to Glory, Mulatto, Soul Gone Home, Little Ham, Simply Heavenly.

189. Hurrell, John, ed. *Two Modern Tragedies*. New York: Charles Scribner's Sons, 1961.
Death of a Salesman, A Streetcar Named Desire.

190. Ibsen, Henrik. *Eleven Plays*. New York: Modern Library, 1935.
The Master Builder, The Wild Duck, Peer Gynt, Hedda Gabler, The Pillars of Society, A Doll's House, The League of Youth, Ghosts, Rosmersholm, John Gabriel Borkman, An Enemy of the People.

191. ———. *Ghosts and Three Other Plays*. Tr. Michael Meyer. Garden City: Doubleday and Co., 1966.
Ghosts, A Doll's House, An Enemy of the People, Rosmersholm.

192. ———. *Hedda Gabler and Three Other Plays*. Tr. Michael Meyer. Garden City: Doubleday and Co., 1961.
Hedda Gabler, The Pillars of Society, The Wild Duck, Little Eyolf.

193. ———. *When We Dead Awaken and Three Other Plays*. Tr. Michael Meyer. Garden City: Doubleday and Co., 1961.
When We Dead Awaken, The Master Builder, John Gabriel Borkman, The Lady from the Sea.

194. Inge, William. *Eleven Short Plays*. New York: Dramatists Play Service, 1962.
To Bobolink, for Her Spirit, A Social Event, The Boy in the Basement, The Tiny Closet, Memory of Summer, The Rainy Afternoon, The Mall, An Incident at the Standish Arms, People in the Wind, Bus Riley's Back in Town, The Strains of Triumph.

195. ———. *Four Plays*. New York: Random House, 1958.
Come Back, Little Sheba, Picnic, Bus Stop, The Dark at the Top of the Stairs.

196. Ionesco, Eugene. *Four Plays*. Tr. Donald M. Allen. New York: Grove Press, 1958.
The Bald Soprano, The Lesson, The Chairs, Jack, or, The Submission.

197. ———. *Hunger and Thirst and Other Plays.* Tr. Donald R. Watson. New York: Grove Press, 1969.
The Picture, Anger, Salutations, Hunger and Thirst.

198. ———. *The Killer and Other Plays.* Tr. Donald R. Watson. New York: Grove Press, 1960.
Improvisation, or, The Shepherd's Chameleon, Maid to Marry, The Killer.

199. ———. *Rhinoceros and Other Plays.* Tr. Derek Prouse. New York: Grove Press, 1960.
Rhinoceros, The Leader, The Future Is in Eggs, or, It Takes All Sorts to Make a World.

200. ———. *A Stroll in the Air and Frenzy for Two or More: Two Plays.* Tr. Donald Watson. New York: Grove Press, 1968.

201. ———. *Three Plays.* Tr. Donald Watson. New York: Grove Press, 1958.
Amádée, The New Tenant, Victims of Duty.

202. Johnson, Stanley, Bierman, Judah, and Hart, James, eds. *The Play and the Reader.* Englewood Cliffs, N.J.: Prentice-Hall, 1966.
Rosmersholm, Lysistrata, Caesar and Cleopatra, The Madwoman of Chaillot, Oedipus Rex, King Lear, Henry IV, Mother Courage and Her Children, The Chairs.

203. Jones, Willis Knapp, ed. and tr. *Men and Angels: Three South American Comedies.* Carbondale and Edwardsville: Southern Illinois University Press, 1970.
The Quack Doctor, The Fate of Chipi Gonzalez, The Man of the Century.

204. Kalman, Rolf, ed. *A Collection of Canadian Plays.* Vols. 1–3. Toronto: Simon and Pierre, 1972–74.
Vol. 1: Counsellor Extraordinary, Wu-feng, Love Mouse, Meyer's Room, Colour the Flesh the Colour of Dust, Exit Muttering.
Vol. 2: Wedding in White, Three Women, The Devil's Instrument, The Pile, The Store, Inside Out, Westbound 12:01.
Vol. 3: Marsh Hay, The Unreasonable Act of Julian Waterman, The Twisted Loaf, Soft Voices, Vicky, The Vice President.

205. Kaufman, William I., ed. *The Best Television Plays, 1950–1951.* New York: Merlin Press, 1952, out of print.
The Pharmacist's Mate, The Night They Made a Bum out of Helen Hayes, The Kathryn Steffan Story, The Rocking Horse, Vincent Van Gogh, Borderline of Fear, The Goldbergs, The Lottery.

206. ———. *Best Television Plays, 1957.* New York: Harcourt, Brace and World, 1957, out of print.
Requiem for a Heavyweight, Cracker Money, The Five Dollar Bill, The Trial of Poznan, Survival, Lee at Gettysburg, Thank You, Edmondo.

207. ———. *Great Television Plays.* New York: Dell Publications, 1969.
The Big Deal, Requiem for a Heavyweight, Twelve Angry Men, The Final War of Olly Winter, Lee at Gettysburg, The Merry Jests of Herschel Ostropolier.

208. Kernan, Alvin B., ed. *Character and Conflict.* 2nd ed. New York: Harcourt Brace Jovanovich, 1969.
Hedda Gabler, Everyman, Mother Courage and Her Children, The Skin of Our Teeth, Antigone, The Stronger, Hamlet, The Cherry Orchard, Riders to the Sea, The Misanthrope, Tiger at the Gates, Picnic on the Battlefield.

209. ———. *Classics of the Modern Theatre: Realism and After.* New York: Harcourt Brace Jovanovich, 1965.
The Father, The Cherry Orchard, Arms and the Man, Six Characters in Search of an Author, The Ghost Sonata, Corruption in the Palace of Justice, Blood Wedding, Mother Courage and Her Children, The Zoo Story, The Chairs.

210. King, Woodie, and Milner, Ron, eds. *Black Drama Anthology.* New York: New American Library, 1971.
Junkies are Full of (SHHH . . .), Bloodrites, Junebug Graduates Tonight, The Corner, Who's Got His Own, Charades on East Fourth Street, Gabriel, Brotherhood, The One, The Marriage, The Owl Killer, Requiem for Brother X, Ododo, All White Caste, Mother and Child, The Breakout, Three X Love, A Medal for Willie, Ladies in Waiting, Black Cycle, Strictly Matrimony, Star of the Morning, Toe Jam.

211. Koch, Kenneth. *Bertha and Other Plays.* New York: Grove Press, 1966.
Bertha, George Washington Crossing the Delaware, Angelica, Pericles, The Merry Stones, Guinevere, or, The Death of the Kangaroo, The Construction of Boston, The Return of Yellowmay, The Revolt of the Giant Animals, The Building of Florence, The Academic Murders, Easter, The Gold Standard, The Lost Feed, Mexico, Coil Supreme.

212. Kopit, Arthur. *The Day the Whores Came Out to Play Tennis and Other Plays.* New York: Hill and Wang, 1965.
The Day the Whores Came Out to Play Tennis, Chamber Music, The Questioning of Nick, The Hero, Sing to Me through Open Windows, The Conquest of Everest.

213. Kozelka, Paul, ed. *Fifteen American One-Act Plays.* New York: Simon and Schuster, 1961.

Thursday Evening, The Dust of the Road, The Undercurrent, The Man Who Died at Twelve O'Clock, Aria da Capo, The Lottery, Red Carnations, Feathertop, Sorry, Wrong Number, The Still Alarm, Trifles, The Trysting Place, The Neighbors, Impromptu, The Devil and Daniel Webster.

214. Labiche, Eugene. *The Italian Straw Hat and The Spelling Mistakes.* Tr. Frederick Davies. New York: Theatre Arts, 1967.

215. Lagerkvist, Pär. *Modern Theatre: Seven Plays and an Essay.* Tr. Thomas R. Buckman. Lincoln: University of Nebraska Press, 1966.

Difficult Hour 1, Difficult Hour 2, Difficult Hour 3, Secret of Heaven, King, Hangman, Philosopher's Stone.

216. Lahr, John, ed. *Showcase 1: Plays from the Eugene O'Neill Foundation.* New York: Grove Press, 1969.

Who's Happy Now?, The Indian Wants the Bronx, Father Uxbridge Wants to Marry, Muzeeka.

217. Lahr, John, and Price, Jonathan, eds. *The Great American Life Show: Nine Plays from the Avant Garde Theatre.* New York: Bantam Books, 1974.

Cop Out, In the Wine Time, The Serpent, Operation Sidewinder, Slaveship, The Kid, Injun: A Happening, Mysteries and Other Pieces, AC/DC.

218. Lamb, Myra. *The Mod Donna and Scylon Z: Plays of Women's Liberation.* New York: Pathfinder Press, 1974.

219. Lawrence, D. H. *Three Plays.* Harmondsworth: Penguin Books, 1969.

A Collier's Friday Night, The Daughter-in-Law, The Widowing of Mrs. Holyroyd.

220. Levin, Richard, ed. *Tragedy: Plays, Theory, Criticism.* New York: Harcourt Brace Jovanovich, 1965.

Antigone, Coriolanus, The Wild Duck, Murder in the Cathedral.

221. Lid, Richard W., and Bernd, Daniel, eds. *Plays: Classic and Contemporary.* Philadelphia: J. P. Lippincott Co., 1967.

Oedipus Rex, Anthony and Cleopatra, The Man of Mode, Don Juan, The Cherry Orchard, The Doctor's Dilemma, The Glass Menagerie, Maid to Marry, Little Eyolf.

222. Lind, Jakov. *The Silver Foxes Are Dead and Other Plays*. New York: Hill and Wang, 1969.
The Silver Foxes Are Dead, Anna Laub, Hunger, Fear.

223. Litto, Frederic M., ed. *Plays from Black Africa*. New York: Hill and Wang, 1968.
The Rhythm of Violence, Edufu, The Literary Society, Song of a Goat, The Rain Killers, The Jewels of the Shrine.

224. Locke, Alain, and Gregory, Montgomery, eds. *Plays of Negro Life: A Sourcebook of Native American Drama*. New York: Harper and Row, 1927, out of print. Reprinted by Negro University Press.
The Dreamy Kid, The Rider of Dreams, Rackey, The No 'Count Boy, The Flight of the Natives, White Dresses, In Abraham's Bosom, Sugar Cane, 'Cruiter, The Starter, Judge Lynch, Granny Maumee, The Bird Child, Balo, Plumes, The Broken Banjo, The Death Dance, The Emperor Jones, The Danse Calinda, An African Ballet.

225. Macgowan, Kenneth, ed. *Famous American Plays of the Nineteen Twenties*. New York: Dell Publications, 1959.
The Moon of the Caribbees, What Price Glory, They Knew What They Wanted, Porgy, Street Scene, Holiday.

226. Machiz, Herbert, ed. *Artists' Theatre: Four Plays*. New York: Grove Press, 1960.
Try! Try!, The Heroes, The Bait, Absalom.

227. MacLeish, Archibald. *Three Short Plays*. New York: Dramatists Play Service, 1961.
Air Raid, The Secret of Freedom, The Fall of the City.

228. Magarshack, David, ed. *Storm and Other Russian Plays*. New York: Hill and Wang, 1960.
The Government Inspector, The Storm, The Power of Darkness, Uncle Vanya, The Lower Depths.

229. Mandel, Oscar. *Collected Plays*. Vols. 1–2. Santa Barbara: Unicorn Press, 1970–71.
Vol. 1: General Audax, Honest Unbamba, Living Room with Six Oppressions, A Splitting Headache, The Virgin and the Unicorn, Island.
Vol. 2: The Monk Who Wouldn't, The Fatal French Dentist, Professor Snaffle's Polypon, The Sensible Man of Jerusalem, Adam Adamson, Of Angels and Eskimos.

230. Mandel, Oscar, ed. *The Theatre of Don Juan: A Collection of Plays and Views*. Lincoln: University of Nebraska Press, 1963.

The Playboy of Seville, or, Supper with a Statue, Don Juan, or, The Libertine, The Libertine, Don Juan and Don Pedro, or, The Dead Stone's Banquet, The Punished Libertine, or, Don Giovanni, Don Juan and Faust, Giovanni in London, or, The Libertine Reclaimed, Don Juan Tenario, The Last Night of Don Juan, Don Juan (Act II), Don Juan, or, The Love of Geometry (Acts IV and V).

231. Marcel, Gabriel. *Three Plays.* New York: Hill and Wang, 1965.
A Man of God, Ariadne, The Votive Candle.

232. Matlaw, Myron, ed. *The Black Crook and Other Nineteenth-Century American Plays.* New York: E. P. Dutton and Co., 1967.
The Black Crook, Fashion, Francesca da Rimini, The Octoroon, Rip Van Winkle, Shenandoah, Margaret Fleming.

233. McNally, Terrence. *Sweet Eros, Next, and Other Plays.* New York: Vintage Books, 1969.
Botticelli, Next, ¡ Cuba Si!, Sweet Eros, Witness.

234. Melfi, Leonard. *Encounters: Six Short Plays.* New York: Random House, 1967.
Birdbath, Lunchtime, Hallowe'en, Ferryboat, The Shirt, Times Square.

235. Mersand, Joseph, ed. *Three Comedies of American Family Life.* New York: Simon and Schuster, 1961.
Life with Father, I Remember Mama, You Can't Take It with You.

236. ———. *Three Dramas of American Individualism.* New York: Simon and Schuster, 1971.
Golden Boy, The Magnificent Yankee, High Tor.

237. ———. *Three Dramas of American Realism.* New York: Simon and Schuster, 1961.
Idiot's Delight, The Time of Your Life, Street Scene.

238. ———. *Three Plays about Business in America.* New York: Simon and Schuster, 1964.
The Adding Machine, All My Sons, Beggar on Horseback.

239. ———. *Three Plays about Doctors.* New York: Simon and Schuster, 1961.
An Enemy of the People, Men in White, Yellow Jack.

240. ———. *Three Plays about Marriage.* New York: Simon and Schuster, 1962.
Craig's Wife, Holiday, They Knew What They Wanted.

241. Merserve, Walter, and Merserve, Ruth I. *Modern Drama from Communist China.* New York: New York University Press, 1970.
Snow in Midsummer, The Passer-By, Dragon Beard Ditch, The White-Haired Girl, The Women's Representative, Yesterday, Magic Aster, Letters from the South, The Red Lantern.

242. Miller, Arthur. *Collected Plays.* New York: Viking Press, 1957.
All My Sons, Death of a Salesman, A View from the Bridge, The Crucible, A Memory of Two Mondays.

243. ———. *The Portable Arthur Miller.* Ed. Harold Clurman. New York: Viking Press, 1971.
Death of a Salesman, The Crucible, Incident at Vichy, The Price, The Misfits.

244. Miller, Helen Louise, ed. *Gold Medal Plays for Holidays.* Boston: Plays, Inc., 1958.
The Greedy Goblin, A School for Scaring, The Mystery of Turkey-Lurkey, Strictly Puritan, Thanks to Butter-Fingers, Mr. Snow White's Thanksgiving, Mary's Invitation, Turning the Tables, The Miraculous Tea Party, The Forgotten Hero, Vicky Gets the Vote, The Christmas Umbrella, Softy the Snowman, The Birds' Christmas Carol, The Santa Claus Twins, The Christmas Runaways, Santa Claus for President, Mystery at Knob Creek Farm, Melody for Lincoln, The Tree of Hearts, Crosspatch and Cupid, The Washington Shilling, Dolly Saves the Day, Washington's Leading Lady, Bunnies and Bonnets, The Bashful Bunny, Mother's Fairy Godmother, The Magic Carpet-Sweeper, Lacey's Last Garland, The Talking Flag.

245. ———. *On Stage for Teen-Agers.* Boston: Plays, Inc., 1948.
Party Line, Pin-Up Pals, What's Cookin'?, Snoop's Scoop, Cupid on the Loose, Homework, Band Aid, Doctor's Daughter, Say It with Flowers, Papa Pepper's Bombshell, Horrors, Incorporated, The Rummage Rumpus, The Soft Hearted Ghost, Thanksgiving Beats the Dutch, Angel Child, Home for Christmas, The Missing Link, Miss Lonelyheart, The Washingtons Slept Here, Nothing to Wear, A Surprise for Mother.

246. Miller, Jordan Y., ed. *American Dramatic Literature: Ten Modern Plays in Historical Perspective.* New York: McGraw-Hill Book Co., 1961.
The Little Foxes, Camino Real, Command Decision, Porgy, Biography, The Male Animal, The Member of the Wedding, Harvey, Desire under the Elms, The Crucible.

247. Mishima, Yukio. *Five Modern Noh Plays.* Tr. Donald Keene. New York: Vintage Books, 1973.
Sotoba Komachi, The Damask Drum, Kantan, The Lady Aoi, Hanjo.

248. Moe, Christian, and Payne, Darwin Reid, eds. *Six New Plays for Children.* Carbondale and Edwardsville: Southern Illinois University Press, 1971.

The Royal Cricket of Japan, Marlin the Magnificent, The Shoes That Were Danced to Pieces, The Golden Mask, Huck Finn, The Strolling Players.

249. Moody, Richard. *Dramas from the American Theatre, 1762–1909.* New York: World Publishing Co., 1966. Distributed by Houghton-Mifflin.

The Contrast, Bunker Hill, The Glory of Columbia, She Would Be a Soldier, The Forest Rose, A Trip to Niagara, Metamora, The Gladiator, The Drunkard, Fashion, Uncle Tom's Cabin, Po-ca-hon-tas, Francesca da Rimini, Minstrel Show, Across the Continent, The Mulligan Guard Ball, Shenandoah, A Letter of Introduction, A Temperance Town, Shore Acres, The Great Divide, The New York Idea, The City.

250. Moon, Samuel, ed. *One Act: Eleven Short Plays of the Modern Theater.* New York: Grove Press, 1961.

Miss Julie, Purgatory, The Man with the Flower in His Mouth, Pullman Car Hiawatha, Hello Out There, Twenty-Seven Wagons Full of Cotton, Bedtime Story, Cécile, This Music Crept by Me upon the Waters, A Memory of Two Mondays, The Chairs.

251. Mortimer, John. *Come as You Are: Four Playlets.* New York: Samuel French, 1971.

Mill Hill, Marble Arch, Bermondsey, Gloucester Road.

252. ———. *Five Plays by John Mortimer.* London: Methuen and Co., 1970.

Dock Brief, What Shall We Tell Carolina?, I Spy, Lunch Hour, Collect Your Hand Luggage.

253. Mosel, Tad. *Other People's Houses.* New York: Simon and Schuster, 1956.

The Waiting Place, Stars in the Summer Night, Other People's Houses, My Lost Saints, The Lawn Party, The Haven, Ernie Barger Is Fifty.

254. Mrozek, Slawomir. *Six Plays.* Tr. Nicholas Bethal. New York: Grove Press, 1967.

The Police, Out at Sea, Enchanted Night, The Party, Charlie, The Martyrdom of Peter Ohey.

255. ———. *Striptease, Repeat Performance, and The Prophets: Three Plays.* Tr. Nicholas Bethal. New York: Grove Press, 1973.

256. Murdoch, Iris. *The Three Arrows and The Servants and the Snow: Two Plays.* New York: Viking Press, 1974.

257. Nathan, George Jean. *World's Great Plays.* New York: Grosset and Dunlap, 1944.
Lysistrata, The Cherry Orchard, Faust, The Master Builder, The Plough and the Stars, The Emperor Jones, Cyrano de Bergerac.

258. Nelson, Stanley, and Smith, Harry, eds. *The Scene—I: New Plays from Off-Off Broadway.* New York: The Smith, 1973. Distributed by Horizon Press.
Bang! Bang!, Worms, Manitoba, Set It Down with Gold, Harrison Progressive School, Concentric Circles, The Heist, Dr. Franklin.

259. *No Time for Sergeants and Other Plays.* New York: Scholastic Book Services, 1971.
No Time for Sergeants, To Catch a Never Dream, Five in Judgement, Taking Honor.

260. Noyes, George Rapall, ed. *Masterpieces of the Russian Drama.* Vols. 1–2. New York: Dover Publications, 1961.
Vol. 1: Young Hopeful, Wit Works Woe, The Inspector, A Month in the Country, Poor Bride, Bitter Fate.
Vol. 2: The Death of Ivan the Terrible, Power of Darkness, Down and Out, The Cherry Orchard, Professor Storitsyn, Mystery-Bouffe.

261. Oboler, Arch. *The Oboler Omnibus.* Norwalk, Conn.: Leisure Books, 1974.
Strange Morning, The Immortal Gentleman, The Ugliest Man in the World, Ivory Tower, This Lonely Heart, This Precious Freedom, Letter at Midnight, Hate, The Visitor from Hades, The Special Day, I Have No Prayer, Holiday 1948.

262. O'Casey, Sean. *Collected Plays.* Vols. 1–4. New York: St. Martin's Press, 1949–51.
Vol. 1: Juno and the Paycock, The Shadow of a Gunman, The Plough and the Stars, End of the Beginning, Pound on Demand.
Vol. 2: The Silver Tassie, The Star Turns Red, Within the Gates.
Vol. 3: Purple Dust, Red Roses for Me, Hall of Healing.
Vol. 4: Oak Leaves and Lavender, Cock-a-Doodle Dandy, Bedtime Story, Time to Go.

263. ———. *Five One Act Plays.* New York: St. Martin's Press, 1966.
The End of the Beginning, A Pound on Demand, Hall of Healing, Bedtime Story, Time to Go.

264. ———. *Three More Plays.* New York: St. Martin's Press, 1965.
The Silver Tassie, Purple Dust, Red Roses for Me.

265. ———. *Three Plays.* New York: St. Martin's Press, 1966.
Juno and the Paycock, The Shadow of a Gunman, The Plough and the Stars.

266. Olfson, Lewy, ed. *Classics Adapted for Acting and Reading.* Boston: Plays, Inc., 1970.
Rip Van Winkle, Jane Eyre, The Importance of Being Earnest, The Flying Dutchman, The Bishop's Candlesticks, Wuthering Heights, The Transferred Ghost, The Rivals, Around the World in Eighty Days, The Count of Monte Cristo, Through the Looking Glass, A Christmas Carol, The Kidnapping of David Balfour, The Man without a Country, Enoch Arden, The Swiss Family Robinson.

267. ———. *Dramatized Classics for Radio-Style Reading.* Vols. 1–2. Boston: Plays, Inc., 1964.
Vol. 1: Oliver Twist, Sherlock Holmes and the Red-Headed League, The Rivals, Little Women, The Invisible Man, The Prisoner of Zenda, The Doctor in Spite of Himself, The Odyssey, The Canterbury Tales, Alice in Wonderland, Christmas for Cosette, Twenty Thousand Leagues under the Sea.
Vol. 2: Washington Square, Don Quixote, Martin Chuzzlewit, Five Weeks in a Balloon, The Masque of Red Death, The Little Princess, Sherlock Holmes and the Stockbroker's Clerk, The Iliad, The Would-Be Gentleman, The Lady or the Tiger?, Tom Sawyer and Injun Joe, The Crowning of Sir Arthur.

268. Oliver, Clinton S., and Sills, Stephanie, eds. *Contemporary Black Drama: From A Raisin in the Sun to No Place to Be Somebody.* New York: Charles Scribner's Sons, 1970.
A Raisin in the Sun, Purlie Victorious, Funnyhouse of a Negro, Dutchman, Blues for Mr. Charlie, Day of Absence, Happy Ending, The Gentleman Caller, No Place to Be Somebody.

269. Oliver, William I., ed. *Voices of Change in the Spanish American Theatre.* Austin: University of Texas Press, 1971.
The Day They Let the Lions Loose, The Camp, The Library, In the Right Hand of God the Father, The Mulatto's Orgy, Three Beach Plays.

270. O'Neill, Eugene. *Anna Christie, The Emperor Jones, The Hairy Ape.* New York: Grove Press, 1964.

271. ———. *The Later Plays of Eugene O'Neill.* New York: Random House, 1967.

Ah, Wilderness!, A Touch of the Poet, Hughie, A Moon for the Misbegotten.

272. ———. *Nine Plays*. Ed. Saxe Commins. New York: Random
House, 1954.
Strange Interlude, Mourning Becomes Electra, The Emperor Jones,
Desire under the Elms, The Hairy Ape, All God's Chillun Got Wings,
The Great God Brown, Marco Millions, Lazarus Laughed.

273. ———. *The Plays of Eugene O'Neill*. Vols. 1–3. New York:
Random House, 1951.
Vol. 1: Strange Interlude, Desire under the Elms, Lazarus Laughed,
The Fountain, The Moon of the Caribbees, Bound East for Cardiff, The
Rope, The Dreamy Kid, Before Breakfast.
Vol. 2: Ah, Wilderness!, All God's Chillun Got Wings, Marco Mil-
lions, Welded, Diff'rent, Gold.
Vol. 3: Anna Christie, Beyond the Horizon, The Emperor Jones, The
Hairy Ape, The Great God Brown, The Straw, Dynamo, Days without
End, The Iceman Cometh.

274. ———. *Seven Plays of the Sea*. New York: Vintage Books, 1946.
The Moon of the Caribbees, Bound East for Cardiff, The Long Voyage
Home, In the Zone, 'Ile, The Rope, Where the Cross Is Made.

275. ———. *Six Short Plays of Eugene O'Neill*. New York: Vintage
Books, 1964.
The Dreamy Kid, Before Breakfast, Diff'rent, Welded, The Straw, Gold.

276. ———. *Ten "Lost" Plays*. New York: Random House, 1964.
Abortion, The Movie Man, The Sniper, Servitude, A Wife for a Life,
Thirst, The Web, Warnings, Fog, Recklessness.

277. ———. *Three Plays*. New York: Grove Press, 1961.
Desire under the Elms, Strange Interlude, Mourning Becomes Electra.

278. Orzel, Nick, and Smith, Michael, eds. *Eight Plays from Off-Off
Broadway*. Indianapolis: Bobbs-Merrill, 1966.
The General Returns from One Place to Another, The Madness of Lady
Bright, Chicago, The Great American Desert, Balls, America Hurrah,
The Successful Life of Three, Calm Down Mother.

279. Osborne, John. *Plays for England and The World of Paul Slickey*.
New York: Grove Press, 1966.
The Blood of the Bambergs, Under Plain Cover, The World of Paul
Slickey.

280. Owens, Rochelle. *The Karl Marx Play and Others*. New York: E. P. Dutton and Co., 1974.

Futz, The String Game, Homo, Istanboul, Beclch, He Wants Shih!, Kontraption, Farmer's Almanac, Coconut Folk-Singer, The Karl Marx Play.

281. ———. *Spontaneous Combustion: Eight New American Plays*. New York: Drama Book Specialists, 1973.

Sun, Cinque, Dialect Determinism, Sannibel and Captiva, A Quick Nut Bread to Make Your Mouth Water, Schubert's Last Serenade, Ba-Ra-Ka, He Wants Shih!

282. Parker, John W., ed. *Adventures in Playmaking: Four Plays by Carolina Playmakers*. Chapel Hill: University of North Carolina Press, 1968.

Singing Valley, Spring for Sure, A Little to the Left, The Battle of Carnival and Lent.

283. Parone, Edward, ed. *Collision Course*. New York: Random House, 1968.

One act plays: Wandering, Stars and Stripes, Chuck, Skywriting, Jew, Thoughts on the Instant of Greeting a Friend in the Street, Tour, Camera Obscura, Metaphors, The Unexpected Memoirs of Bernard Mergendeiler, Rats, A Lesson in Dead Language, Animal, No Answer, Plaster, Cowboys #2, Mama as She Became but Not as She Was.

284. ———. *New Theatre for Now*. Vol. 2. New York: Dell Publications, 1971.

A³, Pictures, June/Moon, Botticelli, Niagara Falls, Tilt.

285. ———. *New Theatre in America*. Vol. 1. New York: Dell Publications, 1965.

Dutchman, Mrs. Dally Has a Lover, Upstairs Sleeping, Match Play, In a Cold Hotel, The 9:00 Mail, The Rook.

286. Patrick, Robert. *Robert Patrick's Cheep Theatricks*. New York: Drama Book Specialists, 1973.

I Came to New York to Write, The Haunted Host, The Arnold Bliss Show (I: The Actor and the Invader, II: La Repetition, III: Arnold's Big Break, IV: Presenting Arnold Bliss), One of Us Has to Work, Phil and Laura, The P.R. and the V.I.P., Pop People, Verna and Artie, Fred and Harold, Help, I Am a Monologue, Cornered (I: Lights, II: Camera Obscura, III: Action), Still Love, One Person: A Monologue, Joyce Dynel, an American Zarzuela, Pieggin and Liss, The Richest Girl in the World Finds Happiness.

287. Patterson, Lindsay, ed. *Black Theater*. New York: New American Library, 1971.
Take a Giant Step, In Splendid Error, Trouble in Mind, Simply Heavenly, A Raisin in the Sun, Purlie Victorious, Dutchman, The Amen Corner, In the Wine Time, No Place to Be Somebody, St. Louis Woman.

288. Pieterse, Cosmo, ed. *Ten One-Act Plays*. New York: Humanities Press, 1968.
Encounter, With Strings, Yon Kon, The Game, The Occupation, Blind Cycles, The Deviant, Fusane's Trial, The Opportunity, Maama.

289. Pinter, Harold. *The Caretaker and The Dumb Waiter: Two Plays*. New York: Grove Press, 1962.

290. ———. *The Dwarfs and Eight Revue Sketches*. New York: Grove Press, 1968.
The Dwarfs, Trouble in the Works, The Black and White, Request Stop, Last to Go, Applicant, Interview, That's All, That's Your Trouble.

291. ———. *Landscape and Silence*. New York: Grove Press, 1970.
Landscape, Silence, Night.

292. ———. *The Lover, The Tea Party, and The Basement*. New York: Grove Press, 1967.

293. ———. *Three Plays*. New York: Grove Press, 1963.
The Collection, A Slight Ache, The Dwarfs.

294. Pirandello, Luigi. *Naked Masks: Five Plays*. Ed. Eric Bentley. New York: E. P. Dutton and Co., 1958.
It Is So, If You Think So, Henry IV, Six Characters in Search of an Author, Each in His Own Way, Liola.

295. ———. *Pirandello's One-Act Plays*. Tr. William Murray. New York: Funk and Wagnalls, 1970.
The Vise, Sicilian Limes, The Doctor's Duty, The Jar, The License, Chee-Chee, At the Exit, The Imbecile, The Man with the Flower in His Mouth, The Other Son, The Festival of Our Lord of the Ship, Bellavita, I'm Dreaming, But Am I?

296. ———. *To Clothe the Naked and Two Other Plays*. Tr. William Murray. New York: E. P. Dutton and Co., 1962.
To Clothe the Naked, Rules of the Game, The Pleasure of Honesty.

297. *Playbook: Five Plays for a New Theatre*. New York: New Directions, 1956.

The Death of Odysseus, The Ticklish Acrobat, Twilight Crane, The Immortal Husband, A Leak in the Universe.

298. *Plays for a New Theatre: Playbook 2.* New York: New Directions, 1966.
The Long Night of Medea, Methusalem, or, The Eternal Bourgeois, Assault upon Charles Sumner, Wax Museum, Knackery for All.

299. *Pocketful of Wry, A.* Schulenburg, Tex.: I. E. Clark, 1974.
What Will Happen to the Children?, The Knight-Mare's Nest, The Old Oak Encounter.

300. Poland, Albert, and Mailman, Bruce, eds. *The Off-Off Broadway Book.* Indianapolis: Bobbs-Merrill, 1972.
The Great American Desert, You May Go Home Again, A Beautiful Day, What Happened?, Home Movies, Things That Go Bump in the Night, Motel, Birdbath, Why Hanna's Skirt Won't Stay Down, Journey of the Fifth Horse, The Rimers of Eldritch, Saturday Night at the Movies, Something I'll Tell You Tuesday, Moon, The Loveliest Afternoon of the Year, Futz, Gorilla Queen, The Hawk, Lemonade, The Golden Fleece, Clara's Ole Man, Massachusetts Trust, Molly's Dream, Gloria and Esperanza, A Rat's Mass, Invocation of a Haunted Mind, Slave Ship, The Unseen Hand, Bluebeard, Gertrude, or, Would She Be Pleased to Receive It?, Dracula, The Richest Girl in the World, Line, Rainbows for Sale, The Basic Training of Pavlo Hummel, Country Music, Satyricon.

301. Popkin, Henry, ed. *Four Modern Plays.* 2nd series. New York: Holt, Rinehart and Winston, 1961.
Hedda Gabler, Pygmalion, The Emperor Jones, The Cherry Orchard.

302. ———. *Modern British Drama.* New York: Grove Press, 1964.
A Taste of Honey, The Hostage, Roots, Serjeant Musgrave's Dance, The One Way Pendulum, The Caretaker.

303. Powell, Anthony. *Two Plays: The Garden God and The Rest I'll Whistle.* Boston: Little, Brown and Co., 1972.

304. Quinn, Arthur Hobson, ed. *Representative American Plays: From 1767 to the Present Day.* 7th ed. New York: Appleton-Century-Crofts, 1953.
The Prince of Parthia, The Contrast, André, Superstition, Charles the Second, Pocahontas, or, The Settlers of Virginia, The Broker of Bogotá, Tortesa the Usurer, Fashion, Francesca da Rimini, The Octoroon, or, Life in Louisiana, Rip Van Winkle, Hazel Kirke, Shenandoah, Margaret Fleming, Secret Service, Madame Butterfly, The Girl with the Green Eyes, The New York Idea, The Witching Hour, The Faith Healer, The

Scarecrow, The Boss, He and She, Beyond the Horizon, Sun-up, The Silver Cord, Paris Bound, Winterset, Command Decision, South Pacific.

305. Rabe, David. *The Basic Training of Pavlo Hummel and Sticks and Bones*. New York: Viking Press, 1973.

306. Ravitz, Abe C., ed. *The Disinherited*. Encino, Cal.: Dickenson Publishing Co., 1974.
The Escape, or, A Leap for Freedom, The Danites of the Sierras, Skits from the Vaudeville Stage, Fixin's, The Adding Machine, Motel, Waiting for Lefty, Winterset, The Tales of Hoffman, Angela Is Happening, All God's Chillun Got Wings, Soul Gone Home, The King of Soul, Great Goodness of Life: A Coon Show, Everybody's a Jew, Monologues from Division Street, Seyklon Z, Hello from Bertha, Talk to Me like the Rain and Let Me Listen.

307. Reeve, F. D., ed. and tr. *Contemporary Russian Drama*. Indianapolis: Bobbs-Merrill, 1968.
Alive Forever, A Petrarchan Sonnet, The Naked King, It's Been Ages!, A Warsaw Melody.

308. ———. *Nineteenth-Century Russian Plays*. New York: W. W. Norton and Co., 1973.
The Minor, The Trouble with Reason, Boris Godunov, The Inspector General, The Storm, The Power of Darkness.

309. ———. *Twentieth-Century Russian Plays*. New York: W. W. Norton and Co., 1973.
The Seagull, The Lower Depths, The Puppet Show, He Who Gets Slapped, The Days of the Turbins, The Bedbug, The Shadow.

310. Reinert, Otto, ed. *Drama: An Introductory Anthology*. Boston: Little, Brown and Co., 1961.
Oedipus Rex, Everyman, Macbeth, Tartuffe, The Wild Duck, Arms and the Man, The Three Sisters, Ghost Sonata, Purgatory, The Good Woman of Setzuan, The Lesson, A View from the Bridge.

311. ———. *Drama: An Introductory Anthology*. Alt. ed. Boston: Little, Brown and Co., 1964.
Antigone, The Alchemist, Othello, The Misanthrope, The Rivals, Hedda Gabler, Miss Julie, Caesar and Cleopatra, The Cherry Orchard, The Playboy of the Western World, Six Characters in Search of an Author, The American Dream.

312. ———. *Modern Drama*. Boston: Little, Brown and Co., 1966.
The Wild Duck, Arms and the Man, The Three Sisters, The Ghost

Sonata, Six Characters in Search of an Author, Purgatory, The Good Woman of Setzuan, The Glass Menagerie, The Lesson.

313. ———. *Modern Drama.* Alt. ed. Boston: Little, Brown and Co., 1966.

The Wild Duck, The Father, Caesar and Cleopatra, The Cherry Orchard, The Playboy of the Western World, The Hour-Glass, Six Characters in Search of an Author, Chronicles of Hell, The Caucasian Chalk Circle, The Glass Menagerie, The Zoo Story.

314. *Requiem for a Heavyweight and Other Plays.* New York: Scholastic Book Services, 1971.

Requiem for a Heavyweight, Tragedy in a Temporary Town, The White Cane, The Elevator, Appalachian Autumn, The Alley, Noon on Doomsday, Saturday Adoption.

315. Rice, Elmer. *Three Plays.* New York: Hill and Wang, 1965.

The Adding Machine, Street Scene, Dream Girl.

316. Richards, Stanley, ed. *Best Mystery and Suspense Plays of the Modern Theatre.* New York: Dodd, Mead and Co., 1971.

Sleuth, Witness for the Prosecution, The Letter, Child's Play, Angel Street, Dangerous Corner, Dial "M" for Murder, Arsenic and Old Lace, The Bad Seed, Dracula.

317. ———. *Best Plays of the Sixties: A Dramatic Prologue to the Seventies.* Garden City: Doubleday and Co., 1970.

Becket, The Night of the Iguana, Fiddler on the Roof, Here I Come, The Odd Couple, The Royal Hunt of the Sun, The Killing of Sister George, Hadrian VII, The Boys in the Band, The Great White Hope.

318. ———. *Best Short Plays, 1968.* Radnor, Pa.: Chilton Books, 1968.

The Night Nurse, The Call, The Freezer, Dentist and Patient, Husband and Wife, The Shoemaker and the Devil, The Small Private World of Michael Marston, The Man Who Loved God, The Bridal Night, Night with Guests, The Mountain Chorus, Opening Night, The Magic Realists, Every Number Wins, The Wooden Box, A Train Going Somewhere.

319. ———. *Best Short Plays, 1969.* Radnor, Pa.: Chilton Books, 1969. New York: Avon Books, 1970.

The Indian Wants the Bronx, Bringing It All Back Home, Augustus, Blake's Design, A Time to Live, The Tape Recorder, The Corrupters, Midwestern Magic, Clara's Ole Man, Daft Dream Adyin', The Golden Fleece, Please, No Flowers, Stud, Blood-Photo.

320. ———. *Best Short Plays, 1970.* Radnor, Pa.: Chilton Books, 1970. New York: Avon Books, 1971.

Next, The Gentleman Caller, Acrobats, History, All on Her Own, The New Play, The Ruffian on the Stair, Trevor, A Day for Surprises, Funnyhouse of a Negro, Molly's Dream, The Love Course, Things Went Badly in Westphalia, A Pretty Row of Pretty Ribbons, Where Are You Going, Hollis Jay?

321. ———. *Best Short Plays, 1971*. Radnor, Pa.: Chilton Books, 1971. New York: Avon Books, 1972.
Billy's Last Stand, Skippy, I Can't Imagine Tomorrow, Doreen, Bad Bad Jo-Jo, The Burial of Esposito, Steal the Old Man's Bundle, Tribal Harangue Two, The Karl Marx Play, Two Little Gentlemen, Desmond, Sandra and the Janitor.

322. ———. *Best Short Plays, 1972*. Radnor, Pa.: Chilton Books, 1972. New York: Avon Books, 1973.
Slam the Door Softly, Contribution, The Great Nebula in Orion, We're Due in Eastbourne in Ten Minutes, Wine in the Wilderness, Once below a Lighthouse, A Black Mass, The Unknown General, Live Spelled Backwards, Stella, Schubert's Last Serenade, An Interview with F. Scott Fitzgerald, Stay Where You Are, Answers, And the Wind Blows.

323. ———. *Best Short Plays, 1973*. Radnor, Pa.: Chilton Books, 1973. New York: Avon Books, 1974.
Double Solitaire, Chinamen, Circus Lady, What Use Are Flowers, Tira Tells Everything There Is to Know about Herself, Tigers, Gordone Is a Muthah, The Ragpickers, Sam Slade Is Missing, The Colonial Dudes, High Summer, Number 9.

324. ———. *Best Short Plays, 1974*. Radnor, Pa.: Chilton Books, 1974.
An American Sunset, Welcome to Andromeda, The Owl Killer, Let's Murder Vivaldi, The Ladies Should Be in Bed, On Vacation, Present Tense, Vanilla Crescents, Blank Pages, Sitting, The Last Victim, The Wooing of Lady Sunday.

325. ———. *Best Short Plays of the World Theatre: 1958–67*. New York: Crown Publishers, 1968.
The Orchestra, The New House, The Waste-Disposal Unit, Come into the Garden, Maude, Crawling Arnold, The Academy, The Firebugs, The Disposal, Great Goodness of Life: A Coon Show, Benito Cereno, Monica, The Window, Birdbath, The Governor's Lady, Nannie's Night Out, A Subject of Scandal and Concern, Bellavita, White Lies, The Tower, Madame de.

326. ———. *Best Short Plays of the World Theatre: 1968–73*. New York: Crown Publishers, 1973.
Confessional, Visitor from Forest Hills, Day of Absence, A Song at Twilight, Line, Lou Gehrig Did Not Die of Cancer, Episode in the

Life of an Author, Mojo, The Gift, The Chinese, Orange Soufflé, The Male of the Species, Marguerite, Bermondsey, Larry Parks' Day in Court, The Safety Match, Margaret's Bed, The Waiting Room, The Holy Ghostly, The Lennon Play—In His Own Write.

327. ———. *Modern Short Comedies from Broadway and London.* New York: Random House, 1969.
Black Comedy, Visitor from Mamaroneck, Losers, Trevor, The Shock of Recognition, Shadows of the Evening, The Sponge Room, The Diary of Adam and Eve, George's Room, Noon, Bea, Frank, Richie, & Joan, Madly in Love.

328. ———. *Ten Classic Mystery and Suspense Plays.* New York: Dodd, Mead and Co., 1973.
Ten Little Indians, The Desperate Hours, Hostile Witness, Kind Lady, The Innocents, Night Must Fall, An Inspector Calls, Uncle Harry, Ladies in Retirement, Seven Keys to Baldpate.

329. ———. *Ten Great Musicals of the American Theatre.* Radnor, Pa.: Chilton Books, 1973.
Of Thee I Sing, Porgy and Bess, One Touch of Venus, Brigadoon, Kiss Me Kate, West Side Story, Gypsy, Fiddler on the Roof, 1776, Company.

330. Richardson, Willis, ed. *Plays and Pageants from the Life of the Negro.* Washington: Associated Publishers, 1930, out of print.
Sacrifice, Antar of Araby, Ti Yette, Graven Images, Riding the Goat, The Black Horseman, The King's Dilemma, The House of Sham, Two Races, Out of the Dark, The Light of the Women, Ethiopia at the Bar of Justice.

331. Richardson, Willis, and Miller, May, eds. *Negro History in Thirteen Plays.* Washington: Associated Publishers, 1935, out of print.
Antonio Maceo, Attucks, the Martyr, The Elder Dumas, Near Calvary, In Menelik's Court, Frederick Douglass, William and Ellen Craft, Nat Turner, Genifrede, Christophe's Daughters, Harriet Tubman, Samory, Sojourner's Truth.

332. Roloff, Michael, ed. *The Contemporary German Theatre.* New York: Avon Books, 1972.
Now They Sing Again, The Ride across Lake Constance, Hunting Scenes from Lower Bavaria, Home Front, How Mr. Mockinpott Was Cured of His Suffering.

333. Rose, Reginald. *Six Television Plays.* New York: Simon and Schuster, 1956, out of print.
The Remarkable Incident at Carson Corners, Thunder on Sycamore

Street, Twelve Angry Men, An Almanac of Liberty, Crime in the Streets, The Incredible World of Horace Ford.

334. Rowell, George, ed. *Late Victorian Plays, 1890–1914*. 2nd ed. New York: Oxford University Press, 1972.
The Second Mrs. Tanqueray, The Liars, The Mollusk, The Cassilis Engagement, The Voysey Inheritance, Justice, Hindle Wakes.

335. ———. *Nineteenth-Century Plays*. 2nd ed. New York: Oxford University Press, 1972.
Black-Eyed Susan, Money, Masks and Faces, The Colleen Bawn, Lady Audley's Secret, The Ticket-of-Leave Man, Caste, Two Roses, The Bells, A Pair of Spectacles.

336. Rozewicz, Tadeusz. *The Card Index and Other Plays*. Tr. Adam Czerniawski. New York: Grove Press, 1970.
The Card Index, The Interrupted Act, Gone Out.

337. Ryerson, Florence, and Clements, Colin. *Angels Don't Marry and Other One Act Plays*. New York: Samuel French, 1938.
Angels Don't Marry, Farewell to Love, Last Night, Sugar and Spice, Write Me a Love Scene, Her Majesty the King, Gallant Lady.

338. Saffron, Robert, ed. *The Permanent Theatre: Great Farces*. Vol. 2. New York: Macmillan Co., 1966.
Lysistrata, Bourgeois Gentilhomme (The Would-Be Gentleman), The Inspector General, The Importance of Being Earnest, Boy Meets Girl.

339. ———. *The Permanent Theatre: Great Melodramas*. Vol. 1. New York: Macmillan Co., 1966.
The Duchess of Malfi, The Count of Monte Cristo, Secret Service, The Letter, Angel Street.

340. Salerno, Henry F., ed. *English Drama in Transition, 1880–1920*. Indianapolis: Bobbs-Merrill, 1968.
The Liars, The Second Mrs. Tanqueray, The Importance of Being Earnest, Major Barbara, The Admirable Crichton, The Silver Box, Deirdre, The Playboy of the Western World, Our Betters.

341. Sanders, Thomas E., ed. *The Discovery of Drama*. Glenview, Ill.: Scott, Foresman and Co., 1968.
Orange Soufflé, Oedipus Rex, Macbeth, Desire under the Elms, The Latent Heterosexual, Sodom and Gomorrah, Riders to the Sea, Camino Real.

342. Sartre, Jean-Paul. *No Exit and Three Other Plays*. New York: Grove Press, 1947.

The Flies, Dirty Hands, The Respectful Prostitute, No Exit.

343. Schevill, James. *The Black President and Other Plays*. Chicago: Swallow Press, 1965.
The Black President, The Space Fan.

344. Schisgal, Murray. *Five One Act Plays*. New York: Dramatists Play Service, 1968.
Memorial Day, The Old Jew, The Basement, Fragments, Windows.

345. Schotter, Richard, ed. *The American Place Theatre: Plays*. New York: Dell Publications, 1973.
Fingernails Blue as Flowers, Papp, The Cannibals, The Carpenters, Five on the Black Hand Side.

346. Schroeder, Robert J., ed. *The New Underground Theatre*. New York: Bantam Books, 1968.
Promenade, I'm Really Here, The Golden Screw, Red Cross, Sand, Fruit Salad, Istanboul, The Life of Lady Godiva.

347. Schweitzer, John C., ed. *A Variety of Short Plays*. New York: Charles Scribner's Sons, 1966.
The $99,000 Answer, The Monkey's Paw, My Client Curley, Sorry, Wrong Number, The Still Alarm, Trifles, The Million-Pound Note, The Clod, She Walks in Beauty, 'Ile, Native Dancer, The Old Lady Shows Her Medals, To Bobolink, for Her Spirit, The Devil and Daniel Webster, Sammy, The Thinking Heart, The Rising of the Moon, The Man with His Heart in the Highlands, The Browning Version, The Shelter.

348. Settel, Irving, ed. *Top TV Shows of the Year, 1954–1955*. New York: Hastings House, 1955, out of print.
Toys and Science, A Letter to the Boss, Report on Senator Joseph Mc-Carthy, Arthritis and Rheumatism, Elisha and the Long Knives, Native Dancer, The Thinking Heart, Camel News Caravan, What's My Line?, Governor Herman Talmadge of Georgia, Conquest of Pain, The Home Show.

349. Shaw, George Bernard. *Four Plays*. New York: Dell Publications, 1957.
Candida, The Devil's Disciple, Caesar and Cleopatra, Captain Brass-bound's Conversion.

350. ———. *Plays*. New York: New American Library, 1960.
Man and Superman, Candida, Arms and the Man, Mrs. Warren's Profession.

351. ———. *Plays Unpleasant*. Baltimore: Penguin Books, 1961.
Widowers' Houses, The Philanderer, Mrs. Warren's Profession.

352. ———. *Selected One Act Plays*. Baltimore, Penguin Books, 1972.
The Shewing-Up of Blanco Posnet, How He Lied to Her Husband,
O'Flaherty V.C., The Inca of Perusalem, Annajanska, The Bolshevik
Empress, Village Wooing, The Dark Lady of the Sonnets, Overruled,
Great Catherine, Augustus Does His Bit, The Six of Calais.

353. ———. *Selected Plays with Prefaces*. New York: Dodd, Mead and
Co., 1948–57.
Vol. 1: The Doctor's Dilemma, Pygmalion, Major Barbara, Heartbreak
House, Captain Brassbound's Conversion, The Man of Destiny,
Androcles and the Lion.
Vol. 2: Back to Methuselah, Saint Joan, John Bull's Other Island, You
Never Can Tell, In Good King Charles's Golden Days.
Vol. 3: Mrs. Warren's Profession, Arms and the Man, Candida, The
Devil's Disciple, Caesar and Cleopatra, Man and Superman, Fanny's
First Play, The Dark Lady of the Sonnets.

354. Shepard, Sam. *Five Plays*. Indianapolis: Bobbs-Merrill, 1967.
Fourteen Hundred Thousand, Red Cross, Icarus' Mother, Chicago,
Melodrama Play.

355. ———. *Mad Dog Blues and Other Plays*. New York: Drama Book
Specialists, 1973.
The Mad Dog Blues, Cowboy Mouth, The Rock Garden, Cowboy #2.

356. ———. *The Unseen Hand and Other Plays*. Indianapolis: Bobbs-
Merrill, 1971.
The Unseen Hand, Forensic and the Navigators, The Holy Ghostly,
Back Bog Bait.

357. Shroyer, Frederick B., and Gardemal, Louis G., eds. *Types of
Drama: A Critical and Historical Introduction*. Glenview, Ill.: Scott,
Foresman and Co., 1970.
The Frogs, The Matchmaker, Tartuffe, The School for Scandal, Cyrano
de Bergerac, Oedipus Rex, Hamlet, The Glass Menagerie.

358. Side, Greenfield, ed. *On Camera*. New York: Holt, Rinehart and
Winston, 1972.
On Camera 1: Checkmate, Murder, The Patriot Game. On Camera 2:
A Storm in Summer, Five Men for Freedom. On Camera 3: The Male
of the Species, Twelve and a Half Cents, Dynasty.

359. Simon, Neil. *The Comedies of Neil Simon*. New York: Random
House, 1971. New York: Avon Books, 1973.

Come Blow Your Horn, Barefoot in the Park, The Odd Couple, The Star-Spangled Girl, Promises, Promises, Plaza Suite, The Last of the Red-Hot Lovers.

360. *Six Great Modern Plays.* New York: Dell Publications, 1956.
The Three Sisters, The Master Builder, Mrs. Warren's Profession, Red Roses for Me, The Glass Menagerie, All My Sons.

361. Smith, Michael, ed. *The Best of Off-Off Broadway.* New York: E. P. Dutton and Co., 1969.
Forensic and the Navigators, Moon, Dr. Kheal, Charles Dickens' Christmas Carol, Mushrooms, Gorilla Queen, The Next Thing.

362. ————. *More Plays from Off-Off Broadway.* Indianapolis: Bobbs-Merrill, 1972.
Tidy Passions, or, Kill, Kaleidoscope, Kill, Georgie Porgie, XXXXX, The Poor Little Match Girl, Willie the Germ, Flite Cage, Grand Tenement, November 22, A Rat's Mass, Bluebeard.

363. Sokel, Walter H., ed. *An Anthology of German Expressionist Drama: A Prelude to the Absurd.* Garden City: Doubleday and Co., 1963.
Murderer the Women's Hope, The Strongbox, Job, Humanity, Alkibiades Saved, The Immortal One, Cry in the Street, Baal.

364. *Sounder and Other Plays.* New York: Scholastic Book Services, 1975.
Sounder, The Shelter, Survival, Times Change, Say Good-Bye to Jamie, The Boy Who Predicted Earthquakes.

365. Sprinchorn, Evert, ed. *The Genius of the Scandinavian Theater.* New York: New American Library, 1964.
Jeepe of the Hill, The Wild Duck, The Master Builder, To Damascus (Part 1), Crimes and Crimes, Difficult Hour, Days on a Cloud.

366. Stasio, Marilyn, ed. *Broadway's Beautiful Losers.* New York: Dell Publications, 1973.
Look, We've Come Through, The Beauty Part, The Last Analysis, Christmas in Las Vegas, Johnny No-Trump.

367. Strasberg, Lee, ed. *Famous American Plays of the Nineteen Fifties.* New York: Dell Publications, 1968.
Camino Real, The Autumn Garden, Tea and Sympathy, The Zoo Story, A Hatful of Rain.

368. Strindberg, August. *Eight Expressionist Plays.* New York: New York University Press, 1972.

Lucky Per's Journey, The Keys of Heaven, To Damascus (I, II, III),
A Dream Play, The Great Highway, The Ghost Sonata.

369. ———. *Five Plays of Strindberg.* Tr. Elizabeth Sprigge. Garden
City: Doubleday and Co., 1960.
Creditors, The Dance of Death, The Great Highway, Swanwhite, Crime
and Crime.

370. ———. *The Plays of Strindberg.* Vol. 1. Tr. Michael Meyer.
New York: Grove Press, 1970.
The Father, Miss Julie, Creditors, The Stronger, Playing with Fire,
Eric the Fourteenth, The Ghost Sonata, The Storm.

371. ———. *Six Plays of Strindberg.* Tr. Elizabeth Sprigge. Garden
City: Doubleday and Co., 1955.
The Father, Miss Julie, The Stronger, The Ghost Sonata, The Dream
Play, Easter.

372. ———. *Strindberg's One-Act Plays.* Tr. Arvid Paulson. New
York: Simon and Schuster, 1969.
The Outlaw, The Stranger, My First Warning, Motherlove, The Pel-
ican, Simoon, The Bond, Miss Julie, Pariah, Debit and Credit, Playing
with Fire, Creditors, In the Face of Death.

373. Sullivan, Victoria, and Hatch, James V., eds. *Plays by and about
Women.* New York: Grove Press, 1973. New York: Random House,
1973.
Overtones, The Children's Hour, The Women, Play with a Tiger, Calm
Down Mother, The Advertisement, Rites, Wine in the Wilderness.

374. Sweetkind, Morris, ed. *Ten Great One Act Plays.* New York:
Bantam Books, 1968.
Sganarelle, The Bear, How He Lied to Her Husband, Spreading the
News, Riders to the Sea, 'Ile, Something Unspoken, To Bobolink, for
Her Spirit, The Feast, Waiting for the Bus.

375. Swire, Willard, ed. *Three Distinctive Plays about Abraham Lincoln.* New York: Simon and Schuster, 1961.
Abraham Lincoln, The Last Days of Lincoln, Prologue to Glory.

376. Swortzell, Lowell, ed. *All the World's a Stage: Modern Plays for
Young People.* New York: Dial Press, 1972.
Swan White, The Post Office, The Jar, The Tingalary Bird, Your Own
Thing, He Who Says Yes and He Who Says No, The Billy-Club Pup-
pets, The End of the Beginning, The Man with His Heart in the High-
lands, Soul Gone Home, Look and Long, Little Red Riding Hood,

Amahl and the Night Visitors, Poem-Plays, The Genie of Sutton Place, The Thwarting of Baron Bolligrew, Child Honor, The Chief's Bride.

377. Synge, John Millington. *The Complete Plays*. New York: Grove Press, 1960.

The Playboy of the Western World, Riders to the Sea, In the Shadow of the Glen, The Well of the Saints, The Tinker's Wedding, Deidre of the Sorrows.

378. *Teacher, Teacher, and Other Plays*. New York: Scholastic Book Services, 1971.

Teacher, Teacher, A Matter of Pride, The Other Foot, The End of the World, or, Seventeen Years Later, Death after School, The Poet.

379. Terry, Megan. *Three One Act Plays*. New York: Samuel French, 1969.

Sannibel and Captiva, The Magic Realists, One More Little Drinkie.

380. ———. *Viet Rock and Others*. New York: Simon and Schuster, 1967.

Viet Rock, Comings and Goings, Keep Tightly Closed in a Cool, Dry Place, The Gloaming of My Darling.

381. *Three French Farces*. Tr. Frederick Davies. Baltimore: Penguin Books, 1974.

The Happiest of the Three, Let's Get a Divorce, Get Out of My Hair.

382. Trewin, J. C., ed. *Plays of the Year*. Vols. 1–42. New York: Frederick Ungar, 1951–73. (Following volumes are in print)

Vol. 6 (1951): Saint's Day, The Prodigious Snob, The Sane Sky, Who Goes There?, Gunpowder, Treason and Plot.

Vol. 11 (1954): Simon and Laura, The Party Spirit, The Misanthrope, Sganarelle, The Little Glass Clock, Serious Charge.

Vol. 18 (1958): An Other Business, The Queen and the Welshman, The Party, Touch It Light.

Vol. 20 (1959): The Edwardians, Rollo, Heart of Bruce, The Sound of Murder.

Vol. 23 (1960–1): The Irregular Verb to Love, House of Cowards, The Bargain, John Gabriel Borkman.

Vol. 24 (1961): Guilty Party, The Keep, The Tinker, Tersa of Avila.

Vol. 25 (1961–2): The Chances, The Empire Builders, Gordon, The Big Killing.

Vol. 26 (1962–3): Rattle of a Simple Man, To Double Deceit, or, A Cure for Jealousy, Jackie the Jumper, A Cheap Bunch of Nice Flowers.

Vol. 27 (1962–3) : Out of the Crocodile, The Sky Is Green, Difference of Opinion, Say Nothing.

Vol. 28 (1963–4) : The Wings of the Dove, The Poker Session, The Formation Dancers, The City Madam.

Vol. 29 (1964–5) : The Little Clay Cart, A Measure of Cruelty, The Creeper, Don't Let Summer Come.

Vol. 36 (1968–70) : The Prince of Homburg, The Unknown Soldier and His Wife, The Secretary Bird, The Servant of Two Masters.

Vol. 37 (1969) : The Cardinal of Spain, Have You Any Dirty Washing, Mother Dear?, The Black Swan Winter, The Sacking of Norman Banks.

Vol. 38 (1969–70) : Spithead, In Celebration, The Magistrate, Knight in Four Acts.

Vol. 40 (1970–1) : The Contractor, The Jockey Club Stakes, Children of the Wolf, Unaccompanied Cello.

Vol. 42 (1972) : Notes on a Love Affair, Lloyd George Knew My Father, Mr. Sydney Smith Coming Upstairs, The Drums of Snow.

Vol. 43 (1972–3) : Crown Matrimonial, The Day after the Fair, Willie Rough.

383. Tucker, S. Marion, and Downer, Alan S., eds. *Twenty-Five Modern Plays*. 3rd ed. New York: Harper and Row, 1953.
He Who Gets Slapped, The Ascent of F6, La Malquerida, R.U.R., The Cherry Orchard, The Infernal Machine, John Ferguson, The Lower Depths, The Field God, Command Decision, The Rats, The Silver Cord, Rosmersholm, The Coral, Gas I, Gas II, Pelléas and Mélisande, Liliom, The Plough and the Stars, The Great God Brown, The Thunderbolt, Roadside, Cyrano de Bergerac, Light-o'-Love, Comrades, Riders to the Sea, The Importance of Being Earnest.

384. Turner, Darwin T., ed. *Black Drama in America: An Anthology*. New York: Fawcett World Library, 1973.
Emperor of Haiti, We Righteous Bombers, Purlie Victorious, Bayou Legend, Earth and Stars, The Toilet, Take a Giant Step, The Chip Woman's Fortune, Our Lan'.

385. *Twelve Angry Men and Other Plays*. New York: Scholastic Book Services, 1971.
Twelve Angry Men, The Big Deal, The Long Fall, On the Waterfront.

386. *Two Great Belgian Plays about Love*. Tr. Marnix Gijsen. New York: James H. Heineman, 1966.
The Magnificent Cuckold, The Burlador.

387. Usigli, Rudolfo. *Two Plays by Rudolfo Usigli*. Tr. Thomas Bled-

soe. Carbondale and Edwardsville: Southern Illinois University Press, 1971.

Crown of Light, One of These Days.

388. Vidal, Gore. *Visit to a Small Planet and Other Television Plays.* Boston: Little, Brown and Co., 1956.

Dark Possession, A Sense of Justice, Summer Pavilion, Visit to a Small Planet, The Death of Billy the Kid, Smoke, Barn Burning, The Turn of the Screw.

389. Vidal, Gore, ed. *Best Television Plays.* New York: Ballantine Books, 1956.

The Mother, Thunder on Sycamore Street, Man on the Mountaintop, A Young Lady of Property, The Strike, The Rabbit Trap, Visit to a Small Planet.

390. Waith, Eugene M., ed. *The Dramatic Moment.* Englewood Cliffs, N.J.: Prentice-Hall, 1967.

Major Barbara, The Zoo Story, Oedipus Rex, The Summoning of Everyman, King Lear, Volpone, The Misanthrope, Hedda Gabler, The Seagull, The Ghost Sonata, Mother Courage and Her Children, Six Characters in Search of an Author.

391. Walcott, Derek. *Dream on Monkey Mountain and Other Plays.* New York: Hill and Wang, 1970.

Dream on Monkey Mountain, Malcochon, The Sea at Dauphin, Ti-Jean.

392. Warnock, Robert, ed. *Representative Modern Plays: American.* Glenview, Ill.: Scott, Foresman and Co., 1952.

Beggar on Horseback, The Late Christopher Bean, Biography, Mourning Becomes Electra, Valley Forge, Waiting for Lefty, The Glass Menagerie, Death of a Salesman.

393. ———. *Representative Modern Plays: British.* Glenview, Ill.: Scott, Foresman and Co., 1953.

The Admirable Crichton, The Doctor's Dilemma, Loyalties, Riders to the Sea, Juno and the Paycock, The Constant Wife, Blithe Spirit, Murder in the Cathedral, A Phoenix Too Frequent.

394. ———. *Representative Modern Plays: Ibsen to Tennessee Williams.* Glenview, Ill.: Scott, Foresman and Co., 1964.

The Master Builder, Miss Julia, The Seagull, The Doctor's Dilemma, Riders to the Sea, Juno and the Paycock, Desire under the Elms, The Constant Wife, Biography, The Glass Menagerie, A Phoenix Too Frequent.

395. Watson, E. Bradlee, and Pressey, Benfield, eds. *Contemporary Drama: Eleven Plays.* New York: Charles Scribner's Sons, 1956.

Pygmalion, The Green Pastures, The Happy Journey to Trenton and Camden, Ways and Means, Hello Out There, Antigone, The Glass Menagerie, The Madwoman of Chaillot, Another Part of the Forest, Death of a Salesman, Venus Observed.

396. ———. *Contemporary Drama: Fifteen Plays.* New York: Charles Scribner's Sons, 1959.

Hedda Gabler, The Importance of Being Earnest, Uncle Vanya, Dream Play, Man and Superman, Riders to the Sea, Henry IV (Pirandello), Ah, Wilderness!, Blood Wedding, Murder in the Cathedral, Purple Dust, The Skin of Our Teeth, Come Back, Little Sheba, The Crucible, Look Homeward Angel.

397. ———. *Contemporary Drama: Nine Plays.* New York: Charles Scribner's Sons, 1941.

The Hairy Ape, Street Scene, Abe Lincoln in Illinois, Silver Cord, Justice, What Every Woman Knows, The Circle, R.U.R., Cyrano de Bergerac.

398. Weiss, M. Jerry, ed. *Ten Short Plays.* New York: Dell Publications, 1963.

Coming through the Rye, The Case of the Crushed Petunias, The Happy Journey to Trenton and Camden, Suppressed Desires, Triumph of the Egg, Feast of Ortolans, Quare Medicine, Parents Are People, My Client Curly, Visit to a Small Planet.

399. Weiss, Samuel A., ed. *Drama in the Modern World: Plays with Essays.* Lexington: D. C. Heath and Co., 1968.

The Wild Duck, Miss Julie, The Cherry Orchard, Major Barbara, The Playboy of the Western World, Six Characters in Search of an Author, Desire under the Elms, The House of Bernarda Alba, Ondine, The Good Woman of Setzuan, The Glass Menagerie, The Bald Soprano, All That Fall, It Happened in Irkutsk.

400. Wellwarth, George E., ed. *German Drama between the Wars.* New York: E. P. Dutton and Co., 1974.

Job, The Atonement, Christopher Columbus, The Captain of Kopenick, No More Peace, The Last Days of Mankind, Happy End.

401. ———. *New Wave Spanish Drama.* New York: New York University Press, 1970.

The Man and the Fly, The Jackass, Train to H. . ., Bread and Rice, or, Geometry in Yellow, The Halo, The Best of All Possible Worlds, Sad Are the Eyes of William Tell.

402. ———. *Themes of Drama: An Anthology.* New York: T. Y. Crowell Co., 1973.

Lysistrata, The Best of All Possible Worlds, The Rhythm of Violence, The Would-Be Gentleman, Gallows Humor, Incident at Twilight, The Bacchae, Everyman, The Holy Experiment, Anthony and Cleopatra, Round Dance, Mrs. Warren's Profession, Henry IV, Cards of Identity, The Man and the Fly, The Blood Knot, King Ubu, All against All, Open Twenty-Four Hours.

403. Wesker, Arnold. *The Wesker Trilogy.* Baltimore: Penguin Books, 1964.

Chicken Soup with Barley, Roots, I'm Talking about Jerusalem.

404. White, Melvin R., and Whiting, Frank M., eds. *Playreader's Repertory: Drama on Stage.* Glenview, Ill.: Scott, Foresman and Co., 1970.

King Oedipus, The Birds, Everyman, Hamlet, Tartuffe, Ghosts, The Importance of Being Earnest, Arms and the Man, The Cherry Orchard, Six Characters in Search of an Author, Desire under the Elms, The Glass Menagerie, A Raisin in the Sun, Oh Dad Poor Dad. . . .

405. Whiting, John. *The Collected Plays of John Whiting.* Vols. 1–2. Ed. Ronald Hayman. New York: Theatre Arts Books, 1957.

Vol. 1: Marching Son, A Penny for a Song, Saint's Day, Conditions of Agreement.

Vol. 2: The Gates of Summer, No Why, A Walk in the Desert, The Devils, Noman, The Nomads.

406. Whitman, Charles Huntington, ed. *Seven Contemporary Plays.* Boston: Houghton Mifflin Co., 1931.

The Cherry Orchard, Strife, The Sunken Bell, An Enemy of the People, Beyond the Horizon, Cyrano de Bergerac, Riders to the Sea.

407. Wilder, Thornton. *Three Plays by Thornton Wilder.* New York: Bantam Books, 1958.

Our Town, The Skin of Our Teeth, The Matchmaker.

408. Williams, Heathcote. *AC/DC and The Local Stigmatic: Two Plays.* New York: Viking Press, 1973.

409. Williams, Tennessee. *American Blues.* New York: Dramatists Play Service, 1948.

Moony's Kid Don't Cry, Ten Blocks on the Camino Real, The Case of the Crushed Petunias, The Dark Room, The Long Stay Cut Short.

410. ———. *Dragon Country.* New York: New Directions, 1970.

In a Bar of a Tokyo Hotel, I Rise in Flames, Cried the Phoenix, The

Mutilated, I Can't Imagine Tomorrow, Confessional, The Frosted Glass Coffin, A Perfect Analysis Given by a Parrot, The Gnadiges Fraulein.

411. ———. *The Theatre of Tennessee Williams.* Vols. 1–4. New York: New Directions, 1971–72.

Vol. 1: Battle of Angels, A Streetcar Named Desire, The Glass Menagerie.

Vol. 2: The Eccentricities of a Nightingale, Summer and Smoke, The Rose Tattoo, Camino Real.

Vol. 3: Cat on a Hot Tin Roof, Orpheus Descending, Suddenly Last Summer.

Vol. 4: Sweet Bird of Youth, Period of Adjustment, The Night of the Iguana.

412. ———. *Twenty-Seven Wagons Full of Cotton.* New York: New Directions, 1953.

This Property Is Condemned, The Purification, The Last of My Solid Gold Watches, Auto-Da-Fe, The Strongest Kind of Romance, Twenty-Seven Wagons Full of Cotton, The Lady of Larkspur Lotion, Hello from Bertha, Portrait of a Madonna, Lord Byron's Love Letter, The Long Goodbye, Something Unspoken, Talk to Me like the Rain and Let Me Listen.

413. Williams, William Carlos. *Many Loves and Other Plays.* New York: New Directions, 1961.

Many Loves, A Dream of Love, Tituba's Children, The First President, The Cure.

414. Wilson, Edmund. *Five Plays.* New York: Farrar, Straus and Giroux, 1954.

Cyprian's Prayer, The Corpse in the Whistler Room, This Room and This Gin and These Sandwiches, Beppo and Beth, The Little Blue Light.

415. Wilson, Langford. *Balm in Gilead and Other Plays.* New York: Hill and Wang, 1965.

Balm in Gilead, Home Free!, Ludlow Fair.

416. ———. *The Great Nebula in Orion and Three Other Plays.* New York: Dramatists Play Service, 1973.

The Great Nebula in Orion, The Family Continues, Ikke, Ikke, Nye, Nye, Nye, Victory on Mrs. Dandywine's Island.

417. ———. *The Rimers of Eldritch and Other Plays.* New York: Hill and Wang, 1967.

This Is the Rill Speaking, Wanderings, Days Ahead, The Madness of Lady Bright, The Rimers of Eldritch.

418. ———. *The Sandcastle and Three Other Plays*. New York: Dramatists Play Service, 1970.
The Sandcastle, Wandering, Stoop, Sextet.

419. Witkiewicz, Stanislaw Ignacy. *Tropical Madness: Four Plays*. Tr. Daniel and Eleanor Gerould. New York: Drama Book Specialists, 1972.
The Pragmatists, Mister Price, Gubal Wahazar, Metaphysics of a Two-Headed Calf.

420. Woodyard, George, ed. *The Modern Stage in Latin America: Six Plays*. New York: E. P. Dutton and Co., 1971.
The Criminals, The Place Where the Mammals Die, I Too Speak of the Rose, And They Told Us We Were Immortal, The Fan Windows, Payment as Pledged.

421. Wylie, Max, ed. *Writing for Television*. New York: Cowles Book Co., 1970.
A Trip to Czardis, Tarzan, The Flying Nun, Get Smart, The Dick Van Dyke Show, Gomer Pyle, The Price of Tomatoes, Judd for the Defense, Run for Your Life, Twilight Zone, Love of Life, Patrol.

422. Zachar, Irwin J., ed. *Plays as Experience*. Rev. ed. New York: Odyssey Press, 1962.
Three's a Crowd, The Ring of General Macias, The Boor, The Fifteenth Candle, Goodbye to the Long K, The Devil and Daniel Webster, She Walks in Beauty, The Sounds of Triumph, Jacob Comes Home, The Valiant, Sparkin', Back of the Yards, Pawns, Trifles.

Indexes

Players Index

This index lists plays according to the number of men and women required in the cast. Plays requiring children, animals, extras, chorus, or nonspeaking parts in addition to the number of men and women required have been marked with an asterisk. With the exceptions of television plays adapted for the stage, titles appearing before page 68 are one-act or short plays; titles after page 68 are full-length plays. Musical plays and television plays not adapted for stage production have not been indexed.

Topical Index

This index categorizes plays in three major sections: (1) general classification or genre, (2) significant details of setting and characters, and (3) selected themes. Because a given play might be classified in scores of ways, categories lending themselves to a comparative consideration of different plays have received emphasis. With the exceptions of television plays adapted for the stage, titles appearing before page 68 are one-act or short plays; titles after page 68 are full-length plays. Musical plays and television plays not adapted for stage production have not been indexed.

Documentary Plays

Existential Plays

Fantasies

Farces

Folk Plays

Historical Plays

Readings

Religious Plays

Revues

Satires

Situation Comedies

Social Comedies

Verse Plays

Details of Setting, Characters

About a Geographic Region or Locale

The South

The Northeast

New York

My Three Angels, 142
Night Must Fall, 149
No Place to Be Somebody, 70
Petrified Forest, The, 140
Valiant, The, 35

Entertainers (see also the theater)
Great Sebastians, The, 120
He Who Gets Slapped, 78
Home Life of a Buffalo, 36
I Am a Camera, 146
Idiot's Delight, 140
Sunshine Boys, The, 141

High Society: Socialites, Playboys, etc.
Circle, The, 122
Cocktail Party, The, 96
Dark Victory, 87
Dinner at Eight, 113
Entertainer, The, 129
Gigi, 121
Hands across the Sea, 29
Hay Fever, 93
Philadelphia Story, The, 83
Play's the Thing, The, 124
Ring round the Moon, 79
Shall We Join the Ladies?, 25
Ways and Means, 30

Journalists
Case of Libel, A, 94
Front Page, The, 107
Sleeping Dogs, 40

Law: Judges, Lawyers, Trials
Andersonville Trial, The, 120
Caine Mutiny Court-Martial, The, 151
Case of Libel, A, 94
Chalk Garden, The, 81
Corruption in the Palace of Justice, 85
Deadly Game, The, 151
Devil and Daniel Webster, The, 26
In the Matter of J. Robert
   Oppenheimer, 116
Inadmissible Evidence, 130
Inherit the Wind, 119
Ponder Heart, The, 98
Poor Bitos, 79
Shot in the Dark, A, 75
Ten Little Indians, 91
Time Limit, 94
Tomorrow, 178
Twelve Angry Men, 183
Witness for the Prosecution, 91

Little People: Powerless Persons,
   Anonymous Persons
Adding Machine, The, 133
Cave Dwellers, The, 135
Hope Is the Thing with Feathers, 36
Time of Your Life, The, 135
Waiting for Godot, 83

Military Life: Soldiers, Officers, Cadets
Bell for Adano, A, 129
Blood, Sweat, and Stanley Poole, 103
Bury the Dead, 51
Caine Mutiny Court-Martial, The, 151
Catch 22, 107
Chips with Everything, 148
Darkness at Noon, 116
Eve of Saint Mark, The, 77
Golden Fleecing, 137
Hessian Corporal, The, 32
Home of the Brave, 118
Journey's End, 139
Married at Sunrise, 40
Mister Roberts, 107
No Time for Sergeants, 119
Stalag 17, 85
Submerged, 29
Unknown Soldier and His Wife, The,
   146
Viet Rock, 144
We Bombed in New Haven, 108
Yellow Death, 63

Politics, Politicians
Advise and Consent, 121
Best Man, The, 147
Both Your Houses, 77
First Lady, 94
Gang's All Here, The, 119
Girls in 509, The, 144
Hogan's Goat, 76
In the Matter of J. Robert
   Oppenheimer, 116
Out of the Flying Pan, 27
Rivalry, The, 92
State of the Union, 120
Sunrise at Campobello, 136
White House Murder Case, The, 97

Prisoners
Goin' a Buffalo, 68
Hello, Out There, 49
Short Eyes, 131
Sleep of Prisoners, A, 99
Stalag 17, 85
Take Care of Business, 65
Time Limit, 94

Prostitutes
Anna Christie, 127
Owl and the Pussycat, The, 122
Rain, 92
Rattle of a Simple Man, 96
Snowangel, 28
Soul Gone Home, 64

Psychiatrists
Far Country, A, 94
Impossible Years, The, 98
Suppressed Desires, 33

Revolutionaries
And We Own the Night, 63

Situation or Theme

About Perception

Author Index

This index includes authors of original dramatic works; authors of dramatic works based on other sources; authors of plays, novels, poems, or stories used as source material for dramatic works; translators or adaptors from foreign languages; and composers of music or lyrics.

Abbott, George, 154, 173
Achard, Marcel, 75
Adams, Lee, 157, 170
Adler, Richard, 154
Agee, James, 125
Akutagawa, Ryunosuke, 112
Albee, Edward, 24, 75, 76
Aldis, Mary, 29
Alfred, William, 76
Allen, Donald M., 38
Allen, Woody, 76
Alvarez Quintero, Joaquín, 24
Alvarez Quintero, Serafín, 24
Andersen, Hans Christian, 172
Anderson, Maxwell, 76, 77, 78
Anderson, Robert, 78
Anderson, Walt, 78
Andreyev, Leonid, 78
Anouilh, Jean, 78, 79, 80
Apel, Paul, 113
Apolinar, Danny, 157
Apstein, Theodore, 24
Archibald, William, 80
Ardrey, Robert, 80
Atkinson, M. E., 25
Aurthur, Robert Alan, 80, 175
Austen, Jane, 112
Axelrod, George, 80
Ayckbourn, Alan, 80

Bacharach, Burt, 169
Bagnold, Enid, 81
Baker, Elliott, 175
Baker, George M., 25
Baker, Melville, 125
Balch, Jack, 186
Balderston, John L., 81
Baldwin, James, 68
Baraka, Imamu Amiri (LeRoi Jones), 60, 61
Barer, Marshall, 172
Barillet, Pierre, 87
Barrie, James M., 25, 26, 81, 82, 155
Barry, Philip, 82, 83
Bart, Lionel, 155, 166
Bass, Kingsley B. Jr., 68
Batson, George, 83
Beach, Lewis, 26
Beckett, Samuel, 26, 83
Behan, Brendan, 84
Behrman, S. N., 84, 102, 155
Benét, Stephen Vincent, 26
Benson, Sally, 91

Bentley, Eric, 86, 87
Berg, Gertrude, 142, 176
Berkey, Ralph, 94
Berlin, Irving, 158
Berney, William, 134
Berns, Julie, 84
Bernstein, Leonard, 158, 163
Berrigan, Daniel, 84
Besier, Rudolf, 84
Besoyan, Rick, 155
Betti, Ugo, 85
Bevan, Donald, 85
Biddle, Cordelia Drexel, 93
Bissell, Richard, 154
Blitzstein, Marc, 156
Bloch, Bertram, 87
Bock, Jerry, 157, 170, 173
Bolt, Robert, 85
Bolton, Guy, 85
Bond, Nelson, 85
Boothe, Clare, 86
Borodin, Aleksandr, 163
Boruff, John, 86
Bost, Pierre, 87
Bowles, Paul, 136
Box, Muriel, 27
Box, Sydney, 27
Brecht, Bertolt, 86, 87, 155
Breit, Harvey, 136
Brewer, George Jr., 87
Bricusse, Leslie, 156
Bridie, James, 87
Brighouse, Harold, 161
Brinnin, John M., 123
Brontë, Charlotte, 112
Brooke, Eleanore, 115
Broughton, James, 27
Bullins, Ed, 61, 68, 69
Bullock, Michael, 99
Burrows, Abe, 87, 156, 172
Butcher, James W., 61

Caesar, Irving, 161
Cahn, Sammy, 161, 165
Caldwell, Ben, 61
Campton, David, 27
Cannan, Denis, 87
Čapek, Josef, 88
Čapek, Karel, 88
Capote, Truman, 88
Carey, Ernestine Gilbreth, 91
Carlino, Lewis John, 27, 28
Carroll, Paul Vincent, 88

Title Index

The number immediately following the title of a play refers to the page on which the play is described. Numbers in parentheses correspond to the anthologies or collections listed in the appendix and refer to volumes in which the play may be found.